Cosmopolitan Spaces

Routledge Advances in Sociology

For a full list of titles in this series, please visit www.routledge.com

7. Immigrant Life in the U.S.
Multi-disciplinary Perspectives
Edited by Donna R. Gabaccia and
Colin Wayne Leach

8. Rave Culture and Religion
Edited by Graham St. John

**9. Creation and Returns of
Social Capital**
A New Research Program
Edited by Henk Flap and Beate Völker

10. Self-Care
Embodiment, Personal Autonomy and
the Shaping of Health Consciousness
Christopher Ziguras

11. Mechanisms of Cooperation
Werner Raub and Jeroen Weesie

12. After the Bell
Educational Success, Public Policy
and Family Background
Edited by Dalton Conley and
Karen Albright

**13. Youth Crime and Youth Culture in
the Inner City**
Bill Sanders

14. Emotions and Social Movements
Edited by Helena Flam and
Debra King

**15. Globalization, Uncertainty and
Youth in Society**
Edited by Hans-Peter Blossfeld, Erik
Klijzing, Melinda Mills and Karin Kurz

**16. Love, Heterosexuality and
Society**
Paul Johnson

17. Agricultural Governance
Globalization and the New Politics
of Regulation
Edited by Vaughan Higgins and
Geoffrey Lawrence

**18. Challenging Hegemonic
Masculinity**
Richard Howson

19. Social Isolation in Modern Society
Roelof Hortulanus, Anja Machielse and
Ludwien Meeuwesen

**20. Weber and the Persistence
of Religion**
Social Theory, Capitalism and
the Sublime
Joseph W. H. Lough

**21. Globalization, Uncertainty and
Late Careers in Society**
Edited by Hans-Peter Blossfeld,
Sandra Buchholz and Dirk Hofäcker

22. Bourdieu's Politics
Problems and Possibilities
Jeremy F. Lane

23. Media Bias in Reporting Social Research?
The Case of Reviewing Ethnic Inequalities in Education
Martyn Hammersley

24. A General Theory of Emotions and Social Life
Warren D. TenHouten

25. Sociology, Religion and Grace
Arpad Szakolczai

26. Youth Cultures
Scenes, Subcultures and Tribes
Edited by Paul Hodkinson and Wolfgang Deicke

27. The Obituary as Collective Memory
Bridget Fowler

28. Tocqueville's Virus
Utopia and Dystopia in Western Social and Political Thought
Mark Featherstone

29. Jewish Eating and Identity Through the Ages
David Kraemer

30. The Institutionalization of Social Welfare
A Study of Medicalizing Management
Mikael Holmqvist

31. The Role of Religion in Modern Societies
Edited by Detlef Pollack and Daniel V. A. Olson

32. Sex Research and Sex Therapy
A Sociology Analysis of Masters and Johnson
Ross Morrow

33. A Crisis of Waste?
Understanding the Rubbish Society
Martin O'Brien

34. Globalization and Transformations of Local Socioeconomic Practices
Edited by Ulrike Schuerkens

35. The Culture of Welfare Markets
The International Recasting of Pension and Care Systems
Ingo Bode

36. Cohabitation, Family and Society
Tiziana Nazio

37. Latin America and Contemporary Modernity
A Sociological Interpretation
José Maurício Domingues

38. Exploring the Networked Worlds of Popular Music
Milieu Cultures
Peter Webb

39. The Cultural Significance of the Child Star
Jane O'Connor

40. European Integration as an Elite Process
The Failure of a Dream?
Max Haller

41. Queer Political Performance and Protest
Benjamin Shepard

42. Cosmopolitan Spaces
Europe, Globalization, Theory
Chris Rumford

Cosmopolitan Spaces

Europe, Globalization, Theory

Chris Rumford

Routledge
Taylor & Francis Group

NEW YORK AND LONDON

First published 2008
by Routledge
711 Third Avenue, New York, NY 10017

Simultaneously published in the UK
by Routledge
2 Park Square, Milton Park, Abingdon, Oxon, OX14 4RN

Routledge is an imprint of the Taylor & Francis Group, an informa business

First issued in paperback 2011

Typeset in Sabon by IBT Global.

Library of Congress Cataloging in Publication Data
Rumford, Chris, 1958-
    Cosmopolitan spaces : Europe, globalization, theory / by Chris Rumford.
        p. cm. — (Routledge advances in sociology ; 42)
    Includes bibliographical references and index.
    ISBN-13: 978-0-415-39067-5 (hardback : alk. paper)
    ISBN-10: 0-415-39067-2 (hardback : alk. paper)
    ISBN-13: 978-0-203-89143-8
    ISBN-10: 0-203-89143-0
    1. European federation. 2. Globalization Europe. 3. Internationalism. I. Title.
    JN15.R86 2009
    341.242'2 — dc22
    2008009876

ISBN10: 0-415-39067-2 (hbk)
ISBN10: 0-415-89689-4 (pbk)
ISBN10: 0-203-89143-0 (ebk)

ISBN13: 978-0-415-39067-5 (hbk)
ISBN13: 978-0-415-89689-4 (pbk)
ISBN13: 978-0-203-89143-8 (ebk)

For Füsun and Lara

Contents

Acknowledgements   xi

1   Introduction: Cosmopolitanism as a Politics of Space   1

2   From a Sociology of the EU to a Social Theory of Europe   18

3   The Borders and Borderlands of Europe: A Critique of Balibar   37

4   Europe's Cosmopolitan Borders   52

5   'Spaces of Wonder': The Global Politics of Strangeness   69

6   Empire and the Hubris of the 'High Point'   90

7   Postwesternization   110

8   The World is Not Enough: Globalization Reconsidered   133

9   Concluding Thoughts: The Spaces of Critical Cosmopolitanism   152

Notes   157
References   161
Index   173

Acknowledgements

I am very grateful to the following for offering help and advice at various stages of the writing of this book. They have all taken the time to read individual chapters, offer helpful comments, or provide feedback on conference or seminar presentations: Barrie Axford, Gerard Delanty, Olivier Kramsch, Stjepan Mestrovic, William Outhwaite, Roland Robertson, Hasan Turunc, Nick Vaughan-Williams, William Walters.

1 Introduction
Cosmopolitanism as a
Politics of Space

This book offers a critique of various strands of globalization thinking from the perspective of what I am calling 'critical cosmopolitanism'. At the core of this critique is the idea that globalization theories have, over a period of two decades or so, uncritically offered us a strong vision of the singularity of the world, its oneness and 'unicity', to use Robertson's term, a vision which follows from the insistence that globalization makes the world into a single place (and allows us to perceive it as a single place). My revisionist intent is to demonstrate that cosmopolitanism, if it is to retain any critical edge in the social sciences, has to be centrally concerned with generating a multiplicity of perspectives, and consequently allowing for the possibility of many worlds.

As an adjunct to the core argument the book also makes the case for why 'critical cosmopolitanism' is best developed through a study of spaces and borders. A double argument sustains this line of reasoning. One is that cosmopolitanism is at root already a 'politics of space'. In other words, cosmopolitanism is an approach to understanding the social and political world which problematizes, rather than assumes, the spaces with which it is dealing. A very good example of this is provided by the work of Beck (2006) for whom cosmopolitanism engenders a critical distance from what he terms 'methodological nationalism'. In other words, it does not automatically assume that the nation-state is the only or primary unit of political organization. The other argument is that spaces and borders, especially in Europe, have been somewhat disordered by processes of globalization acting upon European nation-state space; the outcomes of this disruption to orderly nation-state existence are difficult to comprehend using conventional social science categories. Cosmopolitanism can provide us with the requisite conceptual 'toolbox' with which to understand the novel spaces and borders emerging in Europe.

Despite its title, this is not a book 'about' cosmopolitanism, Europe, political spaces, or globalization. It is a book about how all of these things are connected and why we need to study them together. In truth, I did not set out to write such a book (see below), but the process of writing has brought together a number of pressing concerns in such a way as to point me in this direction. Some time ago, I discovered that several lines of my research were tending to converge in much the same place. One line of enquiry concerned the aspatial complexion of much contemporary work on the European Union, which tends not to go beyond the idea of 'levels' of governance or agglomerations of pre-existing national space, which coupled with the dearth of penetrative studies on the relationship between globalization and Europe (Rumford, 2006e) seriously limits study on the changing nature of Europe's borders. This suggested to me that a new approach to spaces, borders, and Europe was needed and that a cosmopolitan perspective could be a productive way forward. Another line of research, originally not connected to either Europe or cosmopolitanism in an obvious way, was the ways in which many contemporary configurations of borders and spaces seem to confound all models, theories, and explanations. An interest in transnational and global spaces crystallized into an investigation of Europe's changing spatiality for which tried and tested concepts for thinking about spaces and borders did not seem to 'work'. Again, cosmopolitanism appeared to open up the possibility of news ways of conceptualising spaces and borders which could be used to understand political and societal dynamics in Europe.

A third research interest was the relationship between cosmopolitanism and Europe, and its corollary, the misuse of (or careless application of) notions of cosmopolitanism in studies of contemporary Europe, seeing it for example as something 'belonging' to Europe in a way which appeared to be anything but cosmopolitan. Cosmopolitanism cannot be owned by Europe, and my version of 'critical cosmopolitanism' is an attempt to defend and project a cosmopolitanism worthy of the name. The final strand of research which informs the book is a concern with globalization theory, particularly its cultural strands, which have mainly emerged from sociological interventions over the past two decades or so—in my view the most significant and positive development in sociological thinking in recent times. Specifically my concern is with the way that globalization theorists, in a rare example of consensus amongst a diverse range of thinkers, see globalization as leading to 'one world'. Cosmopolitanism, in my view, should challenge the 'one-worldism' of globalization theory and open itself to a multiplicity of worlds which are possible.

WHY DO WE NEED A BOOK ON COSMOPOLITAN SPACES?

The idea of writing a book on cosmopolitanism and Europe seemed like a very good one when I embarked upon this project a couple of years ago. There was little written specifically on a topic which seemed fresh and vital, the field appeared open and inviting, and academic work in the field of (what has subsequently been termed 'new') cosmopolitanism was beginning to take shape and make some influential contributions to thinking on political identity, post-national citizenship, social transformations, and recasting core concerns associated with the study of globalization. My initial enthusiasm for studying cosmopolitanism in the European context led me to organize a conference,[1] edit and write the *Introduction* for a special issue of a journal, and publish an edited collection (Rumford, 2005, 2007c) all on the theme of 'cosmopolitanism and Europe'. I also co-authored a book (with Gerard Delanty), which concludes with a chapter on 'cosmopolitan Europe' (Delanty and Rumford, 2005). On the back of these projects I planned a monograph on the theme of cosmopolitanism and Europe, was fortunate enough to be offered a contract by Routledge, and settled down to the task of writing my new book.

But something has happened along the way, and it no longer seems like such a good idea to write a book on cosmopolitanism and Europe, or, more accurately, it has become impossible for me to write the book I originally planned to write. The result is that this is not the book I began work on a couple of years ago (nor exactly the book I was contracted to write, so apologies to Routledge in advance). The reason for this change of heart is that my perspective on the core themes has changed significantly during the period in which I have been engaged on this project. In just a few short years 'cosmopolitanism and Europe', a field of study once shinning with promise, has lost some of its sparkle, at least that is my conclusion. It is not that the field is flooded with competing titles. In addition to my own edited volume *Cosmopolitanism and Europe* published in 2007, there has appeared only a small number of books exploring vaguely comparable subject matter, most notably Beck and Grande's recently translated *Cosmopolitan Europe* (Beck and Grande, 2007[2004]), for more on which see Chapter 6, and Delanty's edited volume, *Europe and Asia Between East and West* (Delanty, 2006b), to which I contributed a chapter on 'Borders and rebordering'.

So the field is by no means flooded. What has happened though is that the idea of applying cosmopolitan perspectives to an understanding of contemporary Europe has (in the hands of some commentators) been overtaken by a desire to install cosmopolitanism as Europe's 'big idea', resurrect it as a core component of the European heritage, or parade it as a badge of European identity in dealing with the rest of the world (but mainly the United States). This tendency is most evident in the work of Habermas, but also insinuates itself in the aforementioned book by Beck and Grande, and colours the mainstream and journalistic interpretations of the relationship between cosmopolitanism and Europe—see, for example, Beck and Giddens' newspaper article (Beck and Giddens, 2003), or the work of Rifkin (2004a, 2004b). One consequence of my reservations about the direction that cosmopolitan studies is taking is that my advocacy of cosmopolitanism is more muted than it once was, although as I outline later in the chapter I am keen to develop a more cosmopolitan form of social science.

The 'cosmopolitan spaces' of the title are metaphorical, in contrast to the work of Beck and Grande (2007) who look at the European Union (EU) and find a cosmopolitan reality and a 'cosmopolitan empire', or Daniele Archibugi who looks at the EU and sees 'actually existing cosmopolitanism', or the nearest thing to it. This said, the title is not really misleading, although the focus certainly falls more on attempting to understand Europe's new and emerging spaces than their reality as embodiments of cosmopolitanism. The subtitle is more accurate. The book is centrally about the relationship between globalization, cosmopolitanism, and Europe and the way we theorize this relationship, and importantly, the way in which through theory we can better understand such relations. During the writing of the book the emphasis has shifted from the title to the subtitle. Now it is less an investigation of the relationship between cosmopolitanism and space, and more an exploration of the possibility of 'critical cosmopolitanism'. But there is an important sense in which the book has space at the centre of its concerns. The research for this book has been stimulated by my interest in what I see as some rather unusual spatial developments which have occurred in the past few years. I attempt to capture the unfamiliarity of many spaces in the title of Chapter 5 by using the terms 'spaces of wonder' and the 'globalization of strangeness'. There is a peculiar quality to contemporary political spaces and borders which I believe are not easily apprehended with the tools of conventional social science. Stjepan Mestrovic's comment that 'facts do not speak for themselves, and require theory to illuminate them' (Mestrovic, 1997, 17) summarises this idea very well. The sort of spaces I am thinking of are those stimulated by processes of postwesternization (Chapter 7), which confound conventional expectations of spatial organization and bordering processes, the cosmopolitan qualities of Europe's borders (Chapter 4), and the aforementioned 'spaces of wonder', including global borderlands and 'offshore borders'. It is not that these spaces are cosmopolitan is any literal sense, it is more that they are spaces which can only be properly apprehended through a 'critical cosmopolitanism'.

WHAT SORT OF COSMOPOLITANISM?

In studies of cosmopolitanism and Europe what characterises the current state of play then is less a concern to apply cosmopolitan perspectives to Europe in order to better understand the dynamics of social and political transformation, and more a project of bonding cosmopolitanism to Europe with the hope of making the association natural and compelling. In this sense social scientists are trying to do something the EU has never attempted; create a cosmopolitan Europe. The EU is notably reluctant to describe itself, its project of integration, and its European citizens as cosmopolitan. So despite Daniele Archibugi's characterisation of the EU as 'the first international model which begins to resemble the cosmopolitan model' (Archibugi 1998, 219), the EU does not see itself in these terms. Indeed there appears to be an embarrassing mismatch between the cosmopolitanism of the European

Union as perceived by political scientists and the official position of the EU. In my view there are two plausible explanations for this mismatch (for a full account see Rumford, 2007c, 4–5).

The first (partial) explanation is that while the EU possesses some cosmopolitan qualities (its role in funding humanitarian efforts, the institutionalization of post-national citizenship, and advocacy of global environmental regimes), the EU does not equate these preferences and practices with cosmopolitanism. In other words, the EU may act in a way that can be described as cosmopolitan but that this is not the interpretation or designation favoured by EU institutions, which may prefer the terms 'humanitarian' or 'globally aware'. A second explanation is that, for some reason, the EU is wary of the term and deliberately avoids it. This could be because the EU does not want to promote a cosmopolitan identity or wish for Europeans to feel themselves to be cosmopolitan for fear that this will further dilute their already weak attachment to the European project. It is also possible that the EU sees a difficulty in 'selling' the idea of further integration to member states if European citizens perceive the EU as working on behalf of all humanity rather than promoting the interests of Europeans.

However, none of this should be taken to mean that I have become totally disillusioned with the study of cosmopolitanism and Europe. Despite my deep reservations about the trends in the 'cosmopolitan turn' I do believe that there is something very useful about studying cosmopolitanism and Europe, and the focus of this book falls upon the core of what I see as valuable in this enterprise. I am interested to explore the ways in which cosmopolitanism can be considered a 'politics of space'. As I mentioned earlier, a cosmopolitan perspective contains the potential for a radical questioning and examination of political spaces and the politics of space. This is because cosmopolitanism is centrally concerned with changing relationships between individuals, their communities, and the world, and none of these components or the relationships between them can be taken for granted. Cosmopolitanism causes us to rethink the place of individuals in the world and their relation to the communities to which they may belong (or distance themselves from). The spaces occupied or transcended by these communities cannot be assumed. They may not in fact be spaces at all in any conventional sense, and may be better represented by networks, for example. Importantly, cosmopolitanism causes us to rethink the world itself, particularly the 'oneness' of the world (a significant contribution of globalization theorizing) versus the possibility of a multiplicity of worlds (a theme which we explore in depth in Chapter 8). Cosmopolitanism, unlike nationalism, does not come with a ready-made spatial scale attached. Cosmopolitanism presumes no 'natural' political spaces; looking at something from a cosmopolitan perspective implies that we investigate the spatial dimensions of politics. This seems particularly useful when studying contemporary Europe characterised as it is by changing political scales, the emergence of transnational spaces of both governance and political movements, and the changing nature of borders.

The uncertainty about the political spaces of Europe has led to a plethora of neologisms with which to understand this particular dimension of Europeanization: post-national polity, Europe of the regions, network Europe, European empire, or post-national constellation, for example. With its focus on the politics of space, this book offers both an innovative reading of cosmopolitanism and a novel approach to exploring the spatiality of Europe. What emerges is a fresh understanding of why it is good to study cosmopolitanism and Europe in conjunction. Cosmopolitanism channels us into new ways of thinking about the spatiality of Europe and takes us beyond those tired designations which rely on post-national and multi-level motifs. It does this primarily because it causes us to look at the importance of the changing nature of borders, and their impact upon the spatiality of Europe. The result is that Europe's spatiality can be understood through its 'cosmopolitan borders' (Chapter 4), processes of postwesternization (Chapter 7), and even 'spaces of wonder' (Chapter 5).

Of course *Cosmopolitan Spaces* also has something to say about cosmopolitanism, particularly what a cosmopolitan social science can achieve and indeed why we should be interested in developing social science in a cosmopolitan direction. Other contemporary approaches to cosmopolitanism are directed to questions such as whether people can identify with cosmopolitan ideas and/or acquire a cosmopolitan identity, whether it is meaningful to talk of cosmopolitan citizenship, whether cosmopolitanism can be institutionalized and a world level of governance become a reality, and whether international institutions (such as the EU) can develop a cosmopolitan policy agenda. These are not my concerns in this book. In fact, I think it doubtful that there will ever be significant numbers of individuals who identify themselves as cosmopolitans (or at least who do this *and* agree what they understand to be cosmopolitanism). I think that the quest for cosmopolitan institutions is misguided (and gives a far too normative complexion to social science), and I think it is naïve to think that the EU will ever endorse a cosmopolitan agenda. Indeed, as far as I am concerned these questions are largely irrelevant. What is much more important, and certainly more practical, is that we move towards a cosmopolitan social science, one which is genuinely pluralist, multi-perspectival, and not framed by European priorities and preoccupations. The real value of cosmopolitanism lies in its ability to transform the way we think about the world, formulate new research questions, and do social science better. The book is intended as a modest contribution to this task.

CRITIQUES OF THE 'NEW' COSMOPOLITANISM

I am concerned that mechanical attempts to associate cosmopolitanism with Europe will both blunt attempts to develop cosmopolitan critiques of developments in Europe and turn people off to anything that sounds like a cosmopolitan approach. I am also worried that if the EU can be thought to be cosmopolitan (by accident or design) then cosmopolitanism will become seen as something internal to the integration project (a quality of the EU) and social scientists will be able to obtain no analytical purchase by using the term. In order to distance myself from these tendencies I can outline my own approach to cosmopolitanism in the following terms. People (in Europe and elsewhere) are not cosmopolitan and unlikely to become more so (although I would be happy to see this happen); it is wishful thinking to expect institutions of cosmopolitan democratic governance to spring up; it is pointless to try to reform the EU in a cosmopolitan direction or attribute to it a cosmopolitan identity. We can however strive to create a cosmopolitan social science (which in fact may subsequently lead more individuals embracing a cosmopolitan perspective and forging cosmopolitan political agendas). In my opinion, a cosmopolitan social science is very 'doable' and not idealistic or utopian in the way cosmopolitan projects are often perceived.

There are some important developments in thinking about the cosmopolitanization of social science upon which it is possible to draw, and some of these will be given consideration later in this chapter. However, the approach outlined so far conflicts with a range of approaches to cosmopolitanism developed in recent years, particularly much work which can be placed under the heading 'new' cosmopolitanism. My interest in cosmopolitanism does not embrace world citizenship, institutions of justice beyond the nation-state, and a world of untrammelled mobilities, although it does have a degree of affinity with ideas such as multiple belonging, identification with the other, and borders crossings, all of which are central to the contemporary cosmopolitan agenda. Expressed in different terms, the approach to cosmopolitanism informing the spatial politics of Europe examined in this book shares something with the work of Delanty and (some, but not all, of) Beck's recent output, but little with the work of Held and Archibugi, and next to none with that of Habermas. I do not feel an affinity with normative prescriptions for a cosmopolitan world order (Held and Archibugi), and have problems with attempts to reform the EU in a cosmopolitan direction (Beck and Grande). I do however like the idea of 'critical cosmopolitanism' (Mignolo, Delanty) and to a certain extent 'methodological cosmopolitanism' (Beck).

The 'new' cosmopolitanism has been criticised from a number of perspectives, and it will be useful to review some of these criticisms before offering a more positive assessment of cosmopolitanism, especially 'critical cosmopolitanism', and then proceeding to outline why cosmopolitanism should be conceived as a 'politics of space'. Pheng Cheah (2006) identifies two central concerns associated with contemporary cosmopolitanism; the possibility of developing institutions of global reach, and the emergence of global forms of political solidarity (Cheah, 2006, 486). On his reading these concerns are particularly pertinent in a world where there is a high degree of 'material interconnectedness brought about by global capitalism' (Cheah, 2006, 491). The 'lack of fit' between the networked world and the 'formation of global solidarities' is troubling to cosmopolitans, particularly where the cosmopolitan agenda revolves around the need to regulate the 'excesses of capitalist globalization' and to transcend the particularistic attachments of the nation-state era. Thus, for Cheah the core concerns of cosmopolitanism centre on its potential as a counterbalance to economic globalization and as a form of political consciousness appropriate to the new global order. He offers the following critical characterisation of theories of 'new' cosmopolitanism, which he sees as combing or drawing upon three arguments (Cheah, 2006, 491). First, globalization has undermined the legitimacy of the nation-state to the extent that it can no longer circumscribe visions of political solidarity. Second, the interconnectedness of the world has reached a stage where political institutions with global reach and scope are now possible as are purposive forms of global consciousness. Third, cosmopolitan awareness can lead to 'better' forms of solidarity which can deliver democracy and rights superior to those offered by the nation-state.

As with many broad characterizations of this type, Cheah sacrifices detail and nuance to generalization in order to make his argument. This is not the most pertinent comment to be made about his work, however. Cheah's portrayal of 'new' cosmopolitanism, while useful enough at an introductory level, simply ignores the thrust of many contemporary cosmopolitan arguments. First, although the critique of 'methodological nationalism' is pushed strongly by some theorists (especially Beck and Grande) this does not mean that cosmopolitanism is viewed as superseding nationalism. Cheah suggests that a consensus exists that globalization has weakened the nation-state. In fact, this is a hotly debated area of globalization theory and there is an emerging consensus that globalization has worked to disseminate the nation-state as a model state form and bolstered its legitimacy (Meyer, 2000; Meyer, Boli, Thomas, and Ramirez, 1997). Second, the impression given by Cheah is that both globalization and cosmopolitanism only pertain to those processes and institutional forms which encircle the world. On the contrary, much work on globalization emphases its localized effects (Robertson, 1992; Friedman, 1990, 2007) and how globalization works from within national societies (Beck, 2006). Third, it is also assumed that cosmopolitanism enters the scene subsequent to the nation-state (and also subsequent to globalization). On this reading, cosmopolitanism is both post-national and a reaction to (or protest against) globalization. In fact, given its origins in the ancient world, there is every reason to view cosmopolitanism as pre-dating both. In summary, in portraying 'new' cosmopolitanism in the way he does, Cheah does not offer a satisfactory or accurate account of how the relationship between the nation-state, globalization, and cosmopolitanism are understood in the literature. In particular, he views cosmopolitanism as dependent upon a certain reading of globalization, and assumes a linear historical progression from nation-state to globalization and onwards to cosmopolitanism.

Robert Fine, in his book *Cosmopolitanism* (Fine, 2007), also offers a general critique of the 'new' cosmopolitanism, and its concern to place 'human rights, international law, global governance and peaceful relations between states at the centre of its vision of the world' (Fine, 2007, 1). Fine sees the 'new' cosmopolitanism as 'an identifiable current gravitating around a number of shared commitments' (Fine, 2007, 1–2), of which the following are singled out. First, 'overcoming national presuppositions'; second, the recognition that we live in a world of mutual interdependence; third, the development of 'normative and frankly prescriptive' ideas on world citizenship, global justice, and cosmopolitan democracy. This is a fair characterisation of 'new' cosmopolitanism, in my view, and Fine adds to it a pithy critique: 'New' cosmopolitanism is neither cosmopolitan enough, nor new enough (Fine, 2007, x–xi). By this he means that, on the first count, 'new' cosmopolitanism is rather unambitious; cosmopolitanism is simply 'bolted on' to existing understandings of belonging. 'It leaves intact a conventional notion of belonging, in which individuals know intimately the contours of their world, and it only supplements this sense of belonging with a universal element' (Fine, 2007, x). In this sense, 'new' cosmopolitanism depends upon, rather than existing as an alternative to, the national imagination. It does not adequately capture the 'worldliness' of cosmopolitanism, or the voice which it can give to the marginalized (Mignolo, 2000a, 2000b). On the second count, Fine criticises 'new' cosmopolitanism for being beholden to Kant and the natural law tradition, and as such, 'new' cosmopolitanism has failed to re-invent itself in response to changing times. 'New' cosmopolitanism is merely old cosmopolitanism in disguise. To these we could add another pertinent criticism; it is not pluralistic enough. 'New' cosmopolitanism is always someone's project; it is always the projection of a particular perspective. The someone who possesses this perspective is inevitably western and European. The core concern with human rights, international law, global governance, and peaceful relations rightly identified by Fine are also evidence of a political agenda which is more universalising than universal.

TOWARDS A COSMOPOLITAN SOCIAL SCIENCE

Several sociologists have called for a more cosmopolitan social science, including Beck in a number of recent publications co-written with Sznaider (Beck and Sznaider, 2006) and with Grande (Beck and Grande, 2007). Delanty (2006a) too has advanced the case for a cosmopolitan social science. Compared to the claims of some of the 'new' cosmopolitanism, this is a project with much more critical and analytical potential (although it clearly overlaps with it, and, in the case of Beck, cannot be dissociated from it).

The premise underlying Beck's approach is that we are witnessing a 'cosmopolitanization of reality', the full dimensions of which can only be apprehended once we dispense with the 'methodological nationalism' which pervades the social sciences. 'Methodological nationalism' refers to the ways in which 'social scientists in doing research and theorizing take it for granted that society is equated with national society' (Beck and Sznaider, 2006, 2). This should not be confused with the idea that the end of the nation-state is upon us. Cosmopolitan realism, as Beck and Sznaider term their approach, displays three commitments: a critique of methodological nationalism; the recognition that 'the twenty-first century is becoming an age of cosmopolitanism' (Beck and Sznaider, 2006, 3); and a recognition that what we need is 'some kind of *"methodological cosmopolitanism"*, which can dispense with the dualisms that have informed globalization theory: global/local, national/international, inside/outside' (Beck and Sznaider, 2006, 3).

Beck and Sznaider draw a distinction between cosmopolitanism, which they see as 'a set of normative principles, and *cosmopolitanization* which stands for the 'really-existing processes of cosmopolitanization of the world' (Beck and Sznaider, 2006, 7). In doing this they distinguish themselves from the normative and prescriptive approach associated with the 'cosmopolitan democracy' thesis advanced by fellow 'new' cosmopolitans, Held and Archibugi. Importantly, for Beck and Sznaider, processes of cosmopolitanization do not only proceed from cosmopolitan intentions but may be the result of 'unintended and unseen *side-effects* of actions which are not intended as "cosmopolitan"' (Beck and Sznaider, 2006, 7). A good example of this would be the way in the European Union, through pursuing programmes of integration and enlargement, has resulted in the cosmopolitanization of Europe—supranational governance, post-national citizenship and so on—without setting out with this intention (Beck and Grande, 2007, and see also the discussion in Chapter 6).

The project of methodological cosmopolitanism is an ambitious one, but necessary 'if the social sciences want to avoid becoming a museum of antiquated ideas' (Beck, 2007b, 167). Beck (2000) designates as 'zombie categories' social science staples such as class, family, nation, community—'living dead' concepts which were devised for studying societies which are now radically transformed. They are, in short, concepts which live on despite the societies which they were devised to study having changed beyond recognition. Beck writes,

> Social science must be re-established as a transnational science of the reality of denationalization, transnationalization and 're-ethnification' in a global age—and this on the levels of concepts, theories and methodologies as well as organizationally. This entails a re-examination of the fundamental concepts of 'modern society'. Household, family, class, social inequality, democracy, power, state, commerce, public,

community, justice, law, history and politics must be released from the fetters of methodological nationalism, reconceptualized and empirically established within the framework of a new cosmopolitan social and political science. (Beck, 2007b, 167)

The work of Beck and his various co-authors represents a comprehensive attempt to revise the rules of sociological enquiry along cosmopolitan lines. Beck's work also constitutes a major rethinking of the dynamics of European transformation. Indeed, it is arguably the most important systematic study of Europe from a cosmopolitan perspective, and for this reason alone is of significant interest to the themes of this book. We will look at Beck and Grande's reinterpretation of Europe as 'cosmopolitan empire' in Chapter 6. At this stage we can note that while one might agree with Beck's desire to properly establish a 'transnational science of cosmopolitan reality', there is a danger that Beck's work is, inverting Fine's criticism of 'new' cosmopolitanism discussed previously, rather *too* cosmopolitan. By this I mean that Beck finds cosmopolitanism wherever he looks for it. The logic of 'side effects' means that the EU has brought about the cosmopolitanization of Europe even though this was never the intention. Europe possesses a cosmopolitan reality which 'normal social science' tends to overlook; the 'real Europe' can only be understood through the cosmopolitan lens (Beck, 2008). Beck's belief is that once we have learnt to transcend the restrictions placed on social science by 'methodological nationalism' we will discover ways of studying transnational reality and in doing so discover (cosmopolitan) dimensions to Europe that we never realized existed. It is possible that Beck's cosmopolitan version of Europe is the result of what Philip Schlesinger has recently termed the 'cosmopolitan temptation', whereby wishful thinking about cosmopolitanism gets in the way of clear analysis (Schlesinger, 2007).

The work of Delanty represents one of the most successful attempts to date to advance a cosmopolitan social science. Delanty outlines a 'critical cosmopolitanism' which has in common with Beck a distancing from the idea that globalization is the primary mechanism for promoting cosmopolitanism. According to Delanty, cosmopolitanism is concerned with the 'very conceptualization of the social world as an open horizon in which new cultural models take shape . . . and wherever new relations between self, other and world develop in moments of openness' (Delanty, 2006a, 27). This notion of 'world openness' is important. It enables him to go beyond an idea of 'cosmopolitanism as a particular or singular condition that either exists or does not, a state or goal to be realized' (Delanty, 2006a, 27). Instead cosmopolitanism should be seen as 'a cultural medium of societal transformation that is based on the principle of world openness' Delanty, 2006a, 27). It is also important in the sense that it helps us to move beyond a universalistic conception of cosmopolitanism; a post-universalistic cosmopolitanism presupposes multiple modernities rather than simple pluralities, and eschews the idea of a single world culture. Delanty is keen to reiterate the distance between globalization-inspired understandings of the world and a 'critical cosmopolitanism' perspective. The two cannot be conflated and 'cosmopolitanism does not refer simply to a global space or to post-national phenomena that have come into existence today as a result of globalization' (Delanty, 2006a, 43).

The element of Delanty's 'critical cosmopolitanism' on which I would like to focus is that of 'world openness', as this has a particular bearing on one of the core themes of this book, namely the multiplicity of worlds that cosmopolitanism can represent. These ideas are explored fully in Chapter 8 but a few preparatory comments will be useful at this stage. Central to Delanty's 'critical cosmopolitanism' is the idea that the world is viewed 'in terms of openness rather than in terms of a universal system. This is what defines the cosmopolitan imagination' (Delanty, 2006a, 38). The social world is shaped by the encounters between the global and the local, and the universal and particular. As with ideas of self and other these do not simply play out in relation to each other but are defined in relation to 'the abstract category of the world' (Delanty, 2006a, 37). This is a very important development in the way we think about cosmopolitanism, but one which does not allow for the possibility that cosmopolitanism may lead to the envisioning of multiple worlds. In this regard, Delanty still shares something important in common with the approaches to globalization that he is keen to distance his 'critical cosmopolitanism' from: the idea that the world is singular, and forms a conceptual fixed reference point in our thinking about self, other, and community.

A useful corollary to Beck and Delanty's efforts to develop a cosmopolitan social science is the work of Walter Mignolo, in particular his idea of critical cosmopolitanism, or 'border thinking'. For Mignolo, critical cosmopolitanism comes from the 'exterior of modernity', in other words coloniality (Mignolo, 2000a, 724). Border thinking—'the transformation of the hegemonic imaginary' from the perspective of the excluded—is a tool of critical cosmopolitanism (Mignolo, 2000a: 736–737). Border thinking implies that marginalized voices bring themselves into the conversation, rather than waiting to be invited. In Mignolo's words, 'everyone participates instead of "being participated"' (Mignolo, 2000a, 744). Critical cosmopolitanism is thus designed as an antidote to cosmopolitan projects (of a top-down or universalizing nature) which are coloured by what Mignolo terms the legacy of 'global designs' (Christianity, imperialism, and neoliberalism all being examples).

Placing border thinking as a central component of critical cosmopolitanism has several important consequences, not least of which is the centrality of borders to understanding the world and developing a cosmopolitan social science. This insight also chimes with core themes of this book. Significantly it also means that 'cosmopolitanism . . . can no longer be articulated from one point of view, within a single logic, a mono-logic'

(Mignolo, 2000a, 741). This idea resonates with another strand of the argument advanced in this book, namely the impossibility of a 'high point' or a mono-perspective in cosmopolitan social science (see below, and also Chapters 3 and 6). Mignolo also develops the idea of 'diversality', or diversity as a universal project. It emerges from the experience of coloniality and represents new forms of 'imagining, ethically and politically, from subaltern positions' (Mignolo, 2000a, 743). It leads to a vision of a 'pluricentric world built on the ruins of ancient, non-Western cultures and civilizations with the debris of Western civilization' (Mignolo, 2000a, 745). Mignolo is a key thinker in relation to developing a critical cosmopolitanism. His work combines an interest in globalization, borders, and multiperspectival social science in such a way as to provide a valuable antidote to Euro-centric perspectives on cosmopolitanism.

COSMOPOLITANISM AS A POLITICS OF SPACE

Mignolo's work is also significant from the perspective of interpreting cosmopolitanism as a politics of space, which makes him rare among social theorists exploring cosmopolitan themes. I began this chapter by remarking that writing a book on cosmopolitanism and Europe seemed like a good idea at the time but that subsequent directions in cosmopolitan scholarship had given me pause for thought. What has remained constant throughout is my belief that a study of cosmopolitanism as a politics of space *is* a good idea. What I did not fully appreciate at the outset however was that there was so little written about cosmopolitanism and space, and cosmopolitanism and borders. In relation to cosmopolitanism and space this is starting to change a little, for example Beck and Grande's aforementioned interpretation of Europe as 'cosmopolitan empire'. There is still little written on the theme of cosmopolitanism and borders although there are signs that this may be changing too (Delanty, 2007; Spruce, 2007).

Beck (2008) writes that 'cosmopolitanism . . . is not specified in *spatial* terms; specifically, it is not bound to the "cosmos" or to the "globe"'. What he means by this, I imagine, is that cosmopolitanism does not only signify a concern with processes and activities which have world-wide scope (a similar point was made previously in my critique of Cheah). The point for Beck is that cosmopolitanism, or processes of cosmopolitanization as he would prefer, can work from the inside out; cosmopolitanism is 'globalization from within' (Beck, 2004). But there is a strong sense in which cosmopolitanism is very much about the world, the globe, the 'cosmos'. In particular, the argument developed here is that cosmopolitanism is centrally about the multiplicity of worlds which may exist (see Chapter 8). Moreover, there is a sense in which cosmopolitanism can be strongly associated with spatiality, which brings us back to the title and central preoccupation of the book.

I wish to examine the ways that cosmopolitanism calls our attention to new relationships between the individual, community, and the world—and to the fact that these relationships are fluid and evolving. In other words, cosmopolitanism highlights both the fact that social transformation is occurring and also that there is an increasing awareness that we are caught up in a transformative process (or processes). Moreover, cosmopolitanism signals that there are now a multiplicity of possible ways of imagining the world, and the place of the individual in it, and that these models coexist and may be in conflict. In other words, cosmopolitanism implies a recognition that the world is being transformed and that the direction it takes is open and contingent. Cosmopolitanism thus requires us all to negotiate our relationships to the communities we live in (or live in proximity to), our relationship to others, how these communities are bordered and bounded (or not), and how we move between them. Cosmopolitanism requires us to recognize that we are all positioned simultaneously as outsiders and insiders, as individuals and group members, as self and the other, as local and global. Cosmopolitanism is about relativizing our place within the global frame, positioning ourselves in relation to multiple communities, crossing and re-crossing territorial and community borders. It is also about reconciling increasing self-autonomy with a multiplicity of governance regimes, and about electing to live in some communities while at the same time opting out of others that may make claims on our allegiances.

An argument to be advanced is that the development of a cosmopolitan perspective in the social sciences is driven, in part, by the need to understand the changing spatiality of the political world (the idea of the 'spatial turn' in the social sciences is explored further in Chapter 2). The main dimensions of this transformed spatiality include: the rise of political entities which are neither territorially based not possessing a single centre or origin (designated by terms such as polycentric governance, empire, network society, world polity, global civil society; Delanty and Rumford, 2007); the inversion of the relationship between territory and borders (Balibar, 1998, 220), the blurring of boundaries between and within existing territorial polities, and the resulting centrality of borders to any understanding of political spaces (Chapters 3 and 4); the importance of the idea of 'the world' to political imaginaries, for instance the notion of humanity, the supposed universality of human rights, the global nature of terror threats, the unpredictability of the world, for example world risk society (Chapter 8).

It is important to understand why a cosmopolitan approach is preferable to addressing the same set of concerns through the lens of globalization. In my interpretation, cosmopolitanism and globalization are worlds apart. There are several key differences between understandings of space inspired by globalization theory and a critical cosmopolitan approach. First, globalization has provoked thinking about 'levels'—local, regional, national, European, global—and the changing relationship between them (Brenner,

2003, 2004). Cosmopolitanism takes us beyond the metaphor of 'levels' to new appreciation of the interpenetration of spaces, their fuzzyness, and their multiplicity. Second, globalization is often associated with the 'annihilation of space' (Harvey, 1989) and a borderless world. Cosmopolitanism on the other hand deals with the construction of new political spaces and the proliferation of borders. Finally, and perhaps most important, whereas globalization teaches us that we live in 'one world', cosmopolitanism allows us to imagine the multiplicity of worlds that may exist.

COSMOPOLITANISM IN STRANGE PLACES

When studying cosmopolitanism and Europe we should not assume that the two terms possess a natural affinity. But this does not mean that Europe cannot profitably be studied from a cosmopolitan perspective. In fact, it has already proved to be a productive line of research and should grow into a core element of a multi-disciplinary European studies agenda (Entrikin, 2003; Rumford, 2007c; Stevenson, 2006). The problem comes when cosmopolitanism is seen to be an expression of European identity or when Europeans claim exclusive rights over a cosmopolitan heritage. This tends to happen when the emphasis is placed on trying to understand the new relations between self, Other, and community (belonging) which cosmopolitanism brings to the agenda. In relation to Europe the focus then becomes the blurring of inside/outside, self and other, and the ways in which Europe provokes a post-national response to the threat of globalization. This can be a productive agenda, causing EU scholars to approach the question of Europe's relation with the rest of the globe, for example. But the most productive work which a cosmopolitan approach can generate comes through consideration of the third element of the cosmopolitan triad of self, community, and the world. This is what I refer to as the neglected element, the way in which cosmopolitan approaches tend to downplay the importance of the world (or worlds), in the cosmopolitan imagination. One of the main themes in this book is the need to 'bring the world back in' to cosmopolitan studies in general, and the study of cosmopolitanism and Europe in particular. Thus, the book addresses cosmopolitanism not as an adjunct to globalization, but through the lens of the 'spatial turn' in the social sciences.

There are two main (interrelated) consequences stemming from the decision to highlight the worlds of cosmopolitanism. One is that we need to rethink cosmopolitanism vis-à-vis globalization, the other is that we must respond to the new politics of space which follows from this acknowledgment of the 'openness' of the world, to borrow Delanty's phrase. Cosmopolitanism is often accorded a secondary role vis-à-vis globalization, and we have already noted criticisms of this kind in the work of Cheah, for example. Too often cosmopolitanism is seen as an ideational response to globalization, a consciousness resulting from the perceived 'oneness' of the world, or the heightened awareness of the global nature of environmental and humanitarian problems, for instance. It is certainly the case that a growing awareness of (and theorizing about) processes of globalization is perceived as a necessary condition for the recent upsurge of interest in what is after all at root a very old idea (Rumford, 2007c). Chapter 8 explores the relationship between globalization and cosmopolitan thinking, paying particular attention to a hitherto under-researched dimension of global-ization theory; the way in which many otherwise very different perspec-tives on globalization agree on one thing; that globalization leads to one world (and the perception that we live in one world). The assumption of the singularity of the world goes unchallenged in all variants of globalization thinking. It is argued that a critical cosmopolitanism allows for the possi-bility that several worlds can co-exist and that, in this important sense, we do not live in one world. This is a key issue in terms of understanding the relationship between globalization and cosmopolitanism (and also helps explain why my book on cosmopolitanism is sub-titled *Europe, Globaliza-tion, Theory*).

One result of embracing the 'worlds of cosmopolitanism' is that we encounter a whole range of new spatialities. The key here is the idea of postwesternization (Chapter 7) which, it is argued, is central to both the possibility of a non-Eurocentric cosmopolitanism and the idea that cosmo-politanism can reveal a multiplicity of worlds. In this sense, it is also the cornerstone of critical cosmopolitanism. The book contains several other chapters which explore different dimensions of cosmopolitan spatiality. One spatial idea which has had a significant impact on European stud-ies is that Europe is becoming an empire. The significance of the idea of neo-medieval empire (Zielonka, 2007) or cosmopolitan empire (Beck and Grande, 2007) is that it removes the need to think of the EU as some kind of state. The downside is that it maintains the fiction of the possibility of a mono-perspective on Europe, a singular position from which Europe can be viewed and understood. It is argued that empire cannot serve as a vehicle for understanding the cosmopolitan dimensions of Europe (despite Beck and Grande's best efforts) because it prevents the development of both a multi-perspectival Europe and a critical cosmopolitanism. The themes of mono- versus multi-perspectives which has echoes in the idea of 'one world' versus multiple worlds, is developed throughout the book.

Borders are considered to be central to the transformed spatiality asso-ciated with cosmopolitanism, and are considered vital in developing a spatially aware understanding of contemporary Europe and also a critical cosmopolitanism. We look at borders in three contexts. The first is through a critique of the work of Etienne Balibar, arguably the most important borders scholar currently at work. An examination of his insightful essays on borders, written over a period of more than a decade, reveals a particu-larly interesting dynamic of European transformation. Balibar has taught us that borders are increasingly dispersed throughout society (that they are not always at the border, so to speak), that borders and bordering practices are at the heart of Europe's 'democratic deficit' (although not in the way understood by scholars of EU integration), and what follows from this is that borders are increasingly designed to differentiate those individuals who are not wanted by European counties. In common parlance, borders are gateways for some but barriers to others. Following this we examine the possibility that Europe's borders have become (or are becoming) cosmopolitan, this discussion being set against a background of thinking about borders which offers (unhelpful) images of a borderless world juxtaposed with 'fortress Europe'. The argument here is quite straightforward; Europe's borders are cosmopolitan because it is no longer only the nation-state that decides upon them. In addition to the EU being a very powerful shifter of borders, borders are increasingly constructed (or dismantled) by ordinary people. This 'borderwork' performed by citizens is a key component of cosmopolitanism. The third context in which borders are considered is the idea of 'spaces of wonder' (many such spaces being in fact borders). Chapter 5 examines ways in which opportunities for governance can accompany the emergence of 'spaces of wonder' (such as global borderlands, the United Kingdom's offshore border, and the world itself) particularly when they can be domesticated through familiar, cosy, and reassuring discourses of public safety and common cause. Consideration of 'spaces of wonder' also allows us to explore further the way in which cosmopolitanism presumes a multiplicity of worlds, and the importance of the openness of the world in framing cosmopolitan discourses.

2 From a Sociology of the EU to a Social Theory of Europe

> For many years, the process of European integration was accepted uncritically by mainstream research on Europe: it was criticized, if at all, by the wrong people using (mostly) wrong arguments.
>
> —Beck and Grande, 2007, 27

This chapter examines sociological and other approaches to understanding the novelty of Europe's spatiality, and explores the idea that a focus on transformed political spaces must be central to any understanding of contemporary Europe. It is argued that the only approaches which adequately address Europe's novel spatiality are those generated by social theory (or which are heavily influenced by social theory). Social theory accounts of Europeanization are more satisfactory than sociological studies of the European Union (EU) in this regard, and are also more amenable to combining an interest in space with a cosmopolitan perspective.

One can travel a considerable conceptual distance in the literature on the EU, from accounts which see it wholly in institution-building and policy realm terms to writing which explores the novelty of the EU and the ways in which it does not conform to standard (statist) models employed by political scientists and sociologists alike. Nowhere is this distance more evident than in accounts of Europe's (post-national) spatiality. According to taste, the EU is either a supranational state or post-national polity, or, at the other end of the spectrum, an entity which cannot begin to be captured by this terminology, and for which a new conceptual vocabulary is needed. This has led some, for example Beck and Grande (2007) and Zielonka (2007), to see the EU in terms of 'empire' (see Chapter 6), this term being deemed the best currently available to capture both the spatial variability and 'fuzzyness' of the EU and also its distinct oddness. It is significant that Beck and Grande (2007, 28) come to describe the EU not just as "a great misunderstood phenomenon" but as a "freak" of world history. What is odd about the EU is not so much that its institutions and polity-building are difficult to account for in terms of existing models of the state (although this is certainly the case) but that its spaces defy conventional explanation, and in particular the relationship between its political spaces, its borders, and the forms of governance designed to manage these defy the categories and conventions of social science (Rumford, 2006c).

This chapter explores ways in which it is possible to understand the spatiality of Europe by embracing social theory-informed approaches. It does this firstly by looking at the arguments for an empirical sociology of the EU, as advanced by Favell, and considers what is at stake in this call for a sociology of the EU. Favell's proposal for a sociology of the EU is rejected in favour of the idea of a social theory of Europe, the key arguments being that social theory approaches have already made a substantial contribution to the study of Europe and as such have a track record not matched by more sociological accounts, coupled with the realization that social theory is capable of generating a new agenda for the study of Europe, one which is not in thrall to the need to study the state-like properties of the EU. Moreover, social theory approaches are better placed to study those dimensions of Europe which are most odd or "freaky", in Beck and Grande's sense, that is to say those relating to spaces and borders.

DO WE NEED A SOCIOLOGY OF THE EU?

Sociology maintains a low profile in EU studies. This chapter gives some consideration to why this might be the case, and in doing so departs from the usual explanation given for this state of affairs, namely that sociology, with its traditional focus on nationally bounded societies, is not well suited to the task.

Sociology's modest contribution to EU studies in seen by critics as a failure, in the sense that it demonstrates both a lack of ambition and an unwillingness to engage in a key social science debate. The argument advanced here is that sociologists do not much like the EU studies agenda (although they rarely articulate this dislike sufficiently clearly) and prefer to engage in a different sort of study of Europe, with an alternative focus and a different set of priorities. The real issue is not so much how sociology can best bend itself to better contribute to EU studies but how it can promote its own agenda for the study of Europe. The argument will be developed through a critical reading of two very different recent approaches to the sociological study of the EU. One is the call for an empirical sociology of the EU advanced in the work of Adrian Favell (2007), and Guiraudon and Favell (2007). The other is a recent contribution by Borocz and Sarkar (2005) entitled "What is the EU?", which I believe represents an interesting alternative sociological approach to that laid down by the political science EU studies agenda favoured by Favell.

Before we proceed it needs to be pointed out that sociologists are not oblivious to their low visibility in the field of EU integration studies. This is an issue which has been raised time and time again over the past few years. However, even though the 'problem' has became recognised by sociologists there has still not been a marked shift towards sociological studies of European integration. Sociologists are well aware that they are absent from EU studies, and, it might be inferred, are not unhappy in this knowledge. They also recognise (implicitly if not explicitly) that the questions at the core of European integration studies—the extent to which the EU resembles a state, the progression towards 'ever closer union', the commitment of the United Kingdom to the EU project—are not necessarily the most urgent questions we need to be asking about contemporary Europe. In other words, sociology has very good reasons for not wanting to "get involved and be present in the EU studies debate" (c.f. Favell, 2007, 128).

The 'failure' of sociology to contribute to EU studies should not obscure the fact that sociology is actually rather good at studying issues and processes of great relevance to EU integration, but which remain lower-order concerns on the EU studies agenda. Sociology has made a major contribution to the study of migration (Koopmans and Statham, 2000), citizenship (Soysal, 1994, 1997), social movements (Imig and Tarrow, 2001), to offer just a few examples. More importantly, sociologists are rather good at studying Europe. In fact, they have proved themselves much better at studying Europe than studying the EU, particularly when research is conducted at the social theory end of the sociological spectrum, that is to say where sociology is at its least empirical, at least in the conventional sense. This is borne out by the quality of work on the public sphere and European society, for example (Calhoun, 2003; Offe, 2002; Nash, 2007; Outhwaite, 2005, 2006b; Soysal, 2001). This points to a productive direction for sociological activity: away from the fixation on the EU-as-state (Delanty and Rumford, 2005) towards the development (or problematic absence) of European society. In the light of this the chapter advances two arguments. One is that sociology should recognise its strengths in European studies and work to build upon the very substantial platform which already exists. The other is that sociology should establish its own agenda for the study of Europe, rather than feel obliged to contribute to the (political science-dominated) field of EU studies.

These aforementioned comments should not be taken to imply that sociologists should have no interest in the EU. There is absolutely no reason why sociology should not study EU integration, and Favell (2007) outlines comprehensively the contribution that has been made in this field to date. However, the fact also remains that sociology has always been somewhat marginal to EU studies, despite the pioneering efforts of Etzioni to bring the topic into the sociological mainstream in the early days of the integration process (Etzioni, 1965). As Favell confirms, sociology has not featured strongly in EU studies and its contributions have been "scattered and marginal" (Favell, 2007, 122). According to Favell, the reason why "sociologists barely feature among the participants at mainstream EU conferences" is that they are "still wedded to 'society' as their principle unit of analysis" (Favell, 2007, 122). In other words, when sociologists purport to study society, it is in reality nation-state society, with all the attendant assumptions of cultural distinctiveness, which is the object of sociological enquiry. Sociology's 'methodological nationalism' is the subject of an ongoing debate—see for example, the work of Beck (2006) on the one hand, and Chernilo (2006) on the other. In relation to EU studies, it is a charge that has long been laid at the door of sociology (see Rumford, 2002, especially Chapter 1).

However, we need to be sensitive to the difference between studying Europe and studying the EU and its project of integration. It is clear that sociologists overwhelmingly choose to study the former rather than the latter. There are many sociological studies of European migration, new citizenship forms, transnational social movements, new media and the public sphere, ethnicity, people trafficking, identity politics, and so on. As such, it is not Europe that sociologists are neglecting but integration, narrowly conceived, and this may not in fact be a product of 'methodological nationalism'. Favell assumes that the absence of integration studies is a bad thing for sociology. However, it is not necessarily the case that sociologists are insufficiently committed to studying pan-European processes of institutionalization. Rather, the different focus found in sociology may be the result of the fact that the integration studies agenda has always been external to it, in the sense that it has been generated within and dominated by the disciplines of political science and international relations. Whether by accident or design, the different focus that distinguishes sociological studies of Europe from integration studies can be perceived as a strength rather than a weakness.

Favell draws a rather strict division of labour between sociology (especially 'empirical sociology', of which he approves) and social theory approaches (of which he does not). "For all the theoretical talk among social theorists about transnational or global processes, very few of them have applied these ideas to European integration" (Favell, 2007, 122). But the work of social theorists has contributed greatly to thinking about *how* we should study integration and how to contextualise integration within broader understandings of contemporary change (e.g., Balibar, 2004a; Castells, 2000; Meyer, 2001; Therborn, 1995; Delanty and Rumford, 2005; Persson and Strath, 2007). Favell bemoans the fact that it is "very difficult to systematically study pan- or transnational social structures, because of the way nation-states have carved up the world and its populations, statistically speaking" (Favell, 2007, 122). But it is precisely because social theorists have engaged in the "theoretical talk about transnational or global processes" which Favell disparages, that they have been able to find ways to transcend the 'statistical nationalism' of official databases and the forms of sociological analysis which depend on them. If we were limited to only studying phenomenon for which statistics and official data exist then there would be few studies of the European public sphere, identity politics, and cultural citizenship, for example. Indeed, there would be precious few concepts to work with at all, and ideas such as civil society, cosmopolitanism, and Europeanization, which are widely recognised as an essential part of the European studies landscape, would not be available to scholars of contemporary Europe. It is social theory rather than empirical sociology which has furnished the study of contemporary Europe with many of its key concepts, and it is social theory that has deployed these concepts in such a way as to make them relevant to the study of contemporary Europe.

It is clear that there is a big and important discussion to be had about what it is we should be studying when we study Europe. For Favell, a sociology of the EU should be able to compete on the same terrain as political science and international relations, disciplines that have made EU studies their own by studying integration and the institutional capacity of the EU. He believes that "practising sociologists need to get involved and be present in EU studies debates" (Favell, 2007, 128). Amongst other activities, sociologists should aspire to feature more regularly among the participants at academic conferences which address political aspects of the EU. But there are other Europes to be studied. There are good reasons for sociologists to follow social theorists in studying the broader transformations of Europe, or a Europe not reduced to questions of EU integration (Delanty and Rumford, 2005). There is a substantial social theory platform on which to build: Castells' interpretation of the EU as a network state; Beck and Grande's perspectives on 'cosmopolitan Europe'; Outhwaite and Ray's work on 'postcommunist Europe'; Delanty's idea of postwestern Europe. All advance themes which are important in the study of contemporary Europe, vitally important if we are to understand the social dynamics of the continent and its global dimensions, but which are rendered much less significant by a preoccupation with integration and institutional polity-building.

RETHINKING THE EU

There is an enormous amount of literature published on the subject of contemporary Europe, thousands of new books written annually to add to the tens of thousand that already exist, and a growing number of journals devoted to every aspect of European politics, society, history, and culture. The vast majority of this literature takes as its subject the European Union or 'European integration' and in doing so filters our thinking about Europe through an EU frame of reference. It is clear that, in the opinion of most academic commentators, the important developments in Europe are those associated with 'integration'.

It is for this reason that we need to 'rethink Europe' (Delanty and Rumford, 2005). We need to question the assumption that Europe is being created by the EU's self-styled project of integration and question the assumption that Europe and the EU are one and the same. More importantly perhaps, we need to think again about what it is we should be studying when we choose to study Europe. There is a big difference, I believe, between studying 'integration' and studying Europeanization, for example. Integration presumes a purposive form of institutionalization leading to a Euro-polity, the broad outlines of which are clear even if the details are contested, as are the benefits that the project brings to its nation-state partners. Integration studies also presume that EU integration is inherently a good thing and any deviation from the path of 'ever closer union' (e.g., failure to ratify the Constitutional Treaty) will be rectified in the long run. The implicit teleology in such accounts of EU-building reveals a 'narrative of cohesion' (Rumford, 2000a) within which any contradictory or contested developments in the European Union are rendered intelligible as part of an overall project of polity-construction. Europeanization, on the other hand, points to wider horizons of transformation, to an emphasis on the nonbounded nature of European society, and a constitutive link between Europe and the world. Put simply, we need to 'rethink Europe' because thinking Europe in terms of integration is not enough. It is intellectually limiting, unambitious, and distorts the field. Moreover, looking for evidence of 'European integration' detracts attention from some of the most interesting features of Europe today: unpredictable cultural dynamics, contestations over meaning and identity, disintegrative and fragmentary political trends, and the existence of multiple perspectives on the important issues of the day.

As sociologists we need to draw a distinction between political science and international relations approaches to studying Europe, which we must acknowledge have become the mainstream 'integration' studies, and a more social theory-inspired approach to looking at European transformations and, in doing so, provide a new context for studying the EU and a renewed sense of purpose in studying contemporary Europe.

WHAT IS THE EU?

The article by Boracz and Sarkar (2005) entitled "What is the EU?" is an example of one such possible approach. The article utilizes ideas from very different literatures—globalization, post-colonial studies, and world systems theory—to explore the question of what sort of entity the EU is and, in doing so, sidesteps most of the baggage over which many scholars of the EU eventually stumble. In the early part of the article, the authors do concern themselves with the conventional question of what sort of state the EU might represent, concluding that it is actually "beyond the constraints of the current theoretical language of statehood" (Borocz and Sarkar, 2005). (For an alternative reading, see Delanty and Rumford [2005], especially Chapter 8, "The European Union as a non-state".)

The most original contribution of Borocz and Sarkar's article is made when they begin to situate the EU within a global context. They offer the valuable reminder that many European nation-states are the inheritors of imperial legacies: They are, "the same states that had exercised imperial rule over half the inhabitable surface of the globe outside Europe just two to three generations ago" (Borocz and Sarkar, 2005, 162). The history of colonialism continues to exercise its influence on both Europe and the rest of the world, but this history tends to be excluded from the EU's self image, emerging only in discussions of the flows of peoples into the EU from former colonies (see also Bhambra, 2008). "If the former colonial ties are, clearly, relevant to immigration policy, they must be relevant to all other areas as well—most significantly, perhaps, to the question of what the EU is" (Borocz and Sarkar, 2005, 164).

The upshot of this 'burying' of colonial history is that the EU can remain 'clean' of a direct association with an imperial legacy, just as it can distance itself from other aspects of coercion "by contracting out the burden of strategic defence to NATO, and passing on the 'dirty work' of economic transformation in the former countries of eastern Europe to the 'political elites of those societies'" (Borocz and Sarkar, 2005, 166). The EU's distance from "neo-colonial linkages to the third world" should not mask the fact that these colonial roots "continue to subsidize the EU's accumulation process without the EU ever having to get involved in the messy business of the social and environmental violence associated with the extraction of surplus" (Borocz and Sarkar, 2005, 167). The EU likes to see itself as the 'epitome of goodness' and a force for positive political change in the world but in "promoting the ideology of 'European goodness', the political process of identity construction tries to hide the corpse of colonialism while it continues, of course, to partake of the material inheritance of the same colonialism" (Borocz and Sarkar, 2005, 167).

These themes are also enunciated in John W. Meyer's (2001) idea that "Europe is filled with Otherhood", by which he means that Europe's self-identity is based on a belief in rationalism, liberalism, and reasonableness, fuelled by a recent European past which has engendered interdependence and cooperation. *Otherhood* suggests a preoccupation with seeking the universal good rather than narrow self interest and a commitment to progress, rational organization, and human rights *for all*, not just Europeans. According to Meyer (2001), "Europe is all Otherhood and no action". In other words, Europe wants to be seen to embody goodness and does not want to get 'dirty hands' in its dealing with other parts of the world. The Otherhood claimed by the EU is at odds with the colonial legacies of its member states. It also sits rather uncomfortably alongside the fact that the EU works hard (or enlists others to work on its behalf) to forcibly exclude non-Europeans from its borders. As Balibar points out, EU borders are aimed at the 'global poor' who "need to be systematically triaged and regulated at points of entry to the wealthiest territories. Borders have thus become essential institutions in the constitution of social conditions on a global scale" (Balibar, 2004b, 113), leading to a form of 'global apartheid'.

The contribution of Borocz and Sarkar is notable for three reasons. First, it poses the familiar question of what sort of entity the EU might be in unfamiliar terms. Whereas most attempts to address this question would proceed along the lines of thinking about the EU in terms of *some* kind of state, Borocz and Sarkar focus on how it is able to operate in the way it does while distancing itself from the normal state trappings. Even though they fail to disentangle their investigation into what the EU might be from more conventional attempts at state-spotting, they manage to invest this pursuit with fresh impetus, and crucially find it unsatisfactory to resolve the question 'What is the EU?' in statist terms. Second, they bring into focus the foundational violence upon which the EU was constructed and continues to be maintained. European national states continue to conduct wars, and continue to divide the world into us and them, 'haves' and 'have nots'. These divisions are to a large extent constructed on a world order whose basic pattern was consolidated in the age of imperialism. Bhambra (2008) makes the point that viewing the genesis of the EU solely in terms of preventing future war on the continent is rather naïve. She writes, the "representation of an inclusive Europe, formed around a project of peace, effaces the history of domination in the past, as well as exclusions (of both territories and citizens) in the present".

Third, Borocz and Sarkar approach the question of the EU without feeling the need to justify why they choose not to address the conventional EU studies agenda. They construct their argument from their reading of critical literatures which are not generally considered to speak directly to understanding the EU. In doing so, they shift the question of what the EU is onto an intellectual terrain informed not by political science but by social theory. They have taken a different route into EU studies from the one advocated by Favell: They have chosen to initiate their own EU studies debate rather than take part in the one founded by other academic disciplines, and in doing so they affirm that sociology can generate its own agenda for studying the EU. Furthermore, they remind us that a sociology of the EU can benefit from a range of existing social theory literature which has generated a vibrant research agenda for the study of the social and political transformation of Europe. In the next section of this chapter I outline ways in which sociological studies of the EU can productively work alongside social theory-inspired attempts to map the broader contours of Europe.

TOWARDS A SOCIAL THEORY OF EUROPEAN TRANSFORMATIONS

In the novel *Measuring the World*, Daniel Kehlmann (Kehlmann, 2007) narrates the interlinked stories of two great nineteenth century German scientists, Alexander von Humboldt and Carl Freidrich Gauss. Humboldt is a natural scientist, an aristocratic explorer and adventurer who travels the globe in order to conduct experiments, collect specimens of exotic creatures, and to measure the dimensions of the world he 'discovers'; mountains, rivers, jungles. In doing so he becomes one of the great intellectual celebrities of his day. Gauss is a mathematician and physicist of Newtonian stature, but because of his humble background and reluctance to travel beyond his immediate province he remains little known outside the scientific community. The high profile nature of his work means that Humboldt's findings are disseminated widely. However, it is Gauss who makes the more significant contribution to science—understanding the nature of the universe from his desk, so to speak—while some of Humboldt's findings are shown to be 'wrong' and his enduring contribution to natural science diminishes as a consequence. The achievements of Gauss reminds us that it is possible to 'measure the world' in different ways. Empirical observation and recording of findings is one way, another is to theorize the properties and dynamics of a universe, most of which is unobservable and not amenable to direct measurement.

Without stretching matters too far, it might be possible to draw an analogy with contemporary debates on the merits of empirical sociology versus social theory contributions to understanding Europe. There are those, travelling in the wake of Humboldt, who wish to discover new facts about Europe, measure the degree of integration, map the new Europe, find its edges, and determine its mass. There are others who believe that 'Europe' is too large and too complicated to map in a conventional way, and the transformations which are currently taking place are of a nature that cannot be fully comprehended by 'normal social science'. When scholars talk about *postwesternization* or *cosmopolitanization* they are suggesting not that these shifts need to be observed, recorded, and classified by correctly calibrated social scientific instruments, but that there are processes at work which are transformative in nature, bear on our everyday lives, but for which we have an inadequate conceptual toolbox. In short, that we need to have adequate ways of thinking about a world which would otherwise escape comprehension. It is for these reasons that we need social theory approaches to Europe; empirical social science will not reveal the full dimensions of European transformations, nor the scope of Europe's integration with the rest of the world.

The debate between social theory and more conventional sociological studies of Europe do not take place within EU integration studies which, as we have seen, is still dominated by the institutional agenda favoured by the disciplines of political science and international relations. To the extent that they take place at all, they do so within the discipline of sociology, between those wedded to empiricism and those advancing social theory explanations. This helps explain why they do not impact more forcibly on EU studies. In a recent contribution, Guiraudon and Favell (2007) wish to stem the tide of social theory approaches to studying Europe. They argue for an empirical sociology of integration, believing that examining the "social bases of European integration" would place "the biggest sociological question of all" within the mainstream of EU studies (Guiraudon and Favell, 2007, 4). They are concerned that European sociology in general and the sociological work on the EU in particular, is being dominated by social theory: "sociology in Europe is not dominated by empiricists but by social theorists" (Guiraudon and Favell, 2007, 4). They see as 'regretful' the identification of sociology with debates in social theory which, in their view, does not aid the development of an empirical sociology of European integration. The complaint which they lay at the door of social theory is formulated as follows (Guiraudon and Favell, 2007, 5–6):

> It is quite remarkable how little all the grand talk of contemporary social theory—about transnationalism, cosmopolitanism, mobilities, hybridity, identities, public spheres, governmentality, risk societies, modernity, postmodernity, reflexive modernization, or whatever—has to offer to studying contemporary Europe or the EU in empirical terms that have anything in common with how mainstream EU scholars approach the field.

There are several points that could and should be made in response. One is that the 'grand talk' is not as removed from empirical studies as they believe, as evidenced by the Foucault-inspired governmentality studies of William Walters, for example the book *Governing Europe: Discourse, Governmetality and European Integration* (Walters and Haahr, 2005), and also Jensen and Richardson's *Making European Space: Mobility, Power and Territorial Identity* (Jensen and Richardson, 2003). From a different theoretical perspective, the analysis of postcommunist change in Eastern Europe advanced by Outhwaite and Ray (2005) in *Social Theory and Postcommunism* deserves a mention. Another is that it makes no sense to lump together the 'grand talk of contemporary social theory' as if it were a coherent school of thought. Castells' work on network Europe does not fit seamlessly alongside Meyer's cultural globalization approach to Europe's Otherness, or Beck's work on the cosmopolitanization of Europe. Social theory approaches have given rise to a disparate body of work which shares few common reference points. This is born out by the enormous variety of recent work on topics such as mobilities, hybridity, governmentality, risk society, the public sphere, post-national citizenship, Europeanization, and borderlands, for example. However, the main criticism of Guiraudon and Favell would be that, in their desire to fit into the mainstream of EU studies, they rather miss the point that social theory approaches, on the whole, choose to study European transformations rather than EU integration. In other words, whereas Guiraudon and Favell advance a political sociology of EU integration, social theorists turn their conceptual lens on a broader set of questions occasioned by European transformations, of which the integration process is but a part.

HOW NOT TO DO EU STUDIES

Jean Monnet is reputed to have said, when reflecting upon the creation of the original European communities, "If I could start again I would start with culture". In the same spirit, if we were starting EU studies again would it be better to start with culture? Better still, I think, would be to begin with society, but either culture or society would definitely be an improvement on institutional integration. But what prevents us from starting again? Why can't we rethink European studies (Rumford, 2008a)? There are two good reasons why sociology should not feel obliged to adopt the existing EU studies agenda. The first is that there is evidence to suggest that EU studies scholars are becoming frustrated with the rather narrow institutional focus on integration, and this in large part explains the shifts within EU studies towards structures of governance, processes of Europeanization, and an enthusiasm for constructivist approaches (see Favell, 2007). All of these shifts suggest that irrespective of whether or not sociology chooses to embrace the EU studies agenda it has already taken a more sociological turn. Ironically this may make it more, not less, difficult for sociology to enter the field of EU studies on its own terms: Presumptions about what sociology can contribute to the study of the EU may become an unhelpful constraint on new directions of study. This point should not be underestimated.

The second good reason why sociology should not feel obliged to adopt the EU studies agenda is that the strengths of sociology lie in European rather than EU studies, and there is considerable potential in developing lines of enquiry opened up by recent work on citizenship, networks, mobilities, identities, and so on. This is a productive agenda which sociology shares with some lines of enquiry coming out of geography, planning studies, anthropology, and cultural studies, for example, but which overlaps less with the preoccupations of mainstream EU studies. The issue for sociology is not how best to embrace EU studies but to become aware 'how not to do EU studies'. Only in this way can sociologists decide on the most productive lines of enquiry in the study of contemporary Europe.

There are parallels between the situation sociologists find themselves in and developments within the field of European historical studies, where the EU studies/European studies division is reproduced. There are historians of European integration whose work is dedicated to understanding the origins and development of the EU's institutions, the motivations of its founding fathers, and the key turning points which shaped the process of integration (Dinan, 2004; Milward, 1993; Gillingham, 2003). The work of these historians is annexed to the integration literature. Commentators on the development of the single market, institution building, and the development of public policy domains rely upon the histories written by Dinan, Milward, and Gillingham because their field is EU history. At the same time there are many historians of modern Europe, many of them eminent in their field, whose work rarely, if ever, gets referred to by EU studies scholars, even though the work of these historians covers the same historical period and geographical scope, and they even devote chapters to the history of European integration. However, the work of Norman Davis, Tony Judt, and Harold James, to name but three, rarely gets a mention in political science accounts of European integration. See for yourself. Pick up an EU studies textbook and check the index and the bibliography; it is likely that you will find Milward but not Davis, Dinan but not Judt, Gillingham but not James.

When we read modern European history we have a choice. Either we want historical accounts which range across both Eastern and Western Europe, examine the processes that shaped the politics and society of the continent, and explore the unresolved tensions that 50 years of 'integration' have produced, or we are happy to work with more solipsistic accounts of how the EU made itself and/or 'rescued the nation-state'. The resources for reinventing European Studies are rich and abundant. Similarly, sociologists need to decide whether they want to be able to study the impact of globalization on Europe, the role of mobilities in creating European identity, the development and consequences of European borderlands, or whether they are content to chart the rise of institutions of multilevel governance, debate the power of the Court of Justice, and measure the 'deficit deficit'.

To be "in with the 'in' crowd" or else languish in relative obscurity is of course not such an attractive choice. Thankfully, we are not faced with only these two options: a sociology of the EU or a social theory of Europe. There is no reason why the two cannot coexist and enrich each other. Another reason why we are not so constrained is that the study of both Europe and the EU are in any case multidisciplinary affairs. This is particularly important when we give consideration to the 'spatial turn' which has helped reorient the social sciences in recent years, and has enhanced the study of Europe in many ways.

THINKING ABOUT EUROPEAN SPACES

The shift from EU studies to European studies, from political science to social theory-inspired interpretations, argued for in the previous sections is by itself not enough. What is needed is not just a refocusing of attention from the EU to Europe: If we are not expected to treat the EU as a 'given' why should we treat Europe as unproblematic, when it may well be a much more arbitrary and shadowy formulation? What is needed at this juncture is to introduce the idea of space, and in particular a perspective on why thinking about space is important when thinking about contemporary Europe. It is argued here that a focus on the relationship between spaces, borders, and governance is one way in which social theory-inspired approaches can take us beyond the limited and limiting agenda imposed by EU studies which still tends to distil discussion of spatiality into a question of multiple levels of governance (local, national, supranational). The

EU is then seen to organize existing spaces differently—through networks, mobilities, and governance structures—rather than creating new types of political spaces. Thus, the question of the spatiality of Europe is turned into a non-question: European space is but a reorganization of pre-existing national spaces. However, this is by no means the only way that space can be viewed, and a there exists a rich and informative literature which addresses and attempts to understand the dynamics of Europe's transformed spatiality. The starting point is the idea that space is neither unproblematic nor simply the back-drop against which Europeanization is played out. Too many approaches in EU studies treat "spatiality as no more than a descriptive category, explaining nothing about social processes" (Axford, 2007, 325). On the contrary, space is constitutive of social relations and political processes. Europe's spaces are undergoing profound transformation and they are impossible to account for using standard EU studies' models. The problem is that EU studies have embraced the governance turn, but largely ignored the spatial turn. What is needed then is a more sophisticated understanding of Europe's spatiality—its transborder regions, its polycentric organization, its networked mobilities, its borderlands.

Europe no longer (if it ever did) comprises only nation-states, or even subnational regions, aggregated together in a common project. In contemporary Europe, pan-European spaces coexist with national territories, borderlands soften the sharp outer edges of the EU, and networks are indifferent to borders as they connect Europeans to each other and to the wider world. Borders have undergone dramatic changes, not only in terms of their extent and range: Enlargement has massively lengthened the EU's borders and projected them beyond the former Iron Curtain. On some accounts, Europe has been 'rebordered' (Andreas, 2000); the external borders of the EU protect a borderless single market within which internal space mobility is greatly enhanced. On other accounts, borders are themselves networked, mobile, and diffused throughout society (Balibar, 1998; Rumford, 2007b). These changes have also impacted upon structures of pan-European governance which combine the management of genuinely European spaces and Commission-sponsored Euro-regions with more traditional levels of national governance. These shifts point to important transformations in the relationship between European spaces, borders, and governance. The spaces of European governance—and particularly the relationship between spaces, borders, and governance—have never been so complex, nor in need of thorough academic reappraisal.

The spatial novelty of Europe, and attempts to apprehend and understand this novelty, can also be seen very clearly in the terms and concepts with which contemporary Europe is described and analysed. In the past few years, a whole new lexicon of spatial politics has been incorporated into EU studies: polycentricity (multiple centres encouraging diffused growth rather than core-periphery distinctions); 'network Europe' (an EU characterised by connectivity and mobility); territorial cohesion (the balanced distribution of economic activities across the Union); multi-level governance (partnerships between EU institutions, national governments, and regional and local authorities); borderlands (zones of interaction between countries rather than 'hard' frontiers); Europe-as-empire (the non-state-like organization of the EU comprising an internal 'variable geometry' and flexible, expanding frontiers). The brief mention of these terms and concepts makes it clear that spatiality is an increasingly important dimension of the study of contemporary Europe. By the same token, there has been a reordering of Europe's spatial hierarchies leading to the competitive role of regions and cities being enhanced vis-à-vis that of the national state, and a 're-scaling of space' (Brenner, 2004) wherein cities and regions become networked within pan-European space and transborder networks assume a greater importance. In addition, European borders (nicely captured by the idea of 'borderlands') are deemed to have their own spatiality and, as such, require their own regimes of governance. In short, the new spaces of European governance are intimately related to the processes of bordering and rebordering, often associated with securitization, that have proceeded alongside the processes leading to a removal of the internal (national) borders which for so long prevented the emergence of a genuine European space.

THE 'SPATIAL TURN' IN EU STUDIES

The 'governance turn' in EU studies is well documented (e.g., Marks, Scharpf, Schmitter, and Streek, 1996; Jachtenfuchs and Kohler-Koch, 2003, Bache and Flinders, 2005) but has largely ignored the transformation of space that this entails; the governance turn cannot be blind to the 'spatial turn' (Berezin, 2003). Space is much more important, and much more complex, in understanding the EU than suggested by either the idea of multilevel governance or networked polity. Rather than being primarily concerned with state-building or the institutionalization of governance structures, the EU is centrally concerned with the construction of European spaces. Put simply, the EU actively constructs European spaces which it alone is capable of governing. Stated in different terms, the EU works to create new policy networks and governance spaces within which it can deploy European solutions to European problems (see Delanty and Rumford, 2005, especially Chapter 8).

The recent EU studies agenda, highlighting such processes as Europeanization, rebordering and securitization, network Europe, and polity-building has latterly responded to the 'spatial turn' by exploring the processes by which governance spaces are constructed and the way space is constitutive of social and political relations. Not surprisingly, this concern with European spaces has not emerged from within the conventional EU studies literature generated by the academic disciplines of political science and international relations. Exploration of the spatiality of European governance has a multidisciplinary provenance, the acknowledgment of which points to some interesting general shifts in the way the EU is being studied. One of these is the recognition that, in order to understand the dynamics of contemporary European transformation, EU studies must encourage a greater diversity of (theoretical) perspectives (Bourne and Cini, 2006). Another is the recognition that developments in Europe are best studied within a global framework, thereby ameliorating the more solipsistic readings of the EU as the sole author of European developments. Third, and most important in the context of the present discussion, is the increasing awareness amongst scholars of the EU that Europe's new spaces are being studied productively in other social science disciplines.

The key publications exploring the spatial dynamics of Europe have not emerged from within conventional EU studies and the emerging agenda has been largely shaped by the contributions from the fields of geography, sociology, urban studies, anthropology, and spatial planning. A good example of a publication which draws upon many of these disciplines is Berezin and Schain's (2003) edited volume *Europe Without Borders: Remapping Territory, Citizenship and Identity in a Transnational Age*. This volume is paradigmatic of the 'spatial turn' and addresses many central themes: the supercession of territoriality, the changing role of borders, the transnational foundations of Europe, cosmopolitanism. In addition, it focuses on the societal dimensions of integration (as reflected in the subtitle), the public sphere, national/European identity, and transnational networks. Even so, the book can be criticised for taking a rather conservative approach to the question of Europe space, interpreting the spatial recalibration of Europe as a reorganization of existing spaces.

More radical is Neil Brenner's (2004) *New State Spaces: Urban Governance and the Rescaling of Statehood*. Brenner offers an account of the 'post-national' spaces of European governance, particularly the way states now mobilize urban space to develop a competitive advantage in the global capitalist economy, thereby accounting for the relation between supranationalism and the resurgence of urban and regional economies in a globalizing Europe. From a different perspective, Jensen and Richardson's (2003) *Making European Space* critically examines EU attempts to construct a single European space, or what they term a 'monotopia.' The Single Market and single currency are examples of a concerted attempt to create Europe as 'one space' made possible by networks of mobility. In the terms employed by Castells, the EU has, through enhanced mobility and connectivity, attempted to construct a Europe of global competitive flows to replace of a Europe of territorial places (Rumford, 2004). These interventions have been complemented by a range of other texts which are all centrality concerned with Europe's novel spatiality. Donald McNeill's (2004) *New Europe: Imagined Spaces*, Novoa and Lawn's (2002) *Fabricating Europe: the Formation of an Educational Space*, and Walters and Haahr's *Governing Europe: Discourse, Governmentality and European Integration* (Walters and Haahr,

2005) all examine the ways in which the EU has constructed European spaces as a technique of governance.

EUROPE'S NOVEL SPATIALITY

To further the case for a social theory of Europe, and the way that social theory approaches offer a better understanding of spatiality, it will be instructive to look at three attempts to apprehend the novelty of European space: the EU as a monotopia, borderlands, and polycentric development.

As Jensen and Richardson (2003) point out, the EU conceives of itself as a 'monotopia', a single, common space within which all constraints to the movement of goods, peoples, services, and money have been removed. The EU as a realm of freedom and mobility means that Europe is increasingly interconnected and its various component parts (member states, subnational regions) are seamlessly woven together. The monotopic vision is central to the EU's governance of European space:

> this idea of monotopic Europe lies at the heart of new ways of looking at European territory . . . a rationality of monotopia exists, and it is inextricably linked with a governmentality of Europe, expressed in a will to order space, to create a seamless and integrated space . . . which is being pursued through the emerging field of European spatial policy. (Jensen and Richardson, 2003, 3)

The EU's view of Europe as a monotopia is rather optimistic (Delanty and Rumford, 2005, Chapter 7). It fails to acknowledge that European space is dynamic and changing; the EU added ten more members in 2004 and then two more in 2007, and this massive addition of European space and its degree of connectivity and integration is variable at best. Future enlargements will further test the monotopic 'smoothness' of the EU's internal space. Also, the image of Europe as a monotopia conveniently ignores the fact that European space is not contiguous: non-EU countries are embedded within 'European space' (Switzerland, the Russian enclave of Kaliningrad, for example), and both France and Spain posses territories which are not actually in Europe (but in Africa and South America).

The idea of the EU as a monotopia also leads to some rather simplistic ideas about Europe's borders, particularly the assumption that they can be easily superseded by mobility and connectivity. However, it does encourage us to confront the flexibility of borders, their increasingly differentiated and partial nature, and the degree to which they can work to connect as well as divide (Rumford, 2006a). On the latter point, and aligned with the idea that EU borders are constantly shifting, what were previously borders between the EU 15 and the candidate countries of Central and Eastern Europe are now, following accession, part of EU space. In the same way, current EU borders with Turkey and Croatia can be thought of as potential EU space, a space which is already in the process of formation as a result of extensive economic, educational, and communication networks (such as Trans-European road and rail networks and educational mobilities) which traverse those countries, and existing regional and trans-border programmes which are designed to ameliorate problems associated with marginality. Today's external borders represent tomorrow's internal spaces.

The idea that the EU has 'borderlands' at its furthest reaches (especially in the East) has become popular in recent times, in no small part the result of EU attempts to construct a 'new neighbourhood' policy and develop a 'ring of friends' with those countries to the east and south who are unlikely to ever become candidates for formal accession talks.[1] (Lavenex, 2004; Rumford, 2006b; Scott, 2005). The EU has become aware that the imposition of 'hard' borders at the outer perimeter of the EU is likely to create problems for both those EU countries on the periphery (increased insecurity beyond the border) as well as neighbours who find themselves on the other side (economic disadvantage, curtailment of historical patterns of local trade, movement of people etc.). The EU seeks to ameliorate these problems by 'softening' the more abrasive edges of its external borders by, for example, increasing networking opportunities with non-members and allowing for localized and routine cross-border traffic (circuits of local trade etc.). The development of this new neighbourhood policy is seen as a very positive foreign policy tool by the EU and offering access to EU markets and other networking opportunities is viewed as a means of encouraging democratization and the restructuring of economies according to the EU's market principles. In relation to theorizing the spatiality of Europe the idea of borderlands is an important one because it signals the spatiality of borders themselves; no longer simply lines on a map or a physical frontier between nation-states, borders have their own space and have become zones of exchange, connectivity, and security (Barry, 2006). Borderlands should not be though of as simply a development at Europe's borders. Extending the point that borders have become dispersed throughout society Balibar argues that Europe itself can be thought of as a borderland, a zone of transition and mobility without territorial fixity (Balibar, 2004a, see also Chapter 3).

The notion of polycentricity has become a useful way of thinking about the decentred, deterritorialized, and dynamic nature of Europe. The term polycentricity has a much wider applicability to political and societal transformations under conditions of globalization (Scholte, 2004; Delanty and Rumford, 2007). Polycentricity refers to forms of non-territorial politics which emanate from a multiplicity of sites and which cannot be reduced to a single centre. On this reading, the EU is not a superstate or suprastate, or even a form of multilevel governance, but a more decentred (or multicentred) spatial arrangement. For example, the EU is deemed to have a polycentric capital city structure (Hein, 2006) with different functions being carried out in different 'centres': Brussels, Strasburg, Luxembourg,

Warsaw. The idea of polycentricity has also been important in moving away from the idea that the EU has been unsuccessful in preventing the exacerbation of a core-periphery pattern of disadvantage and unbalanced growth (Rumford, 2002, Chapter 7). The EU now encourages polycentric development, with a large number of centres of growth within Europe, and indeed with individual member states, in tandem with aiming for greater territorial cohesion. In this sense, the idea of polycenticity has a clear connection with the self-image of the EU as a monotopia, discussed earlier. In relation to theorizing borders, the spatial notion of polycentricity points us in the direction of the shifting borders of economic governance, borders that are being rescaled away from the traditional 'levels' found within the national state and towards the European city, the assumed centre of growth and site of the accommodation of the global. Urban growth, cast in terms of the desirability of polycentric development is the main consequence of the rescaling of the state (Brenner, 2004). Brenner advances the argument that spatial Keynsianism (dominant until the mid-80s) has given way to more entrepreneurial forms of governance, focused on urban growth centres and aimed at building the global competitive advantage of European city regions. The post-Keynesian competition state has responded to the challenges of globalization and Europeanization by working to enhance the "supranational territorial competitiveness of major cities and city-regions" (Brenner, 2004, 259). The idea of polycentric development can be thought of as an attempt to reconcile the contradictory goals of increasing competitiveness at the same time as securing greater social and economic cohesion (Atkinson, 2001; Brenner, 2003; Rumford, 2000a).

CONCLUDING COMMENTS

Europe's transformed spatiality is becoming a key theme in contemporary European studies. This shift in focus is the product of greater multidisciplinarity and the result of EU scholars coming into contact with a range of literature from a broader field of European studies which was hitherto seen as peripheral: planning, anthropology, geography, education, sociology, cultural studies. The most significant developments to emerge from this multidisciplinary exchange are twofold. First, there is the recognition that distinctly European spaces are emerging, but that the properties, dynamics, and potential of these spaces are not sufficiently understood. The corollary of this is that these European spaces cannot be reduced to the interconnectivity of previously existing places or agglomerations of member-state space. Second is the idea that the EU represents a complex configuration of spaces and borders which have created the need for unique forms of spatial governance. EU governance works by constructing European spaces which the EU alone is capable of managing. In other words, EU governance is concerned with the construction and management of European spaces, borders, and networks, as distinct from the territorial places and spaces characteristic of the nation-state.

European spaces—that is to say, spaces that are genuinely European rather than aggregations of nation-states—are synonymous with EU integration. The most familiar European spaces, for example the Single Market, Euroland, a European education space, are all spaces organized by the EU. But there is another dimension to European spaces not captured by the EU's narrative of integration. Put simply, European spaces do not map neatly onto the space of the EU. There is not always a good fit between the European spaces constructed by processes of integration and the EU to which they belong. For example, Europeanized spaces such as the Single Market, Euroland, or Schengenland, in addition to promoting the idea of deeper EU integration, also make us aware of the incomplete nature of this processes (the Single Market extends beyond the borders of the EU; not all EU members share the single currency; not all EU members comprise Schengenland, which also incorporates non-EU countries). Similarly, the idea of network Europe suggests both dynamic processes of pan-European connectivity, and, at the same time allows for the possibility of breaking down barriers between Europe and the rest of the world, and blurring the distinction between Europe and beyond, between EU and non-EU space.

This chapter has promoted a social theory-inspired study of European transformations in preference to a sociology of integration. Not only is it more valuable to study Europe in its totality rather than develop a narrow focus on the EU and its institutions, it is further argued that it is only work deriving from the concerns associated with social theory that can adequately conceptualize the changing spatiality which is at the heart of European transformations. These arguments rest on the idea that the conceptual innovation and breadth of vision which the study of contemporary Europe requires cannot emerge from within a sociology of the EU which slavishly adheres to an intellectual agenda composed by researchers in other disciplines. To have any purchase on the study of Europe or the EU sociology must develop its own European studies agenda and it can best do this by drawing upon two key resources. One is the research agendas promoted by social theorists who can demonstrate both a long-standing interest in the transformation of Europe and a track record of theoretical innovation in conceptualizing change. For evidence of this, one needs only to look at the contents page of almost any issue of the *European Journal of Social Theory* published in the past decade. The other is the existing strengths of sociology in researching key elements of EU policy, transnational politics, and the cultural dimensions of the European project. Rather than viewing these as adjuncts to the biggest questions in the integration puzzle, sociologists should be more assertive in suggesting the impossibility of understanding Europe and/or the EU without first coming to terms with post-national citizenship, transnational social movements, the formation of European publics, and the cultural dynamics of post-secularism.

3 The Borders and Borderlands of Europe
A Critique of Balibar

Among the key themes in studies of the transformation of contemporary Europe are questions of identity and belonging, the meaning of transnational citizenship, the democractic deficit of the EU, and the need to understand the new spaces of Europe and the processes of bordering associated with them. Each of these themes has generated a huge literature. The work of Etienne Balibar is distinctive in that he links all of these themes (and more besides) within a cogent account of Europe's transformations. His work is also notable for the priority he accords borders in the study of democracy, citizenship, and the question of European identity (Outhwaite, 2006a). Etienne Balibar is arguably the leading theorist of Europe's borders, although paradoxically his influence has not been great on 'mainstream' EU studies, or, for that matter, on border studies. This neglect[1] is rather puzzling given the numerous articles and chapters he has written on the theme of borders in Europe over the past decade or so, forming a remarkable corpus of work which deserves closer scholarly attention. It is less difficult to understand however, if one considers the inward-looking nature of EU studies and the lack of interest displayed by scholars of integration in embracing work from other disciplines such as geography, and especially sociology and social theory.

This chapter critically examines Balibar's contribution to the study of borders in Europe and, to this end, focuses on three key themes in his work. The first of these is the changing nature of borders. According to Balibar, borders are no longer where we expect to find them; they are increasingly found at multiple points within a polity, markedly so as societies become increasingly securitized. Thus, as the old borders internal to EU space have diminished in importance (at border crossings between nation-states, for example) new bordering points including those at airports, at railway stations, and along motorways have risen in importance. Banks, internet cafes, travel agencies, and supermarket checkouts can also perform border functions. Balibar's work on the diffusion of borders and their polysemic nature, allowing easy passage for some while working to exclude others, has over the past decade or so set the agenda for the social scientific study of Europe's transformed borders, but as suggested earlier, the take up of his idea across different disciplines has been somewhat uneven (Bialasiewicz and Minca, 2005, 368).

The second key theme examined here is Balibar's idea of Europe as a borderland. Balibar employs this figure both as a critique of essentialist notions of European identity—Europe is a borderland rather than an entity that has borders (Balibar, 2004a, 220)—and to draw attention to the new spatiality of Europe beyond nation-states where the relation between territory and borders is 'inverted'. It is a radical interpretation of Europe's internal transformation and also its role in the world. As a borderland Europe does not possess a clearly defined interior and exterior and as such is not separated from other parts of the world. This allows Europe to become a 'mediator' between different cultures and civilizations which can meet and interact within 'European space'.

The third key theme is the democratization of borders, which should not be taken to mean advocacy of their removal (Balibar is no believer in a borderless world). Balibar argues for the need for greater multilateral control over borders and increased reciprocity in entitlements to cross them. The democratization of borders is linked to the democratization of Europe, which can never be a true democratic space while it excludes others with such force, and practices a form of apartheid towards those who are labelled 'undesirable' and who remain shut out by Europe's securitized frontiers.

This chapter advances the argument that Balibar's work represents a signal advance in our thinking about the nature and dynamics of borders in Europe. Nevertheless, I also want to identify limitations with respect to some of Balibar's core ideas. For example, it is argued that a particular issue is that despite advancing the idea that borders are polysemic (meaning different things to different people, or having a differential effect on different groups) he believes a border will always be recognised as a border by all parties concerned. In other words, the same border may be interpreted differently but it nevertheless remains a border in every interpretation. He does not allow for the fact that borders do not always appear as borders to every individual and group who encounter them. Borders can remain invisible to the many while bordering out the few. Thus, recognising the polysemic nature of borders is not enough. It is not just that borders can represent walls to some and bridges to others. There are still other groups who see neither walls nor bridges, only a featureless landscape. This point will be expanded upon later in the chapter.

Another criticism advanced here concerns the notion of Europe as a borderland. While representing the most innovative reading of borders in relation to Europe, the idea of Europe-as-borderland also works to privilege Europe in relation to the rest of the world. Not only does Balibar's account of Europe-as-borderland give Europe an unmatched level of connectivity with other parts of the world, it also gives Europe a privileged role as mediator between civilizations. According to Balibar, Europe's lack of fixed identity offers the possibility for it to occupy a unique role in translating between different cultures, and thereby offering solutions to emerging crises in the new world order.

Finally, while Balibar's concern to link bordering process and democratization is exemplary, particularly his awareness of the problems associated with exercising democractic control over the controllers of borders (Balibar, 2002, 85) his preferred solution to the democratic deficit inherent in Europe's borders is for reciprocal mobility between peoples from different regions of the world and for greater multilateralism in the management of borders. This is a radical view of borders but at the same time a statist view of borders. It is argued that Balibar neglects the extent to which citizens (and non-citizens) are able to engage in 'borderwork', constructing, maintaining, and erasing borders. In Europe it is no longer the nation-state that is solely responsible for bordering and rebordering. The EU also performs this function and has the ability to switch the location of the important borders of Europe to a degree never dreamed of by nation-states. At the same time, a range of actors are able to engage in borderwork activities—creating new economic zones to regulate economic production, contesting the legitimacy of the borders imposed by others, becoming citizen-detectives employed in the fight against terrorism, monitoring the movement of other people within local communities—and in doing so creating new democratic (and indeed non-democratic possibilities) for the management of borders (Rumford, 2007b).[2] This particular theme is taken up again in Chapter 4 when we look at Europe's cosmopolitan borders.

THE CHANGING NATURE OF BORDERS

In his article 'What is a border?' Balibar reminds us that borders and the meanings attached to them change over time; "it is clear that the border of a European monarchy in the eighteenth century . . . has little in common with those borders the Schengen Agreement is so keen to strengthen today" (Balibar, 2002, 75). In the contemporary context borders no longer mark a strict separation between inside and outside. Borders are now internal to the state and can take the form of "*invisible borders*, situated everywhere and nowhere" (Balibar, 2002, 78).[3] In order to further understand these shifts, Balibar outlines "three major aspects of the equivocal character of borders in history"(Balibar, 2002, 78). These are (1) their overdetermination, (2) their polysemic character, and (3) their heterogeneity.

What Balibar means by overdetermination is that any border can have a significance that goes beyond its ability to mark out territory in a particular location. In this sense, local borders are also endowed with a global function. "They have always served not only to separate particularities, but always also at the same time, in order to fulfil this 'local' function, to 'partition the world' to configure it . . . Every map in this sense is always a world map, for it represents a 'part of the world'" (Balibar, 2004a, 220–21). Moreover, a national border is not always only a border between two states. Such borders can be reinforced or overlain by more significant geopolitical demarcations. The borders which separated West from East Germany or Austria from Hungary during the Cold War were both national borders and at the same time borders between the Western world and the Eastern world (and therefore between antagonistic ideological blocs, or civilizations) whose representation took the form of an 'Iron Curtain'. In the contemporary context, such overdeterminations continue to be important. The 'Green Line' separating Northern Cyprus and the Republic of Cyprus has been reinforced by a new border between the EU and non-EU member states. The border between Poland and the Ukraine now has significance greater than in previous years, marking as it does the division between EU and non-EU (and possibly the limits of EU expansion in the east). Balibar elsewhere talks about the 'Great Wall of Europe' constituted by a number of borders and bordering activities at Europe's southern periphery (Balibar, 2006). Overdetermination can either work to strengthen existing nation-state borders (as with the Cyprus example) or weaken them, as in the case of the overdetermined national borders at the (current) edges of the EU-27 being denationalized as they become replaced by the common European borders regulated by a EU agency, Frontex (Vaughan-Williams, 2008).

Balibar acknowledges that the contemporary borders of nation-states are not implicated to the same extent in geopolitical demarcations nor overdetermined by the borders of super-blocs working to partition the world. Contrary to expectations perhaps this has led to an unsettled period for nation-states and their borders. Not all nation-state borders have survived the transition to a post-Cold War world, those of Yugoslavia and Czechoslovakia, for example. Many new national borders have been created as a result of the collapse of previously overdetermined nation-state borders (those of the Soviet Union being paradigmatic), and other borders have changed significantly, for example those of Germany. The situation regarding nation-state borders will remain fluid while there exists "uncertainty regarding . . . the nature and location of the geopolitical demarcations which may overdetermine borders" (Balibar, 2002, 81). This is certainly true with respect to the possible future enlargement of the EU.

The idea that borders are overdetermined certainly does not have the same purchase in a post-national, post-Cold War Europe in which bordering processes and border crossings proliferate alongside processes of debordering and rebordering. There are two crucial developments which have resulted in the decline in importance of overdetermination. The first is that, in the Cold War world, there was a sense, shared strongly between the blocs, of what constituted the important borders of Europe. Both sides had a common interest in militarizing and securitizing the same borders. Equally, both sides had a common understanding both of what constituted an important border and the hierarchy of borders that existed to divide the world (between East and West). In contemporary Europe there is no way of knowing whether a border is important or not in anything but a provisional and/or local sense and, as Balibar shows us, borders take many forms and can be found at so many different points within a society that they are all but impossible to classify and rank. The second development follows on from this. The idea of overdetermination presupposes a world where nation-state borders are the most significant borders. The changes to the nature of borders outlined by Balibar, particularly the multiplicity of bordering points within a society, the shifting of the border 'away from the border' and the diffusion of the border through the body of the social takes us away from a concept of borders as national frontiers. One corollary of the dispersal of borders and their polysemic nature has already been noted; a border can take many forms and operate on different groups in different ways.

The idea of the 'polysemic nature' of borders is one of Balibar's most significant contributions to border studies, and speaks to some of the issues raised previously. Borders do not have the same meaning for everyone. Borders actively "differentiate between individuals in terms of social class" (Balibar, 2002, 82) and in doing so create a different experience of the border for the businessman, the academic travelling to a conference, and the itinerant agricultural or unskilled worker. States have come to operate their borders "in the service of an international class differentiation" and as "instruments of discrimination and triage" (Balibar, 2002, 82). Broadly speaking this idea has become central to our understanding of borders today (although the emphasis on borders as a mechanism for distinguishing between classes is not carried through into the border studies literature). Indeed, it is widely acknowledged that the most significant feature of borders nowadays is that they are designed to allow for the free movement of some while curtailing the mobility of others. This is thought to be especially true in respect of EU borders. In Balibar's evocative terms, for a "rich person from a rich country" the border is crossed at a "jog-trot" while for the "poor person from a poor country" the border presents an "obstacle which is very difficult to surmount" and a crossing may not be possible at all (Balibar, 2002, 83).

The idea of polysemic borders now echoes throughout the literature. That borders are increasingly discriminatory and designed to allow easy passage for some while forming a barrier to the movements of others (especially refugees, terrorists, traffickers, or simply the unwanted) has given rise to the idea of "asymmetric membranes" (Hedetoft, 2003) or "firewalls" (Walters, 2006a, 151–54), to choose the best examples. But there is still a dimension of bordering processes not captured by Balibar's term. When we say that borders have a polysemic nature we are pointing to the fact that they mean different things to different people and represent either barriers or gateways depending on who we are. Balibar's idea of the polysemic nature of borders is founded on the assumption that although a border may treat people in different ways it will still be recognised as a border by all concerned. This has much in common with his assumption about overdetermined borders: that contending groups will mutually recognise the important borders, indeed that they will have a mutual interest in consolidating and reinforcing such borders. What is different about the current situation, I would suggest, is that borders may not appear as borders to all concerned. Some borders are only apparent to those who are being bordered out; the rest of the population may remain indifferent to (or even oblivious to) the workings of a border, even one in their midst. This, I think, is what Balibar hints at (but never develops further) when he talks of "invisible borders" situated "everywhere and nowhere" (Balibar, 2002, 78). Borders can be highly selective and work so insidiously as to render them invisible to the majority of the population, for whom no border is deemed to exist. A few examples will help to illustrate these points.

There are many borders existing in our midst but about which we have no awareness unless we are the recipient and target of the bordering practice. What I am suggesting here goes beyond the familiar experience of academics passing through an airport at a 'jog-trot', to borrow Balibar's phrase, while observing other passengers being targeted for baggage checks or attracting the attention of immigration officers because of ethnic markers which work to single them out as somehow different or potentially 'dangerous' (see Chapter 5). What is different is the degree to which borders have ceased to exist for some while looming large for others, coupled with a 'democratization' of the ability to border, or engage in what I term 'borderwork' (Rumford, 2008b). There are many examples of such borders in our midst. Training shoes dangling from telegraph wires in a suburban street may signal nothing to the majority of us but to members of youth gangs they demarcate territory and warn members of other gangs to 'keep off their patch'.[4] The EU's rules governing Protected Designation of Origin allow for the construction of borders beyond which certain products such as Parma Ham, Champagne, or Newcastle Brown Ale cannot be produced. These borders are unlikely to impinge on our lives unless we are in the business of producing rival goods or choosing a location for economic activity. The transport zoning of London has created borders which can condition mobility: If you drive a car you may be discouraged from paying the £8 per day charge payable upon entering the congestion-charging zone. For pedestrians or those using public transport (or those living nowhere near the capital) these borders are of no practical concern. National borders may also share these qualities. Passing from England to Scotland may be marked by nothing more substantial than a tourist signpost and souvenir shop and does not represent a meaningful border except that it demarcates a region within which prescription charges or student fees are payable (or not). We would certainly notice the border if we fell on the wrong side of it in respect of exemption/non-exemption from such charges.

The third major aspect of the equivocal nature of borders pointed to by Balibar is the heterogeneity and ubiquity of borders, which he does not examine at great length in the chapter entitled "What is a border?", although he does so elsewhere and it is possibly the idea with which his work on borders is most commonly associated. Borders are no longer at the border; they form a grid ranging over social space. Borders are found "wherever selective controls are to be found" (Balibar, 2002, 84–85). The idea that borders are concentrated in particular places and along well-defined lines is one that should be associated with the nation-state's bordering preferences, rather than being features of borders *per se*. It was the project of the nation-state to make political, cultural, and economic borders coincide, but their ability to do this is "tending today to fall apart" (Balibar, 2002, 84) under the rubric of globalization. But globalization is not leading to a "borderless world". "Less than ever is the contemporary world a 'world without borders'. On the contrary, borders are being both multiplied and reduced in their localization and their function, they are being thinned out and doubled, becoming border zones, regions, or countries where one can reside and live. The quantitative relation between 'border' and 'territory' is being inverted" (Balibar, 1998, 220).

The dispersal and diffusion of borders in the way advanced by Balibar has become one of the key themes in studying borders in the past few years, particularly the securitization of borders that has been so evident since the events of 9/11. That borders are 'vacillating' has important ramifications. Such borders work differently on 'things' and 'people', and, to reinforce the point about the polysemic nature of borders, "they do not work *in the same way* 'equally', for all 'people', and notably not for those who come from different parts of the world" (Balibar, 2002, 91). As has already been mentioned, the ubiquity of borders outlined by Balibar is one of the signal advances in the study of borders in recent years. It also raises some interesting issues which Balibar's work does not fully address. In the same way that borders may not just mean different things to different people but may only exist for some rather than all, so too is the ubiquity of borders only evident from some perspectives but not all. In other words, the idea that borders are ubiquitous should not be taken to imply that they are perceived as ubiquitous by all concerned. Indeed, a corollary of the ideas outlined thus far by way of a critique of Balibar—that there is no consensus in respect of what constitutes an important border and not all borders exist for all people—is that the apparent ubiquity of borders is a result of a particular perspective. The thinning out and dispersal of borders will lead to the formation of borders "wherever selective controls are to be found" as Balibar put it. These controls may be so selective as to make the border appear invisible, as with the internal borders which Balibar suggests are 'everywhere and nowhere'. Borders which can take many forms and whose existence is not necessarily evident to all are impossible to map. With respect to such borders there can logically be no vantage point from which their ubiquity can be demonstrated.

As with the ideas of overdetermined and polysemic borders, the ubiquity of borders points up the tendency in Balibar's work to assume a shared and reciprocal knowledge of the existence of borders and their location within, or throughout, a polity.

EUROPE AS A BORDERLAND

It has already been noted that the 'spatial turn' in European studies has tended to prioritise the study of Europe's supposed novel spatiality at the expense of studying the relationship between spaces and borders. Balibar's work is distinctive inasmuch as it not only acknowledges the border–territory nexus, but offers an innovative advance with the idea that the "relation between 'border' and 'territory' is being inverted" (Balibar, 1998, 220). Moreover, Balibar attributes spatiality to borders themselves and in doing so moves us away from the idea that borders are 'lines in the sand' and towards an understanding which sees them as becoming diffused throughout society. Thus, borders "are no longer entirely situated at the outer limit of territories; they are dispersed a little everywhere, wherever the movement of information, people and things is happening and is controlled" (Balibar, 2004a, 1). The fullest development of the idea of the spatiality of borders (and also of the idea of the inversion between territory and border) is Balibar's notion of Europe as a borderland. The ubiquity and multiplicity of borders is not only a feature of national societies but can be identified with Europe:

> we are not living on the *edge* of a simple borderline, as . . . during the Cold War . . . Rather, we are situated increasingly in the midst of an ubiquitous and multiple border, which establishes unmediated contacts with virtually all "parts" of the world . . . (Balibar, 2004b)

Thus, Balibar not only alerts us to a radically transformed European spatial order but points in the direction of Europe-as-borderland having a privileged role in the new global order.

Balibar's ideas on borderlands emerge from an extended consideration of the relationship between political spaces and borders. In his Alexander von Humboldt Lecture at the University of Nijmegen in November 2004 (Balibar, 2004b), he outlines what he calls four "schemes of projection of the figure of Europe within the global world", in order to address different "dilemmas concerning the 'construction' of Europe *as part of the world*" (Balibar, 2004b). The four visions of Europe as a political space, or 'four patterns' as he terms them, are (1) the Clash-of-Civilizations pattern; (2) the Global Network pattern; (3) the Centre-Periphery pattern; and (4) the Cross-over pattern (Europe as a borderland). According to Balibar, these are contending and conflictual visions which are largely incompatible but are all directly linked to the representation of European borders and relations between borders, political spaces, and globalization. Balibar is critical of the first three patterns, which he points out have serious limitations, while favouring the Cross-over pattern which introduces the idea of Europe-as-borderland.

The first 'pattern' is termed 'Clash-of Civilizations', after Huntington. This involves a redrawing of civilizational borders based on religious conflict, and can lead to a situation, as in Europe, where civilizational fault lines can cut through national-states and, more importantly, Europe itself; "it is *Europe* as such which now appears as a 'fault line' or an intermediary zone of competition between rival civilizations" (Balibar, 2004b). At the same time as outlining the weaknesses of this model Balibar makes the point that it has begun to influence representation of a Euro-American divide which can be discerned in terms of differences in economic preferences and the political role of religion. This 'divide' or 'clash' has been pointed to by other writers including Kagan, for whom 'Americans are from Mars and Europeans from Venus' (Habermas and Derrida, 2003; Heins, 2005; Pieterse, 2003; and Beck, 2007a).[5] For Balibar,

> the fact that there is now a deep uncertainty as to whether Europe and America belong to a single "civilizational" *Grossraum* or they belong to separated *Grossraume* clearly enhances, and not diminishes the relevance of the *Clash-of-Civilization pattern* for many of its current supporters on both sides of the Atlantic.[6]

This uncertainty also has implications for thinking about borders. The overdetermined borders which Balibar identifies as being to integral to Cold War thinking would continue to be accorded significance in a Europe patterned according to Clash-of-Civilizations.

Balibar's second pattern is termed Global Networks. A world which is increasingly networked is less easy to represent on a map and points to the "limit of traditional representations of political spaces". He points to two antagonistic conceptions of Global Networks. The first, associated with the work of Castells and Sassen, posits global linkages of commercial and communication networks. This equates to a world of global flows which connect together nodes in a network—cities, enterprises, subnational regions—in such a way as to confound the political spaces associated with a world of nation-states. The other focuses on globalization from below and is associated with the activities of social movements and advocacy groups forming networks of 'heretogenous struggles (ecologist, feminist, urban, pacifist etc.)'. These versions of Global Networks are competing with each other to capture the political space of virtual communication and hence the resources with which to shape public debate. The internet and related technologies gives rise to the idea that "the 'virtual' has become today the 'real' of politics" (Balibar, 2004b). In relation to Europe, the pattern of

Global Networks (in both variants) is important in that the idea of Europe as a political, economic, or social reality is undermined by networks which "cross its territory, invest its cities and workplaces, but do not elect it as a permanent or specific site. Europe is not only de-territorialized, but also de-localized, put 'out of itself', and in the end deconstructed" (Balibar, 2004b).

In other words, the communicative and organizational networks which have the potential to reconfigure political space at the global level are also very capable of eroding the territorialized spaces within which policy choices and political action have traditionally been played out. The idea of 'network Europe', beloved of the Prodi Commission and many political commentators can constitute a vision of Europe appropriate to the 'global age' but represents a threat to Europe as a meaningful and coherent actor in the world.

The third pattern is the Centre-periphery model, which for Balibar is an enduring feature of attempts to understand the political space of Europe. It features today in attempts to conceptualize Europe (and the EU) in terms of successive enlargements and the location of its 'security border'. For example,

> the idea that Europe comprises concentric circles: the core EU countries possessing the single currency ("Euro-land"), the broader circle other countries who cannot or refuse to adopt the Euro, and the "periphery", which is not "part of Europe" but should be as closely associated as possible with it, for economic and security reasons. (Balibar, 2004b)

This centre-periphery model relies on some rather conventional assumptions about political spaces; that distance from the centre leads to problems of border control, that peripheries exacerbate economic inequalities, that 'non-European' influences at the peripheries could halt the process of Europeanization. Balibar's point is that thinking about centre and periphery in such ways reproduces some rather tired assumptions about European space. "Notions of interiority and exteriority, which form the basis of the representation of the border, are undergoing a veritable earthquake" (Balibar, 2004a, 5). One implication of this is that Europe's 'peripheries' are not marginal to the constitution of European space but are in fact at the centre.

The fourth pattern offered by Balibar is the 'Cross-over'; Europe comprising three overlapping political spaces; euro-mediterranean, euro-atlantic, and euro-asiatic. What is distinctive about Europe is this overlapping of an East, a West, and a South (Balibar, 2002, 99). This pattern is an improvement upon the centre-periphery model because it allows for each region being a centre in its own right, "because it is made of overlapping peripheries, each of them 'open' to influences from all other parts of Europe, and from the whole world" (Balibar, 2004b). This takes us away from the idea that Europe can ever have a 'pure' identity, and allows for the recognition that European identities depend upon encounters between civilizations that take place in European space. These overlapping and open spaces of Europe constitute it as a borderland. In Balibar's words, "'Borderland' is the name of the place where the opposites flow into one another, where 'strangers' can be at the same time stigmatized and indiscernible from 'ourselves'". Europe as a borderland cannot possess fixity or identity.

> No European "identity" can be *opposed* to others in the world because there exist no absolute *border lines* between the historical and cultural territory of Europe and the surrounding spaces. There exist no absolute border lines *because Europe as such is a "border line"* (or "a Borderland" . . .). (Balibar, 2004a, 219)

Balibar's thinking on Europe as a borderland throws up some important and challenging issues. The most important of these is to what extent does Balibar see Europe's borders (and Europe as a borderland) as privileged sites in global politics? The overdetermination of borders, which Balibar establishes connect local borders to representations of the world and, on occasions, to geopolitical divisions, may have changed in nature since the end of the Cold War but can still be said to exist today. For example, it could be argued that the debordering and rebordering of Europe which has occurred as a result of the creation of the EU's single market on the one hand, and the securitization in the period marked by post-9/11 and the bombings in Madrid and London on the other, sometimes depicted as a tension between network Europe and fortress Europe (Rumford, 2007b), or between fortress Europe and 'sieve Europe' (Walters, 2004, 676) is being projected onto the rest of the world. A range of European policy preferences, shaped by neoliberalism on the one hand, or post-colonialism on the other, still result in the overdetermination of borders. This is the sense in which Balibar can say,

> Europe is the point in the world whence border lines set forth to be drawn throughout the world, because it is the native land of the very representation of the border as this sensible and supersensible "thing" that should be or not be here or there, a bit beyond or short of its ideal "position" but always somewhere. (Balibar, 2002, 88)

In other words, according to Balibar, borders which are decided upon in Europe—as a result of EU enlargement, withdrawal from former colonies, or the break up of formerly sovereign entities—become reproduced in or transmitted to other parts of the world whose ability to construct, shape, or relocate their own borders in a comparable fashion is thereby diminished.

It is possible that Balibar underestimates the contemporary dynamics by means of which borders continue to be overdetermined, albeit in novel ways, and indeed he argues that "globalization is certainly bringing about what can be called an *under*determination of the border, a weakening of its identity" (Balibar, 2002, 93). At the same time he recognizes that "the border is troubled by the recent memory, the insistent afterimage of the . . . *over*determination of borders". The legacy of the overdetermination of borders is that "in Europe . . . state borders have always been immediately endowed with a global signification" (Balibar, 2002, 93). It is entirely possible that while Europe's borders have become underdetermined, the impact of bordering, debordering, and rebordering in Europe continues to overdetermine borders elsewhere.

There are other dimensions to Europe's 'special' status vis-à-vis borders. Being a borderland is at the same time being a 'World-border', offering unmediated contact with the rest of the world. The nature of a 'World-border' means that it is difficult to distinguish Europe from the rest of the world, as the outside and inside are no longer clearly marked, but at the same time "it possesses specific 'European' properties deriving from history, geography and politics" (Balibar, 2004b, 2). In the contemporary context the "specific European properties" are those associated with its role as a "vanishing mediator". This accords Europe the role of "midwife of the future", a transitory institution which is able to "create the conditions for a new society and a new civilizational pattern" (Balibar, 2004a, 133). Balibar sees the possibility "for Europe to use its own fragilities and indeterminacies, its own 'transitory' character in a sense, as an effective mediation in a process that might bring about a new political culture" (Balibar, 2004a, 134). Europe can play the role of mediator because

> there is no—and there cannot be—a European identity that can be delimited, distinguished in essential fashion from other identities. This is because there are no absolute borders between a historically and culturally-constituted European space and the spaces that surround it. (Bialasiewicz and Minca, 2005, 369)

There is an irony here which is that through the recognition that Europe cannot possess borders and therefore cannot become a political entity in the way associated with nation-states, empires, and cities, its nature as a 'borderland' allows Europe to assume a new mantle in global politics which bestows upon it a major new capability as a global actor, one consequence of which is its continued ability to overdetermine (other people's) borders.

THE DEMOCRATIZATION OF BORDERS

Another key theme to emerge from Balibar's work is the need to democratize borders as a way of both constructing Europe as a meaningful political space and also of giving content to the idea of European citizenship. For

Balibar (2003, 43), the "democratization of frontiers" is a necessary "condition (among others) for the construction of a democratic Europe". But Balibar is quick to point out that the democratization of borders, a process which must necessarily have a transnational dimension, is not akin to calling for a borderless world. He writes:

> Such a world would run the risk of being a mere arena for the unfettered domination of the private centres of power which monopolize capital, communications and, perhaps, also, arms. It is a question, rather, of what democratic control is to be exerted on the controllers of borders- that is to say, on states and supra-national institutions themselves. (Balibar, 2002, 85)

Elsewhere he expresses the point rather more dramatically:

> an absolute opening or suppression of borders . . . would only give rise to the extension of a savage capitalism in which men are definitively brought to and tossed out of production sites like commodities, even like simple useful or useless raw materials. (Balibar, 2004a, 176)

We can see that for Balibar a 'borderless world' is neither an attractive proposition in its own right nor a solution to the problem of how to make borders more democratic. In order to prevent the unfettered and damaging mobility of capital we need borders, but at the same time, a laissez-faire approach to borders is not a sufficient condition for democracy (nor indeed a guarantee against the depredations of capitalism). By themselves borders are anything but democratic, working as they do to exclude some while protecting others. What Balibar then proceeds to outline is a radical theory of borders and their relation to transnational or global practices of democracy. Balibar sets out the problem in very clear terms:

> what can be done, in today's world, to *democratize the institution of the border*, that is, to put it at the service of men and to submit it to their collective control, make it an object of their "sovereignty", rather than allowing it to subject them to powers over which they have no control? (Balibar, 2004a, 108)

There are two main dimensions to the democratization of borders. The first concerns the function of borders, the second control over borders. The first dimension points to the power relations inherent in borders; they are instituted and "applied according to someone's or some group's discretion" (Balibar, 2003, p 43). For many people the border is represented by detention zones and filtering systems (Balibar, 2004a, 111). Europe both projects its frontiers far beyond its territory in order to exercise border control and the restrictions on mobility imposed take the form of a "global constraint against the movement of peoples" (Balibar, 2003, 36) and aimed at the "global poor" who "need to be systematically triaged and regulated at points of entry to the wealthiest territories. Borders have thus become essential institutions in the constitution of social conditions on a global scale" (Balibar, 2004a, 113), leading to a form of "global apartheid". These ideas have a clear resonance with the idea of "global borderland" (Duffield, 2005) or "global frontierland" (Bauman, 2002). The unwanted refugees or migrant workers, who are very visible for example, at the fences of Ceuta and Melilla, the Spanish enclaves in North Africa, and elsewhere at points along the 'Great Wall of Europe', are treated as an enemy whose attempts to enter 'our' space must be repulsed. This is a form of apartheid because it involves institutional segregation and a blurring of the distinction between police action and war (Balibar, 2003, 39–40). Balibar's core argument is that a greater freedom to cross and re-cross borders is a prerequisite for democracy. In this sense, a universal right to circulation and residency, "including reciprocity of cultural contributions and contacts between civilizations" is essential (Balibar, 2004a, 116–7).

This leads to consideration of the second, and related, dimension to the democratization of borders, the fact that they are controlled unilaterally rather than multilaterally. The problem with Europe's borders is that they both attract and repel migrants (Balibar, 2004b,15). Borders both act as points of entry but also form sites where migrant populations are controlled and suppressed. Thus, borders form part of an apparatus leading to a "violent process of exclusion" (Balibar, 2004b, 14). Border controls, wherever they are to be found, whether at the edges of a nation-state or in its midst, work to selectively allow transit or deny access. This makes borders "radically undemocratic" because "there is no chance for those who have to 'use' frontiers, individually and collectively, to negotiate as to the manner of administration and the rules according to which one may pass through them" (Balibar, 2003, 43).

CONCLUDING COMMENTS

Balibar's work has done much to advance the study of borders in Europe, and continues to influence social theory accounts of the transformation of Europe, its novel spatiality, and give fresh impetus to the debate on Europe's democratic deficits. Balibar's agenda-setting work the transformation of borders is the contribution for which he is best known, and which has been most influential in the field of border studies. It is now *de rigueur* to hold that Europe's borders are become diffused throughout society or that that borders work as filters, firewalls, or membranes, allowing differential access to groups and individuals. This is one measure of Balibar's achievement. Outside the concerns of social theory however, Balibar's work has not made such a significant impact, despite the overlap with some core concerns of European studies: democratization, Europe's place in the world, and the relationship between spaces, borders, and institutions of governance.

Balibar's work does inform the shape and direction of this book, not least the following chapter on Europe's cosmopolitan borders, where I depart from him in certain respects, particularly my focus on the ways in which borders can be the work of citizens (not just the preserve of nation-states or the EU). There are also other themes explored in this book which have developed in the way they have as a result of Balibar's influence. Chapter 7, on the idea of postwesternization, takes issue with Balibar's assumption that Europe takes the form of a 'vanishing mediator' and is able, because of its status as a borderless realm which contains the whole world within itself, to reinvent itself as a privileged global site of arbitration and dialogue between civilizations. The 'border thinking' associated with critical cosmopolitanism, as developed in the work of Mignolo, stands opposed to Balibar's rather Eurocentric notion of Europe as a borderland. Other themes are taken up in Chapter 8 when we look at some key differences between globalization approaches and critical cosmopolitanism, particularly the idea of the oneness of the world, associated with globalization, and the idea that a multiplicity of worlds may exist, a position which emerges from an engagement with critical cosmopolitanism. As we note in Chapter 6, Balibar adopts a position which endorses a mono-perspectival view of the world: one world coupled with one perspective from which to view that world. This is what in Chapter 6 is designated as thinking from the 'high point'.

4 Europe's Cosmopolitan Borders

From Balibar we heave learnt that borders are changing in many ways, the most important of which is that we can no longer assume that they are only to be found at the edges of a polity; they are becoming generalized throughout society. In common parlance, 'borders are everywhere'—at railway stations, at airports, in internet cafes, along motorways, and throughout city-centers and shopping malls. Everyday life has become heavily securitized and the presence of surveillance equipment in public spaces and along transport networks has become commonplace. In addition, we are habituated to routine security checks and the need to obtain 'access' (Rifkin, 2000) in order conduct key elements of our lives: shopping by credit card, arranging travel abroad, surfing the internet. For John Urry, this securitization of everyday life equates to living in a 'frisk society' in which travelling through public spaces has come to resemble our experience of the passing through the airport (Urry, 2007b, 149).

The idea of 'frisk society' is useful in helping to interpret the following news story which appeared in *The Independent* in March 2007.[1] The newspaper carried the story that the UK security and intelligence service M15 had been training supermarket checkout staff to detect potential terrorists. According to the article, the aim of the training was to enable supermarket staff to identify 'extremist shoppers', clues being the mass purchase of mobile phones or bulk buying of toiletries 'which could be used as the basic ingredient in explosives'. Shock value aside, there are two aspects of this story which are particularly interesting. The first is the obvious desire demonstrated by agencies of the state to be seen to be doing something in order to appease public anxieties in the face of heightened perceptions of a terrorist threat. The other is the suggestion that the supermarket checkout now resembles a border crossing or transit point where personal possessions, goods, and identities are routinely scrutinised. More pertinently perhaps it suggests that the techniques and practices regularly employed at the border are being introduced to the supermarket. In this case, the supermarket checkout has come to resemble a border; a border in the midst of society.

The study of borders, and more particularly the changing nature of borders, is a central component of any attempt to understand contemporary

European transformations. This is because many key European developments, especially those associated with the European Union such as the
establishment of the single market, the Eurozone, Schengenland, and recent
enlargements to the East, have both multiplied the borders of Europe and
substituted new borders for old ones (Rumford, 2006b). The centrality of
borders is also evident from a range of popular designations for contemporary Europe—post-western Europe, Fortress Europe, network Europe,
post-national Europe—all of which suggest that it is no longer enough to
focus on national borders, and alert us to the importance of a multiplicity
of new types of borders and bordering processes.

This consideration of changing borders and processes of bordering is
much more than inward-looking self-scrutiny or an identity-fuelled search
for an answer to the question, 'where does Europe end?' Recent thinking
on borders, bordering, and de-bordering has made it impossible to pretend
that Europe is separate from the rest of the world, as in the once-popular
idea of 'Fortress Europe' (Diez, 2006). Nevertheless, studies of the EU have
been noticeably reluctant to place Europe in the context of global processes,
choosing instead to see globalization as something 'out there' beyond
Europe's borders, posing a threat to the European nation-state, and against
which post-Maastricht integration has been a necessary defensive response
(Rumford, 2002). This chapter seeks to place Europe within a global frame,
and argues that Europe's borders increasingly exhibit cosmopolitan qualities, a claim which requires careful qualification. Cosmopolitanism cannot be limited to questions of world citizenship, identification with the
'Other', choosing to belong to (or not belong to) particular communities, or
establishing justice beyond the nation-state. Nor can cosmopolitanism be
reduced to a generalized mobility (Rumford, 2006c). However, cosmopolitanism does imply a particular kind of mobility: the ability of individuals
to cross and re-cross borders. Importantly, this view of the relationship
between borders and cosmopolitanism assumes not borderlessness but a
proliferation of borders.

Cosmopolitanism has long been associated with mobility and transnational solidarity but for much of its history (particularly in the modern age)
this has been associated with the rootlessness of the aristocracy or those
peoples, such as the Jews, who have been positioned as marginal members
of national societies (Kofman, 2005). In a world where identity was defined
by national belonging, cosmopolitans were treated with suspicion. If today
it is not only 'tourists and vagabonds' (Bauman, 1998) who are designated
as cosmopolitans there remains a strong suspicion that cosmopolitanism
is an elitist lifestyle aspiration enjoyed by the lucky few; business tycoons,
media executives, and conference-attending academics. The idea that
Europe possesses cosmopolitan borders can counter this perceived elitism;
border crossing (and indeed border-making) is not only the business of
elites, it is part of the fabric of everyday life for a great many Europeans
(as it is for people elsewhere). At the same time it must be remembered that

Europe's cosmopolitan borders are not experienced in the same way by everyone—Balibar's polysemic borders—leading to what we might call a 'cosmopolitan paradox'. That borders are diffused throughout society, differentiated, mobile, and networked, also increases the chance that they are experienced differently by different groups, some of who encounter them as anything but cosmopolitan.

The case being made for Europe possessing cosmopolitan borders is a straightforward one. Control over bordering and rebordering is no longer solely in the hand of nation-states. Borderwork has been passed upwards from member-states to the EU. National borders can also be European borders and pose a problem for governance that requires the sort of spatial solution that only the EU can provide (Delanty and Rumford, 2005, 146–154). To this end, the EU has created Frontex, a regulatory body designed to 'coordinate the operational cooperation between Member States in the field of border security' (website blurb).[2] Borderwork has also shifted downwards, not only to regional and urban levels, but has become the business of a whole range of societal actors: interest groups, citizens, enterprises, residents' associations, etc. Thus, the issue of *who* conducts borderwork in Europe is centrally important. The idea that Europe possesses cosmopolitan borders reflects the involvement of a range of individuals, groups, and non-state actors in the creation and dissolution of borders, and in making decisions over where new borders might be placed. It is no longer only the nation-state that is responsible for deciding on the location, recognition, and maintenance of many borders. The important borders in Europe—the Europe-defining ones—are becoming determined less by European nation-states than by the EU, which has the power to shift, dismantle, and construct new borders to an extent never possessed by the nation-state, through for example, successive enlargements and regular re-definition of where the EU's Eastern border might lie.

In sum, there are various dimensions to Europe's cosmopolitan borders. First, a whole range of actors now participate in borderwork and borders are not easily owned by political elites and/or institutions of the state. Second, there exists a multiplicity of borders (not only supranational, national, and subnational, but those belonging to the various 'Europes' formed by Schengen, Council of Europe, EEA, etc.). The post-Cold War period has witnessed the multiplication of borders, and types of borders. Third, there is a 'fuzzyness' or blurring of borders in Europe resulting from a lack of distinction between inside and outside, the borderlands at the edges of the EU polity, and the fact that national borders can become EU borders. As pointed out by Balibar (2002, 78), in terms of borders 'each member state is becoming the representative of the others'. Fourth, there exists a great deal of mobility across borders (for some, but not all). Many Europeans cross borders with ease, indeed borders can enhance mobility within the EU space of commercial and information flows. Borders are not necessarily the enemy of mobility.

NETWORK EUROPE AND 'NETWORKED BORDERS'

The idea of cosmopolitan borders has the advantage of taking us beyond the two perspectives that have come to dominate discussion of European borders in recent times: securitized borders associated with the process of 'rebordering' (Andreas, 2003), and borderless Europe (the single market and its associated mobilities). While rebordering highlights the increasing securitization and impermeability of borders associated with the 'Schengenland' model of enhanced mobility within a common space protected by 'hard' external borders, the idea of 'undivided Europe' posits an extended communicative and economic space represented by the popular notion of 'network Europe'. Linked to this development, the idea of network Europe has started to replace the more conventional idea of Europe as a 'space of places' (Castells, 2000), not least in the European Commission's own view of the EU (Prodi, 2001).[3] On this view, Europe should not be thought of as an aggregation of pre-existing territorial spaces (nation-states) with fixed centres and spatial hierarchies (core and periphery, developed and underdeveloped regions, for example) but rather as a network polity linked by new forms of connectivity prompted by global flows of capital, goods, and services and the concomitant mobility enjoyed by persons, enterprises, and forms of governance.

While the idea of 'network Europe' has struck a chord with commentators (Leonard, 1999) attempting to come to terms with the rapid and fundamental transformation of Europe in the post-Cold War period there exist other, conflicting accounts of the reconfiguration of Europe which emphasise the development of 'hard' external borders as a corollary of the increased internal mobility associated with the EU's single market and single currency (Zielonka, 2002). This is the idea of Europe as a 'fortress' protecting Europeans and their economic gains from a predatory outside world. In its contemporary manifestation the idea of 'Fortress Europe' is represented by 'Schengenland', a model of unrestricted internal mobility coupled with 'hard' external borders designed to control flows of terrorists, criminals, and illegal immigrants (Maas, 2005). This has encouraged the idea that borders are becoming less significant between EU member states at the same time as the EU's external border is increasingly heavily policed, creating a defensive shell designed to prevent seepage of the economic gains made by the EU in the face of economic globalization, and the unwanted influx of migrants from the near abroad.

The unresolved tension between ideas of Schengenland and networked Europe has opened up the possibility of a more nuanced account of Europe's borders, in particular an awareness that the EU's borders are becoming differentiated and can vary in scope and tightness (Hassner, 2002). For example, the EU's security borders are more heavily fortified than the corresponding economic, telecommunication, and educational borders, which are designed to facilitate rather than reduce mobility. The rebordering thesis advanced by Andreas and others focuses on the perceived need to reinforce and securitize borders (particularly in the post-9/11 context) and promotes a rather undifferentiated notion of borders, which are intelligible only in terms of policing and security and a defence against external threats (the mobility of illegal immigrants, terrorists, and traffickers in people and drugs). Thus, it downplays the role of borders in encouraging various kinds of mobility, particularly for certain categories of immigrants, migrant workers, and students (Rumford, 2006b; Walters, 2006b).

The idea of a rebordered Europe sits uneasily beside the differentially permeable borders of network Europe. At the same time, the idea of a Europe defined by flows and networks downplays the importance of territorial bordering and the ways in which political priorities can result in some borders being more important than others: What was previously the EU border with eastern Europe (along the line of the Iron Curtain) has become relatively unimportant when compared to the enlarged border with Belarus, Ukraine, and Moldova. The idea of 'network Europe' and the 'smooth' internal space of the single market has changed the way we think about territorial spaces, but ironically has tended to work with conventional notions of borders. It is argued that 'network Europe' can only be properly understood in conjunction with a notion of 'networked' or cosmopolitan borders.

In particular, the idea of 'networked borders' draws attention to the ways in which Europe's borders are increasingly mobile and diffused throughout society (Balibar, 1998). Such borders are not fixed in the way territorial borders are, rather they can be modulated within and between existing administrative entities. European borders are periodically dissolved, constructed afresh, shifted, reconstituted, and so on, and common European borders have replaced a collection of national borders. However, this is not the only sense in which Europe can be said to possess 'networked borders'. Europe's borders are increasingly networked in the sense that they attempt to manage mobility, and, as such, are constructed in locations where mobility is most intense: at airline check-in desks and Eurostar terminals, along Europe's motorways routes and trans-European road networks. Migration controls exist along motorways where haulage operators are required to check their trucks for illegal immigrants. This means that, in effect, the motorway system operates as a 'networked border' (Amoore, 2006; Walters, 2006b).

WHOSE BORDERS ARE THEY ANYWAY?

As introduced previously, an important facet of Europe's cosmopolitan borders is that they are no longer determined by nation-states alone. Europe's borderwork is increasingly carried out by the European Union, especially in relation to decisions on what constitutes the defining borders of Europe, and also by a diverse range of actors including urban authorities, organized crime interests, citizens, and social movements. In short, a whole range of actors are involved in 'borderwork'; the business of making, dismantling, and shifting borders.

For example, organized crime is involved in the business of bordering, and not just in terms of moving illicit goods across national borders. The breakaway republic of Transdniester is a region of Moldova bordering Ukraine over which the Moldovans have largely lost control (in part, because they decline to patrol the border on the basis that this would amount to recognition of the breakaway region). It is renowned as a centre for the illegal trafficking of weapons.[4] According to Moises Naim, Transdniester is 'not your typical break-away region with deep grievances or a popular liberation movement. It's a family-owned and operated criminal smuggling enterprise . . . The state is a criminal enterprise and vice versa." (Naim, 2006, 58). A few years ago the EU became so concerned about arms smuggling across the Transdniester/Ukraine border that with the agreement of the Moldovan and Ukrainian governments it began to monitor the border in November 2005 (the EU providing 70 border policemen and customs officials).[5] This, it is worth noting, is a very good example of the EU extending its borders beyond the limits of its polity. As is the case of Kaliningrad, a Russian enclave which shares all its land borders with EU countries (Poland and Lithuania). The 2004 enlargement of the EU effectively rebordered Russia, but not only in the sense that the EU now possesses borders with that country. The Russian enclave of Kaliningrad has been separated from the rest of Russia by EU enlargement. To travel to Russia from Kaliningrad one must now pass first through Lithuania and then through either Latvia or Belarus. This degree of separation emerged as a big issue in Russia–EU relations just prior to the 2004 enlargement as a consequence of the EU's proposal to require Russians travelling to and from Kaliningrad to apply for a full visa in order to travel through EU territory. In the event, after negotiation, the EU offered a compromise solution which required Russians travelling to Kaliningrad to obtain a transit document rather than a full visa. In both cases, Transdniester and Kaliningrad, the EU has become influential over borders for which it has no formal responsibility and which fall beyond its obvious or 'natural' jurisdiction.

Urban dynamics also reveal some interesting borderwork, and cities can possess their own bordering processes. Since 2003, UK cities have been able to introduce 'dispersal zones' as a result of powers given to the police under the Labour government's anti-social behaviour legislation. The introduction of 'dispersal zones' in parts of Aberdeen, Southampton, London, and Sheffield for example, allow police to disperse groups of (young) people and prevent them from returning for 24 hours, and impose a 9 pm curfew on people who are under16 years old[6] European or national borders may not be the most significant (or difficult to cross) in the lives of many individuals, and urban and local borders can be substantial barriers to mobility. Some examples from London are illustrative. Since the completion of the Channel

Tunnel, the 'continent is no longer cut off from Britain', and it is now possible to travel from London to Paris by train in slightly over two hours. The Channel Tunnel and the Eurostar rail link have not only enhanced London's links with the rest of Europe but have contributed to the Europeanization of the South-East of Britain (McNeill, 2006). But as some borders diminish in importance others are erected. In London itself, the congestion charging zone creates a new map of the capital, new boundaries, a new division between inner and outer London, and consequently a new spatial experience of the capital.[7] Congestion charging not only reformulates our 'mental maps' of the capital, it also works to transform the way people move around London, creating new reasons to travel (or not travel), and new incentives to visit certain places (and avoid others). Congestion charging has transformed the spatiality of London through a new process of bordering. For many Londoners, the boundaries of the congestion charge zone may present a more significant border and restriction on mobility than that traditionally represented by the English Channel.

In fact, London has been zoned and bordered in many different ways in recent years. The security cordon around the City of London, known as the 'ring of steel', introduced by the Metropolitan Police in 1983 in response to the threat of bombing campaigns by the IRA, was extended again in 1997, and on a further two occasions since the events of 9/11 (Coaffee, 2004). In 1996, the same approach was adopted in the Docklands business district around which a 'collar of steel' was constructed. In 2005, the Serious Organized Crime and Police Act became law and allowed the police to enforce an 'exclusion zone' preventing unauthorized protests within a half-mile radius of the Houses of Parliament. Not only do these new securitized spaces reborder London in a major way and create new patterns of mobility and immobility, but they also connect London to the world in new ways. Terrorist attacks on London confirm London as a global city at the same time as reinforcing its symbolic position as the capital of the United Kingdom. As Le Gales reminds us, globalization is associated with a world of flows, especially in respect of finance, communications, persons, diseases, pollution, social movements, terrorism. "Cities are, of course, the places that function as initial entry points for these flows" (Le Gales, 2002, 89).

It is also important to consider the extent to which individuals can engage in borderwork. Citizens may apply pressure on governments and political parties to adopt stricter immigration policies and apply more rigorous border controls. Conversely they may campaign against the use of detention centres in the United Kingdom to house asylum seekers as is the case with the campaign group *No Borders*, 'a social movement opposed to borders, immigration controls, detention centres and forced migration'.[8] In a very different context, the Pope has recently lobbied to border Europe according to Christian values by setting a limit to further enlargement of the EU, thereby excluding Turkey. Business interests are also engaged in borderwork across Europe, for example when lobbying EU institutions for exclusive rights to market a certain type of produce such as Parma ham, or champagne. In the United Kingdom, the Melton Mowbray Pork Pie Association has sought to establish a 2,880 sq km zone around the town, beyond which pies branded 'Melton Mowbray' cannot be produced. Judges hearing the case in the Court of Appeal have agreed to refer the decision over the geographical extent of the exclusion zone to the European Court of Justice.[9]

When the question of 'whose borders?' is considered in the European context the emphasis is usually placed on the transfer of sovereign bordering power upwards, from the member state to the EU level. As I have already indicated this is indeed one important dimension of Europe's cosmopolitan borders. However, I would like to give further consideration here to another important dimension. The 'borderwork' conducted by ordinary people is a seriously neglected theme in the literature but, as the brief examples just mentioned indicate, an area of growing importance and deserving of detailed investigation. The extent to which our societies are cosmopolitanized, to borrow a phrase from Beck, might be gauged from the involvement of citizens (and non-citizens) in bordering and debordering processes.

CITIZENS AND BORDERWORK

David Newman makes a perceptive point when he writes, 'any border research agenda should also deal with the basic question of "borders for whom?' Who benefits and who loses from enclosing, or being enclosed by, others?" (Newman, 2003, 22). To this we can add that, in any consideration of borders, we need to ask further questions such as who is doing the enclosing and who is in a position to create a border? In short, who performs the borderwork?

Borderwork is very much the business of citizens, of ordinary people. Citizens are involved in constructing and contesting borders throughout Europe: creating borders which facilitate mobility for some while creating barriers to mobility for others; creating zones which can determine what types of economic activity can be conducted where; contesting the legitimacy of or undermining the borders imposed by others. Borderwork can take place on any spatial scale from the geopolitical (knocking down the Berlin Wall) to the local (constructing zones which control flows of people into a local neighbourhood, such as the 'cold calling exclusion zones' and 'respect zones' which have been established in many UK towns and cities).

THE DESIRE FOR BORDERS

Balibar's idea that borders are polysemic is a prerequisite for understanding the dynamics of borderwork as is the insight that borders are diffuse, differentiated, and networked. A degree of consensus exists that borders proliferate under conditions of globalization, at least in Europe, and that there is no prospect of a 'borderless world' as the more enthusiastic globalists once predicted. A corollary of this is that as citizens we have become accustomed to borders, many different kinds of borders, as part and parcel of everyday life, and new borders are forever being constructed at the same time as others are erased. Furthermore, we fully expect that borders—even those borders which are designed to increase security—are things which can be traversed and negotiated, sometimes with the greatest of ease if we have the right credentials and documentation. In this sense, borders do not always constrain us. We are also acutely aware that national borders can be rather impotent in the face of terrorists, drug smugglers, and people traffickers despite their high tech, highly securitized (and polysemic) nature. It is not simply that we are becoming blasé about borders: accustomed to the regular appearance of new borders—the creation of new nation-states in the decade following the collapse of communism, the continued expansion of the EU's external land border and, at a more local level, the securitization and the transport zoning of cities, for example—but we also tend to support their creation (in the name of national or personal security). Some people go further and call for greater immigration controls or restrictions on the mobility of workers from new EU member-states, or support the creation of a new border police force (in the United Kingdom), while others choose to live behind the borders of gated communities.

How we respond to this endless round of bordering and debordering very much depends on who we are. Not everyone experiences borders in the same way, and some people are more comfortable with borders than others. Borders constitute openings and opportunities—the starting point for a business trip or a holiday abroad—and for many of us (although by no means all) border crossings have become a routine part of our lives. Some of us no longer (if we ever did) see borders as restrictive, oppressive, and controlling; borders are becoming quite popular in some quarters. But there is more to this than seeing the border as a high-tech turnstile granting preferential mobility to privileged Europeans.

Borders have always been favoured by those such as smugglers and traffickers in people who make a livelihood from exploiting the financial opportunities offered by illegal border crossings. In this context, borders are big business and criminals are often more adept at exploiting gaps in security than police forces are in locking them down (Naim, 2005, 2006). But there are others who welcome the border. There is a 'desire for border management' as van Houtum and Pijpers (2003) explain. It is not so much that people desire borders *per se*, rather they desire a particular kind of border, the kind that allow for selective personal mobility and which are able to differentiate between the 'good citizen' and the unwanted or undesirable, the kind of border designated by Hedetoft (2003, 152) as an 'asymmetric membrane'. In terms of immigration, van Houtum and Pijpiers argue, the EU wants to encourage immigrants with the rights skills and professional knowledge while at the same time, prevent the entry of 'redundant fortune seekers'. Thus, the 'desire for border management' is driven by a need to open and close the borders selectively, and to manage effectively the 'desirability and undesirability of immigration' in order to protect the EU's 'internal comfort zone'. In view of this, they suggest that the EU cannot be understood in terms of 'Fortress Europe': "much more than a fortress, the European Union is beginning to look like a 'gated community'". It is increasingly concerned with the "purification of space, by shutting the gates for the 'outside' world under the flag of privacy, comfort and security".

UNDERSTANDING BORDERWORK

The various shifts and advances in the study of borders and bordering over recent years have not, to any significant degree, embraced the idea that people, not just states, engage in bordering activities. Before proceeding to further examine the dimensions of borderwork it will be useful to examine the ways in which the relationship between citizens and borders, and in particular the ability of citizens to impact on borders, is dealt with in a selection of the existing literature.

Donnan and Wilson (1999) in their book *Borders: Frontiers of Identity, Nation and State* are concerned with state borders (Donnan and Wilson, 1999, 15), that is to say they examine the borders that form the margins of a polity and work to divide nation-states from each other. Borders, on this reading, are expressive of state power. At the same time, borders are also "meaning-making and meaning-carrying entities, parts of cultural land-scapes which often transcend the physical limits of the state and defy the power of state institutions" (Donnan and Wilson, 1999, 4). Local cultures found in borderlands (the territory on one or other side of a border) can either work to reinforce state-defining borders, or they can work to subvert them. Local cultures in border regions are important in the sense that bor-ders are places where the people interface with the state. The state imposes itself upon a territory and its population whose cultural values and local activities may give legitimacy to the border or, alternatively, to erode that legitimacy. Also, local cultures may extend beyond the state boundary (for historical reasons, or because of shared ethnicity, for example). As such, local cultures are not necessarily passive entities; they can be active in the constructions of nations and states (Donnan and Wilson, 1999, 53). The authors note that ethnic and national identities can be configured differently at borders and that this can have an effect on the 'visibility or invisibility of the border'. In the case of the "Irish border, like borders everywhere, [it] is as much a matter of local communities' national and ethnic identities as it is a result of the structures of the state" (Donnan and Wilson, 1999, 75).

For Donnan and Wilson citizens can, under certain conditions, have an impact on state borders through their cultural predispositions. However, any influence they do exert is on the external borders of nation-states. Donnan and Wilson do not address the ability of citizens to engage in any other dimensions of borderwork and they do not concern themselves with borders which may be diffuse and generalized. Borderwork is thus limited in scope and, to the extent that it exists at all, is confined to borderlands. People may be able to transform the meaning of the state's border through crossing and re-crossing for the purposes of shopping, tourism, or job-seeking but they have no ability to determine the location and the nature of the border, or have any real say over who moves in and out.

Liam O'Dowd, a leading sociologist of borders, examines the changing significance of European borders in the context of increasing cross-border cooperation (O'Dowd, 2003). He argues that the transformation of European borders needs to be understood within the context of the "development of the EU as an institutionalized mediator between global markets and national states" (O'Dowd, 2003, 14). One good example of this is that, in the drive towards greater economic integration in the 1990s, borders became perceived as barriers to the completion of the EU's Single Market, and the need to allow free movement of goods, people, services, and finance required the abolition of borders within the EU and a strengthening of the external borders. One consequence was that borders between member states came to be seen as bridges to cooperation and cross-border collaboration. More importantly, from the perspective of borderwork, borders can, according to O'Dowd, serve as an economic resource for a range of actors who aim to benefit from "bridging and barrier functions simultaneously" (O'Dowd, 2003, 25). This is another way of expressing the idea, referred to earlier by Donnan and Wilson, that although regular crossing and re-crossing can have a transformative effect on borders, or the meaning of borders, the smugglers, shoppers, tourists and others who do the crossing actually require the border in order to operate; "a whole range of legal and illegal activities exist for which the border is the *raison d'etre*" (O'Dowd, 2003, 25). Thus, the same activities that transform the experience of the border also work to consolidate it.

The work of O'Dowd emphasizes the dual nature of borders in Europe (or 'European borders', as the author prefers) as both barriers and bridges, and that the symbolic nature of these borders is changing to emphasize the openness and cooperation which characterizes the rhetoric of the EU project. He also recognizes that "regional borders may be valorized at the expense of state borders" (O'Dowd, 2003, 25), thereby breaking with the notion that borders are only to be found at the limits of the nation-state. It is acknowledged that a range of actors can utilize borders and that some groups and individuals benefit more than others from the opportunities represented by the changing nature of Europe's borders. However, it is not acknowledged that actors other than the nation-state can work to shape borders or that borders have important societal as well as state dimensions.

The borderwork dimension is more pronounced in the work of Lahav and Guiraudon (2000), who write about 'borders which are not at the border' and which are subject to what they term 'remote control'. Importantly for the authors, 'reinvented' forms of border control use "local, transnational, and private actors outside the central state apparatus to forestall migration at the source or uncover illegal migrants" (Lahav and Guiraudon, 2000, 55). Although this suggests the possibility of borderwork, Lahav and Guiraudon emphasize that 'remote control' is in fact a strategy employed by central state agencies to tighten control over migration. So, co-opting "non-state actors in the performance of the migration control 'function' (i.e., security agencies working for airline companies) serves to 'shift liabilities' from central state to private actors such as employers, carriers, and travel agencies" (Lahav and Guiraudon, 2000, 58), but does not alter the fact that it is the central state that is in charge of the borderwork.

Lahav and Guiraudon's account outlines the privatization of security and immigration measures, but no amount of 'outsourcing' can mask the fact that these are strategies of the state. The borderwork performed by citizens, on this account, is on behalf of the state, not independent of it. "By delegating policy functions, states have been able to reconcile their contradictory interests, defuse public anxiety, reduce the costs of regulation, and occasionally circumvent even the most basic of liberal rights" (Lahav and Guiraudon, 2000, 71). The end result is a rebordering strategy which aims to re-assert state borders and make them (selectively) more difficult to cross. It is difficult to reconcile these developments with the sort of borderwork which is under consideration here.

If other commentators have not accorded importance to the borderwork performed by citizens, does this mean that borderwork is a relatively new phenomenon? It is certainly the case that the visibility of borderwork has increased significantly in the past few years, largely (but not solely) as a result of the recognition that processes of bordering take place throughout a society as well as at its edges. The generalization of the border and an awareness that the physical land frontier is not the only possible site of bordering has allowed for a recognition that, at the same time as borders are changing in their nature and scope, the agencies responsible for constructing and maintaining them have also become more diverse. However, this is not the whole story, as was evident in our brief look at the work of Lahav and Guiraudon. In the following section I examine two related contexts within which we can see borderwork in action: the politics of everyday fear; and 'people power'—the role of civil society activity.

PEOPLE POWER AND 'EVERYDAY FEAR'

Borderwork takes many forms but, as with the example of the gated community, it can be the result of a desire for security and a lifestyle of consumption which, in the view of some, cannot be guaranteed by the state. In this sense, borderwork can result from what Brian Massumi terms the 'politics of everyday fear' (Massumi, 1993). This 'everyday fear' is fuelled by a perception that globalization is responsible for an increase in the insecurities or 'risks' (Beck, 1992) associated with routine existence: concerns about climate change, the threat of terrorist attacks, health scares and epidemics, crime and violence on the street. In particular, a sense of insecurity may be heightened by the perception that globalization (and the global nature of risk society) results in state borders being less secure and more porous (Robertson, 2007). One consequence of this perception is that some people try to replace the ineffectual borders of the nation-state with local borders that work to increase a sense of security. This is what the gated community is designed to do.[10] As Bauman (2006a, 96–7) says there exist "vulnerable populations overwhelmed by forces they neither control nor fully understand". As a result, people become "obsessed with the security of their own borders and of the population inside them—since it is precisely that security *inside* borders and *of* borders that eludes their group and seems bound to stay beyond their reach forever". On this reading, citizens are taking matters into their own hands and attempting to create an experience of security which they no longer look to the state to provide (or believe that the state is capable of providing). But this does not mean that they want to be protected by DIY versions of the Berlin Wall. They are looking for a different type of border, Hedetoft's 'asymmetric membrane', which allows both freedom of movement *and* protection for those who construct it, while forming a barrier to those whose presence is deemed undesirable. In a similar vein, Walters (2006a, 151–4) offers the figure of the 'firewall' as an alternative way of thinking about borders of this kind. The firewall, a term taken from the world of computer security, exists to regulate the connection between a computer or local network and the network beyond. A firewall acts as a "filter that aspires to reconcile high levels of circulation, transmission and movement with high levels of security" (Walters, 2006a, 152). The firewall metaphor captures nicely the bordering dilemmas to which 'everyday fear' gives rise: People seek access to and engagement with the wider world but are apprehensive of doing so. The firewall allows elites the freedom to engage with the world on their own terms and affords them the comfort of doing so from a position of safety.

The idea of 'globalization from below' has become an important adjunct to thinking about global civil society. Events such as the worldwide anti-war demonstrations of 15 February 2003, the humanitarian response to the Asian Tsunami in 2005, the Live 8 demonstrations in 2005, and various incarnations of the World Social Forum over the past few years have given additional substance to the rather vague notion of global civil society. These events are all reminders that 'people power' can be a significant force in global politics. It can also add a significant dimension to borderwork. 'People power' was very visible at the time the Berlin Wall came down, indeed this still represents the most potent symbol of ordinary people remaking the borders of the state. But do citizens acquire additional borderwork capacity as a result of the rise of global civil society? It might be argued that the transnational networking which is at the heart of global civil society is bound to provide greater opportunities for eroding or remaking borders. The more dense the networks and the greater the amount of cross-border activity the greater the potential erosion of national and other official borders.

But this is not the whole story. Rather, global civil society stands in a rather ambivalent relation to borders and borderwork. Some civil society actors work to erode borders while others work to reinforce them or to create new ones. On the one hand, transnational social movements and advocacy networks are indifferent to borders, working across them without intending to challenge them (although an indirect effect of their activity may be to undermine or weaken existing borders) but they do not, on the whole, have bordering or debordering as their primary or even secondary aim. There are exceptions of course, and some social movements such as 'No Borders', 'No One is Illegal', or 'Brides Without Borders', target the restrictive and discriminatory nature of borders and the way they are policed. It is certainly the case that some civil society groups do work to ameliorate the impact of borders. For example, but from outside Europe admittedly, Fronteras Compasivas (Humane Borders) is an NGO working at the 'tortilla curtain', the border between Mexico and the United States, where it installs water stations in the desert in order to pride succour to those attempting to cross the desert into the United States (Doty, 2006). On the other hand, borderwork is often exclusionary and by no means always works for democratization or humanitarian ends. It could be argued that the borderwork that leads to gated communities, dispersal zones in city centres, or 'no cold calling zones' in residential neighbourhoods, are undemocratic in that they mobilize societal resources in favour of some while seeking to exclude other sections of the population. This is what Bauman has in mind when he talks of "people trying to exclude other people to avoid being excluded by them", or what Rifkin identifies as a contemporary manifestation of personal freedom in the "Age of Access", the ability to exclude others (Rifkin, 2000,12). The key, it appears, is to 'get your borderwork in first' before you become excluded and bordered out by others. The question remains as to whether this kind of 'people power' accords in any sense with the spirit of civil society. Certainly the civil benefits of this kind of bordering are not that readily apparent. 'Bottom up' globalization, grass roots and neighbourhood campaigns, the politics of identity and societal autonomization are all key dimensions of civil society. However, on their own they do not necessarily lead to acts of civility, although they do point in the direction of an increased amount of borderwork.

CONCLUSION: FROM 'BORDER SICKNESS' TO COSMOPOLITAN BORDERS

In the novel *Divided Kingdom* (Thomson, 2005), Rupert Thompson depicts an alternative United Kingdom (the Divided Kingdom of the title) which, in the interests of social harmony, has been rebordered not along the lines of region, class, ethnicity, or religion, but according to personality type: sanguine, melancholic, phlegmatic, or choleric. To achieve this 'rearrangement' of the population, families are divided and forcibly relocated, and the four personality types are forbidden from mixing. "In an attempt to reform society, the government has divided the population into four groups . . . [t]he land, too, has been divided into quarters. Borders have been established, reinforced by concrete walls, armed guards and rolls of razor wire" (publishers website blurb). As the story unfolds, the novel's central character crosses and re-crosses these new borders in an attempt to recover his past, his family history, and his role in society. The central theme of the book is that borders work to divide us from ourselves, as well as from others. The experience of the central character is that crossing borders can be harmful to the self; in crossing borders one can become "depleted by the experience [and] . . . one might lose part of oneself" (Thomson, 2005, 85). Indeed, the experience of the rebordering resulting from the dismembering of the country is said to have led to "whole sections of the population . . . suffering from what became known as 'border sickness'" (Thomson, 2005, 23). It is not until he visits another Quarter and discovers the mysterious Bathysphere club (which offers alternative ways of travelling across borders) that he begins to recover his sense of self taken away by the 'rearrangement' and the borders that sustain it; "I seemed to have crossed a kind of border in myself, and . . . for the first time I'd had a real sense of the person I used to be, the person I was first, before everything changed . . ." (Thomson, 2005, 192).

The borders depicted in the novel *Divided Kingdom* are unlike the cosmopolitan borders of Europe that are the subject of this chapter. The borders of *Divided Kingdom* are more akin to those found in Cold War Europe, divided Berlin most obviously. Cosmopolitan borders are different. They do not always take the form of physical barriers, they do not necessarily pose the same threat to our subjectivity or psychic wellbeing, nor do they divide us from ourselves. Rather, borders and border crossings can constitute a resource for identity construction, self-actualization, and sense of belonging. In order to live in multiple communities or to be at home with multiple identities we must be comfortable with and adept at crossing and re-crossing borders. A cosmopolitan lives in and across borders. Borders connect the "inner mobility" (Beck, 2000, 75) of our lives with both the multiplicity of communities we may elect to become members of and the cross-cutting tendencies of polities to impose their border regimes on us in ways which compromise our mobilities, freedoms, rights, and even identities.

However, it would be a big mistake to see all European borders as cosmopolitan (and indeed all Europeans as cosmopolitans). As Zygmunt Bauman points out, there exists a new stratification between those who cross borders with ease and those to whom this freedom is denied.

> Progressively, entry visas are phased out all over the globe. But not passport control. The latter is still needed . . . to set apart those for whose convenience and whose ease of travel the visa have been abolished, from those who should have stayed out—not meant to travel in the first place. (Bauman, 1998, 87)

In this way, the external borders of the EU can constitute a gateway for some but a barrier to others. For example, many Africans die each year attempting to cross illegally into Spain via the Canary Islands. According to the Mauritanian Red Crescent, at least 1,200 people died trying to make the trip between November 2005 and March 2006.[11] Such attempts at border crossings, whether across sea or land, are increasingly located away from the EU's networked borders, those borders constituted by airports, railway stations, motorways, and maritime ports, as these 'smart' borders constitute a serious barrier to the mobility of those lacking proper travel documentation (Rumford, 2006a). Those seeking illegal entry to the EU must rely on the relative porosity of the land and sea borders, which may be increasingly securitized but where crossing is still, for some, a distinct, if potentially lethal, possibility.

So what value is there in asserting that Europe's borders are becoming cosmopolitan? We have already noted that a 'cosmopolitan paradox' exists in respect of borders; the nature of cosmopolitan borders is that they are experienced differentially, and for some, the borders are solid and unmoveable barriers rather than aids to mobility. Does this not stymie the case for the cosmopolitanization of Europe's borders? It is not only cosmopolitan borders that are experienced differentially. With any border the question can be asked: Is it designed to keep people out or in? Every border creates benefits for some and disadvantages for others. Each border is held to be essential to the wellbeing of some people while being indifferent to the lives of others. This is as true for nation-state borders as for the 'new' borders of post-national Europe.

All of this points to another important dimension of the cosmopolitanization of Europe's borders. Not only are borders experienced differentially, as in the case of groups on either side of a common border, but borders can also be highly individual. In addition to the security borders introduced to London mentioned earlier in the chapter, other cities have constructed borders and zones to selectively restrict the mobility of inhabitants. Police in several UK cities enforce exclusion zones to curb drink-related offences in city centres. For example, in December 2005 in Swansea, police introduced an exclusion zone to prevent offenders returning to the city centre.

The exclusion comes into force at the point that an individual is charged at the police station. The miscreant is 'provided with a map of the exclusion zone'[12] and a bespoke border is thereby established.

The 'cosmopolitan paradox' assumes that the same border can be experienced in different ways by different sections of the population (in the sense that some people find it easier to cross a border than others), for whom the border then does not appear cosmopolitan at all. In fact a deeper paradox is emerging with the cosmopolitanization of borders. What constitutes a border may not only vary from person to person, but borders that actively regulate the activity of some may not even be perceived to exist in the case of others and, perhaps more significantly, some people may be engaged in borderwork to the disadvantage of others. That borders are increasingly diffused throughout society, as Balibar teaches us, can lead to bordering processes which work to impose borders on some people while encouraging others to remain indifferent to the establishment of new borders. We have seen how this can work in terms of city centre exclusion zones, but it also operates in the case of passenger profiling (on the basis of ethnic origin and religion) mooted as an adjunct to existing anti-terrorist security measures on airlines. The cosmopolitanization of borders also provides incentives to those wishing to engage in borderwork for their own ends. Why remain passive in the face of other peoples' borders when you can obtain advantage by becoming an 'early-bird' borderer? If borders are networked throughout society and more and more people can participate in borderwork, then the capacity to make or undo borders becomes a major source of political empowerment, and a key dimension of local, national, and global political power relations. In such circumstances, designating borders as cosmopolitan is not an intellectual conceit but an urgent requirement for social and political scientists.

5 'Spaces of Wonder'
The Global Politics of Strangeness

We find ourselves now in a circumstance in which the problem of strangeness is rapidly becoming institutionalized.
—Roland Robertson, 2007, 409

Europe . . . is becoming a place of plural and strange belongings.
—Ash Amin, 2004, 2

This chapter explores themes which, in a bout of recent writing and theorizing, have been placed, unsatisfactorily in my view, under the rubric of 'risk' or 'fear', terms which it would seem have become indispensable to social scientists attempting to both characterise the times we live in ('world risk society', 'liquid fear') and explain the tensions between our securitized forms of governance and the insecurities and anxieties experienced in everyday life. However, accounts of fear and risk offer only partial explanations of an important dimension of the contemporary policy responses to uncertainty and apprehension. This chapter seeks to place the strangeness of (and in) the world at the centre of accounts of insecurity, and examines the role that processes of globalization can play in increasing this sense of strangeness, with particular reference to the strangeness of political spaces, some of which, it is argued, have become 'spaces of wonder'.

The term 'spaces of wonder' refers to emerging social spaces or political domains, often made manifest by processes associated with globalization, which have an unsettling, destabilizing, or disorienting effect in the sense that they are difficult to comprehend or assimilate into understandings of political topography to the extent that they inspire awe or wonder in those trying to apprehend them. It is argued that new opportunities for governance (and perhaps also political opposition) accompany the emergence of these spaces, particularly where political actors are capable of rendering the strangeness of 'spaces of wonder' in very familiar terms. At the core of the chapter is the argument that a focus on the politics of strangeness can provide valuable ways of understanding forms of societal control and new modes of governance not matched by the literature on fear, even those accounts which examine the ways in which fear is increasingly used as an organizing principle for governing social relations (Huysmans, 2006; Robin, 2004).

'Spaces of wonder', and the processes of bordering which help construct and sustain them, are a key feature of globalization. As such, they have their origins in the idea that globalization has undermined the familiar territoriality of a world of nation-states, a notion which has become well established in the social science literature on globalization (Axford, 2007; Rumford, 2000 b). For example, McGrew (1995, 52) writes that "processes of globalization are transforming the very foundation of world order, by reconstituting sovereign statehood and reordering international political space". A range of contributions have bolstered this view, from the more apocalyptic accounts associated with the idea that globalization has led to the 'annihilation' of space, to advocates of 'network society' who see mobilities and flows as being indifferent to territorial boundaries, and the deterritorialized sovereignty of Hardt and Negri's *Empire* (Hardt and Negri, 2000). In all of these approaches the emphasis is very much on the transformed spatiality of the world rather than the strangeness of it, even in accounts where attention is drawn to the link between global connectivity and 'the concomitant rise in the danger of 'strangers' in the modern world' (Robertson, 2007, 404). In other words, the vast majority of accounts of the transformation of spatiality in a world of connectivity focus on the new spaces created by globalization and the flows and mobilities thought to energise them, rather than the processes by means of which our familiarity with those spaces is undermined and the strangeness and unpredictability—unknowability even—of the world has increased as a result. But this under-researched realm of the strangeness of the spaces of globalization is an important one, it is argued, and the focus of attention here. If globalization makes and re-makes the world, it also makes the world increasingly strange.

GLOBALIZATION AND STRANGENESS

What do we mean by 'strangeness', and what is its relation to globalization? In addition to alerting us to the 'oneness of the world' (Robertson, 1992; Singer, 2004) accounts of globalization have also made it possible to view the world as a more uncertain and strange place. This is because at the heart of our understanding of processes of globalization lies a paradox. At the same time as generating an awareness that the world is a single place and encouraging actors to rethink their place in relation to the world as a whole, globalization can also lead to a sense that the world is larger, more complex, and more threatening and dangerous than was hitherto the case. In other words, globalization both compresses the world, and, paradoxically, brings its enormity into focus. While we are increasingly conscious of the compactness of an increasingly interconnected world in ways that bring the globe within the grasp of all individuals, we are also cognizant that the flows and mobilities constitutive of globalization constitute a threat to our familiar nation-state communities as a result of which much economic and political decision-making is removed from democratically elected polities, and the individuals that constitute them. Bauman (2007, 2) neatly summarises these concerns and links them to the uncertainties surrounding political spaces in a global world:

> Much of the power to act effectively that was previously available to the modern state is now moving away to the politically uncontrolled global (and in many cases extraterritorial) space; while politics, the ability to decide the direction and purpose of action, is unable to operate effectively at the planetary level since it remains, as before, local.

In a recent discussion of securitization and the 'open society', Roland Robertson draws attention to the link between increasing global connectivity and the concomitant rise in the danger of 'strangers'. For Robertson, in his now famous formulation, globalization is best understood as both the increasing interconnectedness of the world coupled with the realization that this is so (Robertson, 1992). Both elements of the equation are equally important as 'increasing global consciousness runs in complex ways, hand in hand, so to speak, with increasing connectivity' (Robertson and White, 2007, 56). One dimension of the global connectivity—global consciousness nexus is the way in which globalization results in the institutionalization of difference leading to increased strangeness. We live in a world in which distance is said to have died but it is still one "in which there are many barriers and borders being erected by individuals, communities, societies, regions, and civilizations against 'strangers'" (Robertson, 2007, 404–5). For Robertson, alterity, or strangeness, is the flip-side of securitization, and social cohesion is sustained through the invocation of the threatening 'other'. In other words, strangeness–the radical and threatening difference associated with the Other—is exacerbated by processes of globalization which are perceived as throwing open the doors to the world and leaving us unprotected from threats that come from beyond previously secure borders. The result is that "we live in a world in which we are encouraged to believe in more and more dangers, and an increasing number of 'protections' are offered to help us" (Robertson, 2007, 406). These 'protections' include 'everyday' forms of securitization: CCTV, training on how to survive terrorist attacks, gated communities, and SUVs (Bauman, 2006a, 143–4), all likely to increase our sense of alterity. In addition, the "democratization of surveillance" means that "we are all spies now" (Robertson, 2007, 408) and the upshot is that "we are constrained to be suspicious of all others"; the problem of strangeness is becoming institutionalized (Robertson, 2007, 409). Globalization thus creates the sense that we are living in an open and networked world and, at the same time, increases our perceptions of the threats inherent in such an 'open' world. Our response to this is to create at a local level what we no longer believe the nation-state of being capable of or committed to: our collective security. The increasing securitization of our lives exacerbates our sense of alterity: The world is rendered unfamiliar and is full of strangeness.

Balibar (2006, 3) pursues similar themes but focuses more on the role of borders in the construction and reproduction of strangeness in Europe. He writes,

> increasingly it is the working of the border, and especially the difference between geopolitical, economic and security borders and mere administrative separations, which constitutes, or "produces" the stranger/foreigner as social type. (Balibar, 2006, 4)

In other words, some types of borders are more important than others in producing strangeness—and the borders he has in mind constitute what he calls 'the Great Wall of Europe',

> a complex of differentiated institutions, installations, legislations, repressive and preventive politics, and international agreements which together aim at making the liberty of circulation not impossible but extremely difficult or selective and unilateral for certain categories of individuals and certain groups. (Balibar, 2006, 1–2)

This border is not conceived at the outer edges of Europe but in fact projected beyond Europe's borders, and component parts of the 'Great Wall of Europe' include the Israeli-built wall dividing the West Bank from Israel and the heavily fortified security fences guarding the Spanish enclaves of Ceuta and Melilla in Morocco. What this means for Europe is that citizens from other member states are no longer 'fully strange' (because the borders that separate them from us are of the 'merely administrative' type) while those from beyond 'the Great Wall of Europe' are constituted as full strangers. "'Strangeness' and the various conditions referred to by the category of the Stranger are nothing natural, but they are produced and therefore also reproduced" (by borders) (Balibar, 2006, 4).

BEYOND FEAR AND RISK

This chapter takes as its central theme the ways in which opportunities for governance emerge from the construction of 'spaces of wonder' resulting from the strangeness of the world. This is a little-explored feature of globalization studies and a neglected theme within the literature on global governance and public policy. It is important, it is argued, because the awareness of the strangeness of the world is the basis for techniques of governance in contemporary western (or perhaps we should say postwestern) societies (Delanty, 2006c; Therborn, 2006, and also Chapter 7), the focus in this chapter being Europe and North America.

In pursuing an understanding of 'spaces of wonder' the chapter seeks to distinguish its concerns from two themes which have loomed large in recent sociological and political science literature: fear and risk. There has been a dramatic increase in studies of fear in recent years, a trend fuelled by a much needed recognition that emotions play a larger role in politics than hitherto assumed (Mestrovic, 1997) on the one hand, and by the need to understand responses to the attacks in the United States of September 11th 2001, and subsequent attacks in Madrid and London, and the whole phenomenon of 'global terror', on the other (Bauman, 2006a; Appaduarai, 2006; Robin, 2004). The 'risk society' thesis has been with us a little longer (Beck, 1992) and has become strongly associated with the man-made insecurities resulting from the industrial age's attempts to dominate nature and/or irresponsible use of natural resources. That we are moving towards a risk society increases insecurity in our lives. We find it difficult to rely upon previously authoritative sources, and scientific findings are increasingly contested by a range of societal actors, a fact which also increases our sense of apprehension and fear as we are no longer sure whose 'truth' we can rely upon (Strydom, 2002). Beck argues that we have moved from 'first modernity' characterised by struggles over the production and redistribution of resources and summed up in the concern that 'we are hungry', to a 'second modernity' (risk society) where our insecurities lead us to conclude that 'we are afraid'. Thus, for Beck, risk and fear are connected, and both are a consequence of 'risk society'.

It is argued here that a focus on fear and risk is not sufficient to understand our contemporary insecurities. What is neglected in the current concern with insecurity, apprehension, anxiety, and trepidation is the sense of wonder that many contemporary events evoke. In such cases the world becomes a strange place in which familiar reference points have been erased and a new logic of cause and effect seems to be at work. For example, the response by the US authorities to the devastation caused in and around New Orleans by Hurricane Katrina was seen by many not only as totally inadequate but almost unbelievable in the context of the resource mobilization which the world's most powerful nation-state is capable of (or believes itself to be capable of). The devastation of New Orleans, the paucity and tardiness of the response, the break-down of law and order that ensued, and the fortitude of many who suffered there as a result was truly awe-inspiring and produced the mixture of strangeness and wonder to which I am alluding.

There have been other such wondrous and awe-inspiring events in recent years, all of which have required a suspension of disbelief and a major rethink of what we believe is possible or likely in a social universe within which life usually 'makes sense': the attacks on the United States of

September 11th 2001, the abuses at Abu Ghraib prison, the role played by Guantanamo Bay in the 'war against terror', the 'rendition flights' which implicate European nation-states in acts of torture, and to go back a few years further, the Balkan wars of the early 1990s (Mestrovic, 1994). The realization that the 'crust of civilization is wafer thin' is what Bauman (2006a, 16–17) terms the 'Titanic Syndrome'; the dread inspired by the possibility that civilization could collapse totally. "Calling what happened in and around New Orleans a 'collapse of law and order' cannot grasp the event, let alone its message, fully. Law and order simply vanished—as if they had never existed" (Bauman, 2006a, 13), an image which may call to mind Hobbes' 'state of nature' in which life was 'nasty, brutish and short', but more importantly demonstrates the political potential represented by an 'awesome' event. When our sense of wonder allows us to believe—even for a moment—that nothing makes sense, those who govern us are able to legitimate all kinds of action (and inaction) through, for example, labelling an event an 'emergency' (Calhoun, 2006).

This 'sense of wonder' is what in other historical periods has been designated by the term 'the sublime' (Bleiker and Leet, 2006; Rumford and Inglis, 2005) or 'cosmic fear' (Bauman, 2006a). In its original formulation, the idea of the sublime or cosmic fear referred to the awe experienced in the face of the vastness of nature and human frailty in the face of the power of the natural elements. In Bauman's terms, "cosmic fear is also the horror of the unknown: the terror of uncertainty" (Bauman, 2006a, 46). The idea of 'cosmic fear' derives from the work of Bakhtin who viewed it as "the prototype of mundane, earthly power, which, however, remoulded its primeval prototype into *official fear*", human power, man-made, manufactured. In this way it is possible to see how a 'natural' disaster can be constructed so as to manufacture fear, or, as Bauman terms it, the "manufacture of vulnerability" (Bauman, 1999, 60). This suggests that it is insufficient to view fear as simply an emotion: it is best thought of as a "political tool, an instrument of elite rule or insurgent advance, created and sustained by political leaders or activists who stand to gain something from it" (Robin, 2004, 16). A similar conclusion is reached by Huysmans, writing about the securitization to which anxieties about immigration in Europe often give rise, who talks of the 'politics and administration of fear' and the way it provides opportunities for a particular mode of governance. He writes, "fear is not simply an emotion that security framing instigates in social relations. It is first of all an organizing principle that renders social relations as fearful" (Huysmans, 2006, 54).

As Bleiker and Leet (2006, 715) note, awe and wonder can provide antidotes to conventional responses to fear. What they have in mind is the stimulation of the senses and empowerment of the will which the sublime can engender in those who experience the vastness of nature or the horrors of modern disasters. In other words, humans are not merely passive and cowed in the face of the sublime; it can be an energizing, empowering, and even uplifting experience. But there is another sense in which we can understand the idea that wonder can provide an antidote to fear. By looking at 'spaces of wonder' rather than the politics of fear and risk, we can better understand the dynamics of certain dimensions of contemporary governance. But to make this possible we need to further sharpen and hone our understanding of what will otherwise remain rather general and descriptive notions of strangeness and wonder. Strangeness is most evident, I would argue, through the construction of 'spaces of wonder', that is to say unfamiliar spaces resulting from processes of globalization which evoke feelings of trepidation, apprehension, and awe. There is an associated argument which is also very important in the context of the chapter and this is that these 'spaces of wonder' can be utilized as a tool of governance but, as pointed out by Robin (previously), they can also become a resource in political struggles. The important point is that the unfamiliarity of spaces can be engendered and the resulting insecurity and trepidation can be cultivated within policy realms and governance strategies.

The chapter examines three 'spaces of wonder': (1) 'the world', made more uncertain and threatening by accounts of the global nature of terror; (2) the United Kingdom's borders, which, according the government, are now located 'offshore' and controlled remotely from the United Kingdom; (3) and 'global borderlands' where the separation between good and evil, civilization and barbarism, is regulated. These 'spaces of wonder' are intimately related to borders and processes of bordering. Indeed, they suggest a radically different relationship between spaces and borders than is encountered in accounts of the 'realist' borders that divide nation-states. Furthermore, these 'spaces of wonder' (or 'borders of wonder' perhaps) suggest a very different interpretation of the relationship between globalization and borders than advanced by supporters of the 'borderless world' thesis. The changing spatiality of the world under conditions of globalization is most keenly observed in the changing nature of borders which are not only required to act as containers for new spaces, but have acquired a spatiality of their own. As Balibar (2004) states, the relation between borders and spaces has been inverted. Such shifts in the nature and function of borders have contributed in no small way to the strangeness of 'spaces of wonder'.

THE POLITICS OF DANGEROUSNESS

We can now consider our first 'space of wonder', the globe itself, or more specifically the uncertain and threatening world. One key theme in the political responses of Tony Blair, John Reid, and other senior UK politicians to the threat of terrorism in the United Kingdom has been to emphasize the dangerousness of the post 9/11 world; a world which 'no longer makes sense'. Tony Blair was keen to assert that the world has changed post 9/11, and such a world requires a new style of politics: 'a new world order needs a new set of rules' (see also Chapter 8). What is portrayed as particularly new, as Runciman (2004,11) points out in his discussion of Blair's politics, is the risk represented by the future (uncertain, unknowable) and the impossibility of being able to fully assess the risk posed by the world's new strangeness. The supposed dangerousness of the world is a key theme in attempts by politicians and policy makers to frame responses to the threat of 'global terror'. In Albrecht's terms, "demonisation has been replaced by the concept and strategy of 'dangerisation'" (quoted in Bauman, 2004, 56). But dangerousness and 'dangerisation' are not merely new words to describe fears, risks, and insecurities. In addition to the world order being easily portrayed as dangerous and unmanageable and terrorist threats inevitable and unpredictable, dangerisation offers solutions to the problems it identifies.

We can see this more clearly if we examine two policy responses occasioned by the threats posed by the world (dis)order and the idea of 'dangerousness' to which these threats have given rise. These policy responses are good examples of how the perception of globalization as the source of threats has led to the need to create novel forms of protection. One example is the 'control orders' introduced to the United Kingdom by the Blair government and designed to restrict the freedoms of suspected terrorists (without initiating criminal proceedings), the other is a comparable example from the United States. We will start with the latter, which is the case of the suspected bombers detained in Chicago a couple of years ago (six men suspected of plotting to blow up the Sears Tower). Described in news reports as "home-grown terrorists", the men were suspected of Al-Qaeda sympathies (according to the charges brought against them they had "sworn allegiance to al-Qaeda but had no contacts with it").[1] After being charged they were refused bail on the ground that, in the opinion of the judge, they posed a danger to society.[2] This news story is of significance not because it deals with the rather odd circumstances surrounding the arrest and detention of suspected terrorists, but because of the rationale used to detain them.

Although they were thought to pose a danger to society by the judge, US government officials quoted by the BBC said, "they posed no real threat because they had no actual al-Qaeda contacts, no weapons and no means of carrying out the attacks".[3] Another BBC news story reported that officials said the men "posed no danger".[4] The BBC journalists were alert to the fact that US officials were making contradictory statements. One BBC reporter remarked that official statements both confirmed that the alleged plot was not far advanced and the terrorists were "aspirational rather than operational", at the same time as the US Attorney General saw it as evidence that there exists a heightened possibility of home grown terror plots.[5] Mr. Gonzales said that "the lack of direct link to al-Qaeda did not make the group any less dangerous . . . Left unchecked these home-grown terrorists may prove as dangerous as groups like al-Qaeda."[6]

Clearly, those that pose no palpable threat can still be considered dangerous. The 'war on terror' constructs its own temporality, stretching the threat of terror into the distant future. This is because dangerousness is seen as a latent property which may only reveal itself in the future. Judith Butler, in her book *Precarious Life* (Butler, 2004,74–77) makes the point that one line of defence used by the United States for detaining 'enemy combatants' at Guantanamo Bay indefinitely and without the prospect of a trial is that they are 'dangerous people'. Butler demonstrates how, in the eyes of the US authorities, someone detained in Guantanamo Bay could be still deemed dangerous even if a trial found him not guilty of a particular charge. She argues that the determination of dangerousness is extra-legal and according to the new 'post-political' logic at work in these situations, establishing dangerousness trumps the need to prove guilt. According to Butler, "a certain level of dangerousness takes a human outside the bounds of law . . . makes that human into the state's possession, infinitely detainable. What counts as 'dangerous' is what is deemed dangerous by the state" (Butler, 2004, 76).

There are UK parallels in the response to 'dangerousness'. The much-debated 'control orders', introduced by the Blair government in March 2005 in cases where there is insufficient evidence to prosecute suspected terrorists, are motivated by the same need to construct dangerousness. Control orders replaced emergency laws introduced after 9/11 which permitted the indefinite detention of suspects, but were adjudged illegal by the House of Lords in December 2004. The newer control orders are designed to limit the mobility of suspects who to this end are tagged, confined to their homes, and restricted in their communication. Although they are applied to those deemed 'dangerous' the danger that they actually represent has been the subject of much debate. For example, Shami Chakrabarti, director of Liberty (a leading human rights advocacy group), was quoted by the BBC as saying "if someone is truly a dangerous terror suspect, why would you leave them at large."[7]

Moreover, the control orders have themselves been deemed dangerous (to individual liberties), and Britain has been criticised by the Council of Europe for introducing this measure. The legality, or otherwise, of control orders is in fact central to an ongoing debate on the contemporary nature of rights and freedoms in the United Kingdom.[8] Human rights are no longer sacrosanct (a point to which we will return later in the chapter). Some members of the current Labour government portray them as outmoded, brought into being by a Europe in which the memory of 'state fascism' was still fresh (Tempest, 2006). On the contrary, Alvaro Gil-Robles, voicing the views of the Council of Europe, has warned that across Europe (but nowhere more so than the United Kingdom, perhaps) there has been a tendency "to consider human rights as excessively restricting the effective administration of justice and the protection of the public interest" rather than the "very foundation of democractic societies" (quoted in Gillan,

2005). In the contemporary context in which a Home Office minister can suggest the introduction of 'a stronger version of control orders which would depart from the European Convention on Human Rights' the status of 'dangerous terror suspect' in both the United Kingdom and the United States trumps mere criminality.

The extra-legal status of dangerousness is rightly flagged up by Butler as being a development which undermines the rule of law and the quality of democracy which depends upon it. However, the point that I wish to make is of a different nature. Dangerousness—indeed the very language of the fight against terror networks—works to domesticate a global threat and constructs that threat in terms which are familiar and reassuring. What sorts of things are usually described as dangerous? Escaped prisoners, vicious dogs, faulty electrical appliances, freak weather conditions are some examples. 'Dangerousness' renders a global threat into familiar terms and makes the 'spaces of wonder' constituted by global terror networks explicable, manageable, and amenable to policy solutions. The practice of labelling something dangerous is at the same time a strategy to mobilise discourses of safety, and to assuage anxieties and trepidation.

BRINGING THE OFFSHORE BORDER BACK HOME

As Bauman reminds us, one consequence of globalization is that we live in 'open societies' which can no longer easily remain closed to ideas, influences, and trends originating elsewhere. This openness is a double-edged sword, bringing both the promise of freedom and autonomy but also forcing us to acknowledge

> the terrifying experience of a heteronomous, hapless and vulnerable population confronted with, and possibly overwhelmed by forces it neither controls nor fully understands; a population horrified by its own undefendability and obsessed with the tightness of its frontiers and the security of individuals living inside them. (Bauman, 2007, 7)

The openness of borders is highly desirable in some senses (availability of cheap consumer goods and easy foreign travel) but also signals a vulnerability to flows and mobilities which can be perceived as threatening. It is for these reasons that borders and bordering strategies have loomed large in recent anti-terror policy initiatives in the United Kingdom, in Europe, and in North America. The second 'space of wonder' under consideration then is the United Kingdom's border and its changing configuration under contemporary conditions of insecurity. The United Kingdom's border is an exemplary 'space of wonder' because it confounds the understanding of inside/outside or domestic/foreign, which borders traditionally provide.

Peter Andreas (2000, 1) states that, "it has become intellectually fashionable to dismiss borders as increasingly irrelevant to the human experience in the so-called age of 'globalization'". While by no means an accurate reflection of the balance of thinking about borders under conditions of globalization, the idea that globalization equals a 'borderless world' has become lodged in the public's consciousness. In reality, the opposite has happened: We live in a world where borders proliferate but, at the same time, for many of us (but by no means all) these borders have become much easier to traverse (Rumford, 2007b). This is by no means the only way in which borders have been changing. Many commentators have noted that rather than existing as 'lines in the sand' which delineate a legal space and mark the limit of a particular sovereign jurisdiction, borders can now take many forms. No longer only physical presences at the edges of a polity working to regulate movement and protect the domestic realm from outside threats, borders can be everywhere and anywhere; 'smart' borders, relying on high-tech biometric technology, or 'remote borders' located away from domestic ports, airports, and land frontiers (Amoore, 2006). Indeed locating borders has become a key issue in the academic literature in recent years as it has become increasingly evident that borders are not only 'at the border': They can be elsewhere too—at airports, in railway stations, in internet cafes, and along the motorway (Walters, 2006b). Security functions associated with bordering have in many cases been privatized—by offloading security checks to airlines and other carriers, for example (Lahav and Guiraudon, 2000).

In the United Kingdom, the approach to bordering has changed significantly in recent years. In a recent publication entitled 'Securing the UK Border: Our Vision and Strategy for the Future' (Home Office, 2007) the Borders and Immigration Agency takes a far-from-conventional view of where the United Kingdom borders are to be found. No longer is it the goal of border policy to fortify and secure the traditional perimeter (although there is some domestic political momentum for the idea of a new unified border police force). The approach favoured by the United Kingdom now is to move the border rather than fortify it in the standard way. The United Kingdom prefers to locate its borders 'offshore'. "The days when border control started at the White Cliffs of Dover are over", in the words of one Government spokesperson.[9] According to the 'Securing the UK border' document, "border control can no longer be just a fixed line on a map . . . we must create a new offshore line of defence, checking individuals as far from the UK as possible". Moreover, the aim, according to the Immigration Minister Liam Byrne, is to lay the foundation stone for "offshore borders all over the world".

Not only does Britain have 'offshore' borders, it also has 'juxtaposed' borders. The United Kingdom and France have swapped border controls at either end of the Eurostar train route, the UK passport controls being located in Paris and Lille and the French controls at St. Pancras station.

What does having a 'juxtaposed' or 'offshore' border mean, and what are these borders designed to do? According to the Home Office document, offshore borders are designed to combat methods of illegal entry to the United Kingdom by exercising tighter controls on the issue of travel visas throughout the world, fining airlines who carry passengers not in possession of the correct documents, and by preventing clandestine entry at unauthorized entry points such as remote parts of the coast and small airfields. An important development is the 'electronic borders' (e-borders) programme. Travellers to the United Kingdom will be required to submit personal details prior to travel, thus allowing the UK authorities to authorise or deny permission to travel at an early stage.

In developing offshore and remote borders, the United Kingdom relies heavily on the 'e-borders' technology, especially the use of biometric visas and the 'remote control' of passenger carriers. However, the government's problem is that these initiatives do not necessarily increase public confidence that the country's borders are working properly and its population is safe from terrorist attacks, traffickers, and illegal immigrants. Smart borders do not have high public visibility, and the government has to be seen to be doing something reassuring. It is within this context that we can understand the August 2007 announcement that immigration officers at Gatwick Airport have been given new uniforms 'to make it clear to people that they are at a UK border'. Home Office minister Tony McNulty said, "we are determined to improve public confidence in how immigration is managed. Key to this is the creation of highly visible staff at our borders, to deter people who have no right to be here." The 'space of wonder' represented by the United Kingdom's offshore border has been subjected to a policy make-over by familiar and reassuring border images; the clear signage at UK airports confirming that 'you are now at the UK border', and the uniforms worn by officers of the newly created Borders and Immigration Authority. The capacity of these initiatives to fortify the border is questionable: Do smart uniforms really 'deter people who have no right to be here'? The suspicion remains that open borders are rather difficult to close, both in reality and by through policy 'slight of hand'. As Bauman (2006a, 109) states,

> However many border security guards, biometric appliances and explosive-sniffing dogs are deployed at the ports, borders that have already been thrown open and kept open by and for free-floating capital, commodities and information can't be sealed back and kept sealed against humans.

FIGHTING NAZIS IN THE GLOBAL BORDERLANDS

It is not only Europe that is deemed to possess a borderland (Batt, 2003), a feature which in itself further complicates the functioning of the United

Kingdom's border, forming as it does a portion of the EU's external border, which the agency Frontex now works to regulate and harmonize. The EU has introduced Frontex, based in Warsaw, as a new border agency which has responsibility for harmonizing the border control regimes of nation-states in such a way as to create common European borders out of a plurality of national borders (Vaughan-Williams, 2008). The EU has also developed its Neighbourhood Policy (Lavinex, 2004) as a way of softening the outer edges of the EU and preventing the new, enlarged border from producing a new group of disadvantaged regions on either side of the border and increasing stability in non-EU countries beyond the new borders by offering a range of incentives to participate in the EU's single market and trans-European mobility and communication networks, for example. The notion of 'borderland' has become a key motif in understanding contemporary Europe and has added a further twist to the account of the transformed spatiality of Europe under conditions of globalization. Balibar (2004b) has gone one step further and asserted that Europe *is* a borderland, all margin and no centre, a region in which global flows and processes are subject to translation into a European idiom. In this sense, Europe's borderlands could be said to represent 'spaces of wonder' in their own right.

However, the third 'space of wonder' under consideration here is the global borderland or global frontier-land, as Bauman (2007, 37) terms it, a realm beyond the control of states which is a 'global space' not subject to the rule of law. This is a realm where 'global outcasts' reside, refugees, migrants, asylum seekers living in a state of 'permanent transitoriness'. It is these very qualities that make it highly suitable as a realm of global governance. The global borderland can be appropriated by powerful nation-states such as the United States and the United Kingdom to pursue forms of exclusion, create barriers to global mobility, and pursue a 'politics of pre-emption' which would be most unthinkable and unacceptable in conventional domestic politics. Global borderlands are the 'spaces of wonder' within which Guantanamo Bay and Abu Ghraib have become possible, and which also allow thousands of 'illegal' immigrants to perish in the Mediterranean and Atlantic while undertaking journeys by sea or in attempts to cross into the EU at the barbed wire fences erected in the Spanish enclaves of Ceuta and Mellila in North Africa. In some places the global borderland resembles the aforementioned 'Great Wall of Europe' (Balibar, 2006) designed to keep out the unwanted from Europe, while at other time it takes the form of a generalised 'state of exception' (Vaughan-Williams, 2008) which allows for responses consistent with a permanent state of emergency (Calhoun, 2006).

This section will examine one consequence of the attempt to conduct the 'war on terror' in the global borderlands. In the drive to present terrorism as something that both has global reach and importantly originates beyond the borders of (Western) civilization, the UK authorities have drawn attention to the strangeness of both the enemy and also the struggle against them (a new type of war against a new enemy). Importantly, projecting the struggle onto a global borderland has increased our own strangeness: Do we recognize ourselves in the acts that are being perpetrated in our name; at Abu Ghraib, Camp Breadbasket, or the rendition flights that implicate European countries in acts of torture? It is not only the enemy that is increasingly unfamiliar: Our own societies are also becoming 'spaces of wonder'. In an effort to ameliorate this strangeness the Blair government has sought to provide the enemy with a 'familiar face', that of Nazism.

In a speech at Kings College, London, on 20th February 2006 on the topic of the behaviour of UK troops in Iraq (against a background of suspected abuse of Iraqi civilians by British troops) the then Home Secretary John Reid stated that he was not attempting to defend the indefensible. The army must be responsible for maintaining high standards. However, he was concerned with what he sees as a lack of "balance and fairness towards our troops" who today have to fight on a "changed and hugely uneven battlefield" (Reid, 2006). What we fail to comprehend, Reid asserted, is that the enemy are unconstrained by any law and unfettered by any sense of morality: "we intrinsically value life, they do not" (Reid, 2006). The enemy is "the completely unconstrained terrorist" (Reid, 2006).

It should be noted that what starts as a speech defending the actions of British soldiers in Iraq quickly mobilizes the (non-Iraqi) threat of Al-Qaeda in order to frame the difficulties that those troops face. Because of media openness and the access of the terrorists to that media, our troops are under greater scrutiny than ever before. "British troops are forced to operate on what I call 'an uneven playing field of scrutiny'—there is now asymmetric—uneven—scrutiny of warfare" (Reid, 2006). The crux of the matter is that

> it is this uneven battlefield of one-sided scrutiny which has done so much to encourage the perception among our troops that they are increasingly constrained while the enemy is freer than ever to perpetrate the most inhumane practices and crimes. (Reid, 2006)

Reid's message is that we need to be 'slower to condemn, quicker to understand' the forces. He argues his case for not dwelling disproportionately on isolated acts of wrongdoing by British soldiers by appealing to historical experiences of war and, more particularly, to familiar oppositions such as good versus evil, and sacrifice versus freedoms, and also invocations of 'core' values such as 'fairness' (which become counterposed to human rights). The good–evil dichotomy is based on more than a reminder that the enemy are 'beyond the pale' and possess no moral legitimacy, although this is a key motif: "we" fight for what is right and oppose what is wrong, the adversary "revels in mass murder" and "sets out to cause the greatest pain it can to innocent people" (Reid, 2006). To bolster the good–evil distinction, Reid draws upon the enemy imagery of Hitler and the Nazis to point up the magnitude of the evil which Al-Qaeda is capable, unfettered as it is by any sense of morality: "it is the rule of law and the virtue of freedom of expression versus barbarism" (Reid, 2006).

Another key theme in Reid's speech is that of 'sacrifice versus freedoms', which again resonates with resistance to Nazism. "Without the wartime generation that made sacrifices to defeat Hitler, we wouldn't have the means to fight this more modern evil" (Reid, 2006). The freedoms referred to here are press freedoms, and the sacrifices are those associated with a curtailment of press freedom 'in the national interest', which it is assumed the media were happy to go along with during WWII 'in the national interest.' Reid's argument is that Al Qaeda will exploit media images for their own ends; it is the media's responsibility to ensure that in reporting the facts ... it does not fall victim to this campaign (Reid, 2006). The enemy seeks to undermine our public morale by using "our democratic freedom of speech to destroy our will to fight for our democratic values" (Reid, 2006). It is a battle of ideas which, like earlier ideological struggles against communism and Nazism, can be won. In his attempts to mobilize society in the fight against terrorism ("the struggle has to be at every level, in every way and by every single person in this country")[10] he is drawn to equate the terrorist threat to the United Kingdom with the earlier threat of Nazism; "Britain is living in the most threatening time since the second world war".

Reid has reiterated the 'war against the Nazis' theme on other occasions. In a talk at a conference on technology he was reported as saying that the technological race to stay ahead of extremists recalls 'innovators of the past' such as Barnes Wallis or Alan Turing during WWII. These individuals, Reid said, "were vital in the technological battle to beat the then enemy, the Nazis, so we must be able to utilise the skills and expertise of all in our society in the battle against terror".[11] Pursuing another favourite theme, the inappropriateness of human rights legislation in the 'war against terror', Reid stated that 'Europe-wide human rights—such as freedom from detention, forced labour, torture and punishment without trial—had been formulated in the wake of state fascism, but were now threatened by what he dubbed "fascist individuals"'.[12]

Another key theme in his Kings College speech is 'fairness' rather than human rights, and this links strongly with the previously discussed themes of good versus evil and sacrifice versus freedom. As we noted earlier, Reid argues that British troops are operating on an 'uneven playing field of scrutiny': 'We' not only play to the rules, but we have to be seen to be doing so. This has resulted in a "perception among our troops that they are increasingly constrained while the enemy is freer than ever to perpetrate the most inhumane practices and crimes" (Reid, 2006). Reid reiterates that British troops go to great lengths to stay within the law and treat people fairly ("even the enemy"). Fairness is built in to military operations, the problem however is human rights legislation which, "has improved lives in so many areas" but "has also sometimes become the convenient banner under which some who are fundamentally opposed to our Armed Forces, or to the government of the day, or to a particular military conflict, have chosen to march" (Reid, 2006). This is a problem, states Reid, because in the soldiers' perception human rights lawyers and . . . the International Criminal Court are waiting in the wings to step in and act against them' (Reid, 2006). They need to know that they operate under British law not European and International law. Reid opposes 'fairness', an intrinsic decency rooted in the professionalism of an army which "seeks to inject morality—right and wrong—into the harsh reality of warfare" (Reid, 2006), to the idea of human rights, which is portrayed as well-meaning but, in reality, benefiting the enemy. In a striking attempt to portray human rights as being opposed to the 'national interest' Reid states, in a section of his speech devoted to the sacrifices of the WWII generation and the courage of modern troops, "both these groups must sometimes feel that if Lord Haw-Haw was still around today, someone would be telling us that human rights demand that he be given a weekly column in the newspapers".

Former Prime Minister, Tony Blair, has given a clear indication that the struggle against 'global terror' is best fought in the global borderlands. In a speech to the World Affairs Council in August 2006,[13] he stated that success in the battle against global extremism will not come about through force as such, but can be won "at the level of values" where we can show that "we are even-handed, fair and just in our application of those values to the world". In this way, the 'war on terror' becomes domesticated through its translation into a battle over values rather than a war against an enemy which involves killing large numbers of 'unlawful combatants'. Pursuing this theme Blair states, "We could have chosen security as the battlefield. But we didn't. We chose values." The fairness invoked by Blair is both an attempt to de-territorialize the war (thereby exacerbating the global nature of the threat) and to domesticate the struggle by transcribing it within the familiar reference points of war—our decency versus their barbarism—a regular theme of British WWII movies, for example. Similarly, equating the enemy in the 'war on terror' with the Nazis is another attempt to domesticate strangeness, and the British government are happy to be 'still hunting Nazis' (Mestrovic, 1994), this time out of choice, rather than necessity. By conducting the 'war on terror' in the global borderlands (the terrain of values, rather than conflict) it has been given a 'familiar' face; the Nazis are enemies of us all and no one can deny their evil intent or the legitimacy of the struggle against them. In the next section we look further at the domestication of these 'spaces of wonder' and to do so we will draw upon Stjepan Mestrovic's notion of postemotionalism.

FROM CULTURAL TRAUMA TO POSTEMOTIONALISM

'most people try to deal with terror by translating it into a familiar language'
—Diken and Laustsen, 2004

The problem with contemporary analyses of the politics of fear, particularly as they are applied to an understanding of social policy, is that they tend towards a 'humpty-dumpty' understanding of society (Rumford, 2002, 122). The emphasis is very much on the ways disruption to societies caused by insecurities, uncertainties, and traumas can be made good, mended, restored—put back together again—with the right social policies. This tendency is highlighted by Robin (2005, 4), who criticises commentators on the 9/11 attacks in the United States (as well as commentators on a range of historical events from the Russian Revolution to Balkan genocide), who utilize the political fear instilled by the attack as an 'opportunity for collective renewal'. Fear is seen as necessary in issuing a 'wake-up call' to society and to restore cohesive social values. In such cases, fear serves as "the agent of personal; and collective salvation" (Robin, 2005, 13). Fear can easily be mobilized as a governance strategy in order to offer the "hope of beginning, renewing or restoring a robust republic of energetic virtue and galvanizing purpose" (Robin, 2005, 23).

The same 'humpty-dumpty syndrome' underpins the 'cultural trauma' approach associated with the work of Jeffrey Alexander, Neil Smelser, and others (Alexander, Eyerman, Giesen, Smelser, & Sztompka, 2004), which has emerged as a dominant framework for understanding major disasters and events such as the attacks on the United States of September 11th, 2001. According to Alexander (2004, 1),

> cultural trauma occurs when members of a collectivity feel they have been subjected to a horrendous event that leaves indelible marks upon their group consciousness, marking their memories forever and changing their future identity in fundamental and irrevocable ways.

Importantly, this sociological approach emphasises that trauma does not exist in nature but is constructed by society. The approach adopted by Alexander et al., thus differs from 'common sense' understandings of trauma in that it does not assume that the trauma is an intrinsic property of events themselves (Alexander, 2004, 2). The authors reject this "naturalistic fallacy": "events are not inherently traumatic. Trauma is a socially mediated attribution" (Alexander, 2004, 8). And it is "carrier groups" in society—"collective agents of the trauma process" (Alexander, 2004, 11) who construct events as traumas. Specifically, the carrier groups organize the collective response; giving meaning to the group's injury, establishing the victim, attributing responsibility, and establishing the consequences

(Alexander, 2004, 22). Significantly, the process of trauma construction outlined by Alexander and his colleagues works to calm and manage emotional responses by putting them in some explanatory perspective or coherent narrative. In Alexander's words, "once the collective identity has been so reconstructed, there will eventually emerge a period of 'calming down'" (Alexander, 2004, 22).

The cultural trauma approach is important because it draws attention to ways in which traumas can be rationalized, managed, and absorbed by the social system. Alexander and his colleagues outline how the collective acknowledgment of cultural trauma can be the starting point for the societal mobilization of healing mechanisms, and through which society is able to draw strength, and 'move on'. What begins as a massive collective shock which provokes a series of inchoate responses, will, through the process of constructing cultural trauma, become a rational way of managing feelings of distress, anger, responsibility, and guilt, and processing them into a useful and constructive episode of social learning. Thus, through social trauma, emotion is translated into rationality and the 'world turned upside down' is righted once more. In other words, cultural trauma is a societal mechanism for apprehending and understanding the inexplicable, formulating a rational response, and healing the wounds inflicted upon its collective being.

However, the 'cultural trauma' framework of Alexander et al., conforms to Robin's critique of fear as the catalyst of demands for social renewal. In this sense, it does not allow us to properly apprehend the dynamics of 'spaces of wonder' or the attempts to drive social policy through responses to increasing strangeness. In this context, another more satisfactory approach is provided by the American sociologist, Stjepan Mestrovic, and in particular his ideas on 'postemotional society'. For Mestrovic 'postemotional society' is a designation for a society no longer in touch with its emotions, not sure how to respond to traumatic events, and increasingly disconnected from a sense of purpose which would enable it to respond to events with genuine anger, outrage, and feeling. 'Postemotional society' is characterised by a mining of emotional responses from the (distant) past in order to create 'synthetic moral indignation' and other faux-emotional responses to current events. For Mestrovic, postemotionalism indicates not only that emotions are manipulated and mechanised in contemporary public life—"intellectualized, mechanical, mass-produced emotions" (Mestrovic, 1997, 26)—but importantly, dead emotions are recycled (Mestrovic, 1997, 2) and transformed into objects for consumption:

> anger becomes indignation . . . envy an objectless craving for something better. Hate is transformed into a subtle malice that is hidden in all sort of intellectualizations. Heartfelt joy is now the bland happiness represented by the "Happy Meal". (Mestrovic, 1997, 62)

In short, society has lost its collective sense of morality, right and wrong, and what might constitute a genuine emotional response to an outrage or threat. Mestrovic portrays America as a country in which the search for ways to acknowledge a range of perspectives (multiculturalism) and validate a range of experiences (relativism) has led to a form of 'other-directedness' in which politics is designed to speak to everyone but not offend anyone. The result is a range of policy perspectives which are both bland and self-congratulatory.

One central aspect of postemotionalism is the rhetoric of victimhood. Mestrovic makes the case that anger and outrage have been replaced by 'dead' emotions retrieved from history (as is the case with recent episodes of ethnic violence such as occurred in the former Yugoslavia). Victimhood has become a celebrated state—and a licence (Staples, quoted in Mestrovic, 1997, 9). Not surprisingly perhaps, initial responses to both 9/11 and 7/7 emphasised victimhood. With the benefit of a longer-term perspective perhaps the victimhood status of the United States was over-stated, and is rather dismissed by Ulrich Beck: "Fifteen suicidal terrorists armed with carpet knives sufficed to compel the global hegemon to see itself as victim" (Beck, 2006,153). In any case, victim status served the United States well in the early days of the 'war on terror'. As Smelser (2004, 272) points out, the victimization of the United States served as a considerable asset "in mobilizing the support and cooperation of other countries". To illustrate these features further we can focus on one aspect of the United Kingdom's 'victim status' and offer a reading based on Mestrovic's 'postemotional society' thesis. The example I have chosen to focus on is the then Defence Minister John Reid's defence of the actions of UK soldiers in Iraq (made in the light of growing evidence of abuse of Iraqi citizens in and around Basra) outlined in the preceding section.

Reid's Kings College speech discussed at length earlier in this chapter demonstrates a strong postemotional dimension. The message that we need to be 'slower to condemn, quicker to understand' is packaged postemotionally, relying as it does on positioning the United Kingdom as victim (at the hands of one-sided media scrutiny, and over-zealous human rights lawyers). Reid portrays the struggle against the contemporary enemy in postemotional terms, drawing heavily on the fixed emotional reference points associated with WWII and the struggle against Nazism, an enemy whose evil is beyond debate. This allows him to portray the United Kingdom on the right side of the good–evil dichotomy without fear of contradiction. Similarly he positions human rights as inferior to 'gut feelings' about what is right, and quotes with approval Michael Ignatieff's view that "the decisive restraint on inhuman practice on the battlefield lies within the warrior himself". Human rights legislation is no substitute for an innate sense of fairness and the knowledge that we are fighting for what is right. Human rights can only be established by treaties, legislation, and international agreements, and these are in need of 'reinterpretation'. In a more recent speech,[14] Reid argues that the Human Rights Act was designed according to an "old model of war". The world has changed, and nowadays human rights are "helping terrorists escape and fight deportation". On this reasoning, human rights legislation hinders the government in its attempts to protect the public.

CONCLUDING COMMENTS: FROM APPREHENSION TO WONDER

The United Kingdom's borders can also be viewed through the postemotional lens. The future may be 'e-borders' but the United Kingdom's borders are dressed in the trappings of a good old-fashioned frontier post where the guards wear smart uniforms and the crossing is clearly labelled so you are aware that 'you are now at the UK border'. The postemotional response is to 'put a smiley face on the border' and soften the impact of any perceived threat. As Diken and Laustsen remark, it was common for commentators on the 9/11 attacks on the United States to call for enhanced border controls, even extending to a temporary halt to immigration (Diken and Laustsen, 2004, 3). In doing so, they maintain the fiction that the threat emanates from outside, and, indeed, that an outside still exists.

The 'humpty-dumpty syndrome', in common with postemotionalism, highlights a disinclination to confront the magnitude and strangeness of the world: In this sense, both approaches pre-empt any possible experience of the sublime. From a different perspective an experience of terror or the 'spaces of wonder' elaborated here—in other words an encounter with the sublime—could result in a form of empowerment: The individual is able to master the emotions, achieve self-control, and develop a new form of understanding. It follows that experiencing the sublime can be a way of viewing, controlling, and even producing the world (Makdisi, 1996, 67). Thus, confronting 'spaces of wonder' might not be the disempowering experience that fear is thought to represent. Such ideas call into question Furedi's (2004) view that the "culture of fear is underpinned by a profound sense of powerlessness, a diminished sense of agency that leads people to turn themselves into passive subjects who can only complain that 'we are frightened'".

This chapter offers an alternative to the idea of fear as a catch-all category for understanding political choices. It is argued that, through a critical awareness of 'spaces of wonder', we can better understand the ways in which choices are framed in order to reposition global spaces, and the disorientating affects that these can have within the vernacular of everyday politics. We have examined attempts to domesticate 'spaces of wonder' through policy responses which seek to take advantage of the power of the global to create experiences of trepidation and anxiety by encroaching upon the normality of everyday existence. Such policies aim to enfold 'spaces of wonder' in discourses of familiarity. In this way, the threat of global terror is localized in terms of 'dangerousness', the futuristic 'offshore borders' are 'brought back home' through new signage and smart uniforms, and the sliding standards of human rights occasioned by the 'war on terror' are justified by invoking the struggle against Nazism.

The literature on globalization has long emphasised the interconnectedness and resulting 'oneness' of the world. It has also taught us that globalization can bring negative as well as positive developments; new winners and losers, new patterns of inequality, as well as a new world of threats resulting from environmental degradation and overproduction. What is rarely confronted in the literature is that, at the same time as the world is re-made by processes of globalization, the world is also becoming increasingly unfamiliar. Global threats have occasioned a range of solutions which themselves have heightened a sense of insecurity and threat. This is true of the nationalisms which seek to defend the authenticity of culture at the same time as portraying that same culture as being under terminal threat from external forces, and it is also true of the gated communities which offer commoditized safety at the same time as working to remind inhabitants that the world beyond the gates is violent, unpredictable, and fraught with danger. This chapter has sought to take Robertson's idea that globalization has resulted in an institutionalization of strangeness (Robertson, 2007) and used this to explore the ways in which this strangeness or perception of 'stranger danger' has resulted in new opportunities for governance and new strands of public policy which work to offer 'solutions' to everyday trepidation. To understand these social policies, it is argued, we need to focus less on the 'politics of fear' and more on 'spaces of wonder'.

6 Empire and the Hubris of the 'High Point'

> The EU is an empire. Not an empire like the Roman, the British or Byzantine empires . . . an empire can be liberal . . . An empire can be welcoming and modern. An empire can be attractive.
>
> —Hartley, 2006, 6

It was perhaps inevitable that the EU would come to be viewed as an empire, given the vogue for that term. What is surprising, however, is that the idea has been taken up by commentators from such diverse theoretical perspectives. In this chapter we examine the idea that the EU might be best thought of as an empire, looking in particular at Jan Zielonka's book *Europe as Empire: The Nature of the Enlarged EU* (Zielonka, 2007) and Beck and Grande's *Cosmopolitan Europe* (Beck and Grande, 2007), which contains a chapter on "Cosmopolitan Empire". Both books make a strong case for rethinking the EU through the lens of empire, particularly from the point of view of developing a new politics of space and more especially finding a way to understand the EU which does not involve the assumption that it must be some kind of state. (See Delanty and Rumford [2005], particularly Chapter 8).

The introduction of the idea of empire into the European frame also allows us to give consideration to Hardt and Negri's now famous book and their very different formulation of the idea of empire (and very different approach to the politics of space), which, it is argued, provides a valuable global context for understanding European transformations. The chapter concludes that empire (in any formulation) is not a satisfactory framework within which to understand European transformations. The reason for this is that empire works to maintain the fiction of a 'high point', a privileged perspective from which all processes and developments, all spaces and border, all actors and institutions, can be viewed and interpreted. In this sense, empire is but the latest attempt to provide a 'master' viewpoint from which an authoritative analytical position can be established. It is argued that there can be no 'high point', an argument which was first introduced in the chapter on Balibar (and the theme is also taken up again in Chapter 7). In this regard, the idea of the EU as a 'multiperspectival polity', as developed by Ruggie (1993) is a more satisfactory approach, although not one fully appreciated in the literature.

STUDYING THE EU AS EMPIRE

Zielonka's *Europe as Empire* is the most comprehensive attempt to recast the EU as empire. At its root, the argument advanced by Zielonka is simple: The EU is not becoming like a state but it is taking on the form of an empire. The empire-like qualities of the EU should not be understood in terms of imperial designs but rather in terms of its "multiple and over-lapping jurisdictions, striking cultural and economic heterogeneity, fuzzy borders, and divided sovereignty" (Zielonka, 2007, vii). In other words, its polycentric system of governance means that it can be likened to "a neo-medieval empire" (Zielonka, 2007, vii). In short, its spatial characteristics are what make it empire-like: polycentricity, overlapping jurisdictions, 'soft' borders. This means that the notion that the EU is a form of empire is rich in possibilities for thinking about the politics of space.

Europe as Empire is an attempt to step outside the mainstream EU integration literature and find a way of talking about the EU in terms other than that of a state. As such, it represents "a polemical response to the mainstream literature on European integration" (Zielonka, 2007, 2). It is also notable for its commitment to bringing enlargement centre stage in EU studies. Enlargement, "cannot be treated as a footnote to the study of European integration" (Zielonka, 2007, 3). The argument is that enlargement renders the rise of a European state impossible (Zielonka, 2007, 9) and, as a result, EU scholars need to develop new paradigms with which to study integration: state-centric approaches are insufficient.

But why should we be convinced by the idea that the enlarged EU resembles a neo-medieval empire? What, according to Zielonka, are the characteristics of the EU which make it more like an empire than a state? The case for the EU as a neo-medieval empire can be outlined as follows. The EU is diverse, more so than ever after the recent enlargement. This diversity can be discerned in terms of economies ('cascading socio-economic discrepancies') and democratic institutions, as well as history and culture. National minorities and patterns of immigration also add to the diversity. In short, "the current plurality of different forms of governance, legal structures, economic zones of transactions, and cultural identities is striking and bears a remarkable resemblance to the situation in medieval Europe" (Zielonka, 2007, 168).

A second main reason why the EU is neo-medieval is the system of governance, particularly as it extends beyond the EU's borders ('soft borders in flux'). The EU has promoted EU governance in the near-abroad in order to stabilize the region. "Countries such as Bosnia and Kosovo are practically EU protectorates, and there is a long list of countries from Ukraine to Palestine which are following EU instructions on organizing economic governance" (Zielonka, 2007, 169). The EU behaved in an imperial fashion towards its then neighbours, but the "means were civilian rather than military" (Zielonka, 2007, 48). Nevertheless, the enlargement exercise was imperial and geared to "asserting political and economic control over an unstable and underdeveloped neighbourhood" (Zielonka, 2007, 59). The means of exerting this control are "similar to many previous imperial exercises: export of laws, economic transactions, administrative systems, and social habits" (Zielonka, 2007, 59).

Enlargement has increased the diversity of the EU, seen in terms of economic stability, levels of development, democratic sophistication, and cultural practices. Enlargement has made manifest a gradient of systemic differences between the EU 15 and the newer member states. However, the differences are not so large that the new member states are in a different category altogether: "they clearly belong to the same broad category of states, economies, and societies" (Zielonka, 2007, 43). A gradient can also be observed between the new members and those countries further east and south. These countries are

> clearly less stable, less economically developed, and less democratic, but the gap between the ten and the rest of post-Communist Europe is neither sharp nor consistent, and as such it is subject to engineering. (Zielonka, 2007, 43)

The two groups of countries also enjoy many linkages which means that "introducing any hard functional borders between the enlarged EU and its new neighbours is not easy" (Zielonka, 2007, 43). The argument is that the external boundaries of the EU are not marked by sharp differences in levels of economic and political development. The EU and non-EU countries form something like a continuum. These features reflect the neo-medieval nature of the EU, overlapping edges of the EU polity, softer distinctions between us and them, increased networking and connectivity, and polycentric governance regimes.

The democratic culture of the EU, particularly the absence of a public sphere, is seen to enhance the neo-medieval nature of the enlarged EU. Although Zielonka's views on the existence of a public sphere are not always consistent, ranging from a dismissal of the idea that a European public space can emerge (Zielonka, 2007, 21) to an acknowledgement that the European public space is segmented (Zielonka, 2007, 34), the nature of European publics enable him to make some important points regarding the EU-as-empire. In the absence of a unified public, the enlarged EU possesses a greater diversity of political cultures, public spaces, and peoples. This situation is not likely to change as there are "hardly any pan-European agents able to promote greater cultural homogeneity" (Zielonka, 2007, 136), nor movements leading to a convergence of democratic cultures. There remains a plurality of European demoi and nationally contained public spaces which do not join up into a coherent whole. This leads to the conclusion that the diverse and segmented public space reinforces the neo-medieval complexion of the EU. In other words, the EU is not a state and lacks the democratic resources to become more state-like. This is a rather simple conclusion to emerge from a relatively rich and suggestive argument. In many ways, the discussion is driven by the book's overall thesis—that the EU is becoming more neo-medieval in complexion—rather than by the analysis of the public sphere.

Zielonka makes several interesting points about the nature of European public space which are not developed as fully as they deserve to be. For example, there are two insights that could usefully form the nuclei of different debates on the public sphere. One is the capacity of citizens to contest European decisions, the other is the global nature of European civil society. The idea that the EU possesses a democratic deficit is given a fresh twist by Zielonka (2007, 139) who suggests that this criticism is predicated on the assumption that the EU is state-like or should become so. He states that rather than assuming that the EU should or will develop better systems of democratic representation, it is mechanisms of public contestation which are crucial to the democratic development of the EU. He writes, "the capacity of citizens to contest European decisions will be more crucial in a neo-medieval setting than the functioning of institutional channels of representation" (Zielonka, 2007, 139). Popular contestation could lead to greater legitimacy for the EU (Zielonka, 2007, 188). If this is the case, it appears rather odd that Zielonka underplays the importance of the emerging public space, which is constituted by exactly these forms of contestation (Strydom, 2002).

The second insight not developed by Zielonka is that those civil society organizations that do operate beyond national borders "usually see themselves as global rather than merely European movements" (Zielonka, 2007, 133). This is an important point, the significance of which eludes many EU scholars. There are I think two dimensions that could usefully be developed. The first is that it is indeed the case that, according to scholars, there appears to be much more global than European civil society. This, as I have argued elsewhere (Delanty and Rumford, 2005, Chapter 10), is due to the nature of EU studies, which tends to neglect those processes that are not seen as of primary importance in understanding EU integration, or conceived as processes internal to member states, their political elites, and citizens. It is not the case that civil society is underdeveloped in Europe but extensive throughout the rest of the world. Rather, it is the case that EU scholars have certain expectations about civil society, namely that it must be a project initiated or governed by the EU, and that civil society actors must work to develop a pan-EU sphere of operation. This means that a significant proportion of what might count as European civil society 'flies under the radar' of EU integration scholars. The second dimension is linked to the first and is that the search for European civil society is launched from the wrong starting point, the assumption that social movements or advocacy networks must build upwards from the local level, through the national level, to the European level and only then on to the global level.

To understand the dynamics of European civil society, such as it is, it is far more productive to reverse the analytical priority and see as an instance of a global civil society which is continuous with it.

INTEGRATION THROUGH ENLARGEMENT
OR INTEGRATION WITHOUT ENLARGEMENT?

One of the main weaknesses of Zielonka's account is that his assessment of EU governance beyond borders and the neo-medieval nature of the EU's approach to its new neighbours post-enlargement fails to take into account the EU's neighbourhood policy (ENP), an EU policy specifically designed to soften or blur the external borders and promote EU norms, values, and practices in a range of countries not likely to become EU members (or whose candidature is not yet on the EU agenda).[1] This omission is strange given that the nature and ambitions of the ENP could well add support to Zielonka's argument for the EU as empire. However, contrary to the thrust of the ENP, Zielonka (2007: 171) believes that yet further enlargements are likely, driven by geopolitical considerations rather than through adoption of the *acquis communaunitaire* (in other words, the EU would utilize derogations and opt-outs to 'soften the edges' of future enlargement). In fact, the ENP makes integration through enlargement an unlikely future scenario, although this is not to say that a country from the ENP group[2] may not eventually be considered for membership. Quoting from the ENP webpage, "The ENP remains distinct from the process of enlargement although it does not prejudge, for European neighbours, how their relationship with the EU may develop in future, in accordance with Treaty provisions"[3] On the contrary, the EU is more likely to proceed on the basis of integration without enlargement (Rumford, 2006b). By downgrading the importance of the ENP ("inadequate to shape political and economic developments in the EU's unstable neighbours to the south and east", Zielonka, 2007, 173) makes the mistake of believing that the EU "has no other equally effective foreign policy tool to shape its unstable external environment".

The ENP is a significant development in EU foreign policy and is interesting not for what it tells us about the future of enlargement but for how it frames the EU's relationship with the wider world (Axford, 2006). ENP rhetoric has centred on the construction of 'undivided Europe' and the need to ensure that enlargement does not create new divisions in and beyond Europe; "avoiding the emergence of new dividing lines between the enlarged EU and our neighbours" (website blurb). 'Hard' borders are perceived to be problematic due to the difficulty of policing them and the negative consequences for countries consigned to exist beyond the EU's expanded border. In fact creating new borders can result in disadvantaged regions on both sides of the border. To tackle the first problem the EU has created the new border regulatory agency, Frontex, whose job it is to harmonize border control and ensure that national borders are also common European borders (Hein, 2006). To tackle the second problem the EU has launched ENP in order to prevent enlargement from creating new economic instabilities and security problems on the Eurasian frontier.

The result is that countries who are not likely to become official candidates for full membership can be brought within the orbit of the Single Market and other pan-European collaborative projects. The distinction between EU and non-EU, members and non-members, has been replaced by a notion that integration can proceed in ways which do not result in automatic enlargement. Marketization and democratization are the keys to inclusion, not outright membership (Axford, 2006, 173). The ENP offers the EU's neighbours a privileged relationship, building upon a mutual commitment to common values (democracy and human rights, rule of law, good governance, market economy principles, and sustainable development; website blurb). Thus, 'economic integration' is possible through this route as is a 'deeper political relationship'. How far the relationship develops will depend on "the extent to which these values are effectively shared" (website blurb). It is entirely possible that, in the future, a number of countries of the former Soviet bloc and countries in North Africa or the Middle East could be integrated (to differing degrees) within the Single Market. They would not necessarily move closer to full membership of the EU, however. According to former Commission President, Romano Prodi, the EU and its neighbours can share 'everything but institutions' or, in other terms, integration without enlargement.

HOW NEO-MEDIEVAL IS THE EU?

Zielonka makes a strong case for the EU not only resembling an empire but a neo-medieval empire. In his rejection of the 'Westphalian superstate' model, he emphasises that the EU neither resembles a state nor a "neo-Westphalian empire: it does not acquire land by conquest, develop centralized structures of government, rule by coercion and military power, nor does it have sharp borders or a hierarchical core-periphery relationship" (Zielonka, 2007, 14). There are two main problems with the neo-medieval argument. One derives from the utility of the neo-medieval metaphor, the other concerns alternative explanations for the changes that Zielonka places under the neo-medieval heading.

Early in the book Zielonka (2007, 6–7) considers various metaphors which have been employed to help us understand the EU. He reminds us of Puchala's elephant, Wallace's flying geese, and a host of architectural and geometric metaphors. In place of these, he argues, we "need a complex and sophisticated paradigm and not just an inspiring metaphor or fancy term to comprehend the union" (Zielonka, 2007, 7). More than this, he continues, we need a paradigm to replace the statist paradigm which dominates EU studies. Out of this critique is born the 'neo-medieval' paradigm. Zielonka is of the opinion that paradigms and metaphors are mutually exclusive. But one could argue that his use of neo-medieval is still a metaphor, notwithstanding its designation as a paradigm. In fact, Zielonka (2007, 17) acknowledges that other authors have used 'medieval and imperial metaphors' and he draws upon these in his book. Neo-medieval is a metaphor because the societal, economic, and political context is modern, not medieval. As Zielonka states, "I use the term 'neo-medieval empire' exactly to emphasize that the EU's ways of organizing governance and projecting power abroad are not unique, but have been tried in previous stages of European history, even though in an entirely different socio-political context" (Zielonka, 2007,17). In other words, the EU can be said to *resemble* a neo-medieval empire, it shares some similarities, but its socio-political and global context mean that it cannot *be* a neo-medieval empire, although it may be productive to think in such terms.

There is another point about the use of the neo-medieval metaphor that needs to be made. It could be argued that it is a fairly 'tired' metaphor which has been used in the past in an attempt to capture some aspect of the EU. The best example is probably Anderson's work on postmodern and medieval territories. Inspired by Bull's work on neo-medieval political orders Anderson offers the idea of the EU as a system of overlapping authorities and multiple loyalties: local, regional, transnational, and global structures of governance exist alongside those working at nation-state level. The nation-state is no longer the automatic container of all forms of power and authority. Sovereignty is dispersed between different agencies and territory becomes 'unbundled'. Anderson (1996, 151) readily concedes that the concept of neo-medievalism is problematic and needs qualification if it is to be of use in understanding contemporary social and political change. He spells this out, thus. Medieval hierarchies were nested, they sat one inside the other: manor, lordship, kingdom. Nowadays hierarchies are rarely nested:

> people are often directly members of international networks, not via national bodies; small local groups increasingly deal directly with transnational bodies, not via larger intermediaries; regional groups and institutions deal directly with their counterparts in other states without the respective states necessarily having any involvement.

This is an important critique. Can Europe be described as neo-medieval when its enterprises generate global networks, its citizens are connected via global communications networks, and its politics are expressions of global concerns? Zielonka does not acknowledge this limit to the neo-medieval metaphor. He is confident that his neo-medieval paradigm can 'work' even though, as he acknowledges, the EU possesses a 'plurilateral' system of governance. "The EU's governance is increasingly non-territorial, multilevel, and multicentred" (Zielonka, 2007, 179).

The other main problem with the neo-medieval paradigm is that it makes rather grand claims regarding its explanatory power, whereas in fact many of the shifts and changes examined in *Europe as Empire* can be adequately apprehended using other, more familiar, perspectives. For example, many of the changes seen as being at the heart of the neo-medieval empire can be better explained by talking about a shift from government to governance (Rumford, 2002, 52–56). The plurilateral and polycentric model outlined by Zielonka, in which bargaining, coordination, informal contacts, and benchmarking are central to understanding the decision-making process, are key features of EU governance. In other words, what Zielonka describes is familiar to students of EU governance and does not require the neo-medieval paradigm in order to be intelligible.

"EUROPE AS EMPIRE": SOME CONCLUDING THOUGHTS

The cracks in the neo-medieval paradigm are difficult to hide. Indeed the main weaknesses of *Europe as Empire* are less to do with the idea of Europe as empire and mainly to do with the idea that the empire is a neo-medieval one (Beck and Grande, 2007, 70). Nevertheless, the book is well placed to perform a useful service in EU studies, in the sense that it could become the launching pad for a fresh round of thinking on the EU which is not in thrall to the statist paradigm, which Zielonka is right to identify as a major fetter on scholars of the EU. The book also makes a valuable contribution to thinking about the spatial dimensions of Europeanization and the need to place consideration of space and borders more centrally within EU studies. Where the 'neo-medieval paradigm' scores heavily is in its recognition that a key spatial dynamic in Europe is the periodic territorial expansion and the ways in which the new territories can be brought within existing structures of governance. This is also where we find the marriage between the neo-medieval nature of the EU and its imperial dimensions works best (Colas, 2007).

Europe as Empire is rather good on the politics of space, and particularly on the need to understand borders in order to understand space. For example, he holds that we are witnessing the development of a Europe in which

> different legal, economic, security, and cultural spaces are likely to be bound separately, cross-border multiple cooperation will flourish, and the inside/outside divide will be blurred. In due time, the EU's borders will probably be less territorial, less physical, and less visible. (Zielonka, 2007, 4)

He also makes the case for neo-medieval Europe, giving rise to 'soft borders', disjunctures between economic, political, and cultural competencies and territorial authority, blurred relations between core and periphery, the overlap and interpenetration of territorial units, the importance of non-territorial networks, and the dispersal of sovereignty. For these reasons alone, the book makes a significant contribution to rethinking the EU. It makes a convincing case for seeking alternatives to the dominant statist paradigm in EU studies and advances the argument for the centrality of the politics of space to an understanding of contemporary Europe.

BECK AND GRANDE: COSMOPOLITAN EMPIRE

Ulrich Beck and Edgar Grande's (2007) idea of 'cosmopolitan Empire' shares some family resemblances with Zielonka's project. They, too, start from the perspective that study of the EU has been severely hampered by an undue emphasis on the EU-as-state. The need to rethink the EU in non-state terms requires us to "abandon the outdated, state-fixated concepts and develop an alternative understanding of state, society and social structure that overcomes the methodological nationalism of research on Europe" (Beck and Grande, 2007, 53). Like Zielonka, they propose empire as the best term for understanding the new political entity that is the EU. They depart from Zielonka in that they do not favour the neo-medieval thesis, choosing instead to emphasise the 'cosmopolitanization of the state in Europe' (Beck and Grande, 2007, 53) as the driving force behind a 'post-imperial empire'. On this understanding, the EU has possessed "cosmopolitan momentum" (Beck and Grande, 2007, 19) from its inception. The supranational governance structures, beginning with the Coal and Steel Community, have institutionalized cosmopolitanism, as have the intergovernmental arrangements, both of which have taken the EU well beyond the realm of inter-state political cooperation. What this account does not acknowledge is that the EU's self-image precludes cosmopolitanism: There is no sense in which the EU sees itself as a cosmopolitan entity and it eschews the language of cosmopolitanism in documents, reports, statements, and so on. The EU does not see itself, or its citizens, in cosmopolitan terms (see Chapter 1).

Why should the transformation of the European state and the cosmopolitanization of Europe be best thought of in terms of empire? This is because the EU is a 'new political entity' not based on national demarcations and conquest, but on "overcoming national borders, voluntarism, consensus, transnational interdependence and the political added value accruing from cooperation" (Beck and Grande, 2007, 53). The concept of empire has "three significant advantages" according to Beck and Grande (2007, 55). First, as already noted, it takes us beyond state-centred politics. Second, it reminds us that there exists an 'asymmetry of power' between nation-states. Member states are unequal in respect of competitive advantage and political influence. Third, "it historicizes the division between the national and international and hence challenges the axioms on which politics and political science still act and think" (Beck and Grande, 2007, 55). Put simply, it reminds us that the nation-state is not a 'given', it can be placed historically, what Beck and Grande (2007, 55) term the "brief eternity of the national era". Also, they remind us that empires as a type of political entity have a pre-national and post-national history and this allows them to ask the question whether there "exists an affinity between the premodern period and the second [reflexive] modernity" (Beck and Grande, 2007, 53), but this speculation falls way short of embracing a neo-medieval conclusion. Not surprisingly, Beck and Grande also point to the spatial novelty of empire, and how this corresponds to the reality of present day Europe: the transcendence of territorially bound states through external expansion and the flexibility and variability of external borders. Moreover, empires also confound statist presumptions about the distinction between 'inside' and 'outside'.

Beck and Grande (2007, 62–72) identify ten features which are "fundamental to the European Empire". The first of these is the "asymmetrical political order", noted previously, which refers to the fact that EU states are unequal in terms of status, rights, and duties. Some member states belong to the Eurozone or Schengenland while others remain or choose to remain outside. The newer, mainly former Eastern European, members, were not permitted full freedom of mobility for their workers in the early years of membership. The second feature is its open and variable spatial structure, which includes flexible and mobile borders, resulting in "a highly variable, multidimensional geometry of Europe with bizarre spatial structures" (Beck and Grande, 2007, 65). The third feature is "multinational societal structure", which does not take the form of different national cultures subordinated to a "standardized 'European' culture" (Beck and Grande, 2007, 65) but is based on a cosmopolitan approach to difference: "others as different *and* at the same time as equal" (Beck and Grande, 2007, 13). The fourth feature is "integration through law, consensus and cooperation". This reminds us that the EU works not through military subjugation but through consensus and cooperation.

Feature number five is "welfare vs. security". The EU does not enlarge in order to make its territory more secure but in order to increase affluence. Feature six is "horizontal and vertical institutional integration" which speaks to the multi-level and multi-agency governance structures of the EU. Member states continue to play an important role and there exists "highly diverse institutional and material interdependencies among the various levels of policy-making" (Beck and Grande, 2007, 68). Feature seven is termed "network power" and points to the non-hierarchical forms of decision-making and the inclusion of societal actors in governance structures. The 'networked polity' structure of the EU means that it "does not reproduce the straightforward centre-periphery relations of older territorial and colonial empires" (Beck and Grande, 2007, 70). "Cosmopolitan sovereignty" is feature number eight, and a crucial plank in the overall 'cosmopolitan empire' thesis and links with some of the aforementioned features such as asymmetric political order, network power, and variable spatial structure.

According to Beck and Grande (2007, 70–71) the "European Empire is based entirely on sovereignty. It does not mark a refeaudalization of society or a 'new Middle Ages'". It also displays "graduated sovereignty rights" whereby the "greatest losses of formal sovereignty are incurred by those states which constitute the innermost zone of power. The further we move outwards, the greater is the formal sovereignty of the subject states" (Beck and Grande, 2007, 70). This point illuminates the comment made previously concerning centre-periphery relations in the 'cosmopolitan empire'. Sovereignty is being transformed into 'cosmopolitan sovereignty' or 'complex sovereignty': sovereignty beyond the nation-state. Feature nine is the "ambivalence of delimitation and delineation" which is also important in as much as the EU cannot ever assume that it has reached a final, end stage. The EU may aspire to universality but can never achieve it. The practical (or geographical) limits to enlargement should not result in the foreclosure of the debate about where Europe ends. Finally, feature ten comprises "emancipatory vs. repressive cosmopolitanism". The EU has to guard against the latter (a hierarchy of differences) while promoting the former (the "expansion of free spaces"; Beck and Grande, 2007, 71).

Feature number ten, "emancipatory vs. repressive cosmopolitanism", points to a more fundamental issue in relation to the Europeanness of the cosmopolitanism that the 'cosmopolitan empire' is presumed to posses. Beck and Grande (2007, 86) acknowledge a 'contradictory imperative' in the idea of European Empire. The more cosmopolitan the empire becomes, the less exclusively European it can hope to be (this, it should be noted, is one of the reasons why the EU is wary of seeing Europe in terms of 'actually existing cosmopolitanism'). The 'contradictory imperative' is spelt out by Beck and Grande in the flowing terms. Cosmopolitan Europe "is *potentially* universal and includes all countries in the world. *In reality*, however, this is ruled out and the politics of the EU ultimately contracts this non-excludability by constructing high border fences" (Beck and Grande, 2007, 87).

The case for Europe as a cosmopolitan empire rests on the account of the institutionalization of cosmopolitanism offered by Beck and Grande. On their account, the EU has been cosmopolitan all along, moving Europe beyond the era of nation-states by binding European countries together in a common, post-national project, which institutionalized supra-national governance structures, coupled with intergovernmental mechanisms in such a way as to preserve the nation-state while at the same time transforming (and transcending) it. One problem with the 'cosmopolitan empire' thesis is that the authors' account stresses that although cosmopolitanism was politically institutionalized by the EU, it was always a "deformed institutionalized cosmopolitanism" (Beck and Grande, 2007, 5–6). European cosmopolitanism has been shaped from above rather than below, in a technocratic rather than democratic fashion. All of the EU's problems (including the democratic deficit) can be traced back to this design flaw. The result is that Europe needs reforming in a more wholehearted cosmopolitan fashion.

The cosmopolitanization of Europe means "completing the incomplete European project" (Beck and Grande, 2007, 20). This suggests a strong teleological element to the cosmopolitan empire narrative. The cosmopolitanism that the EU does possess is lacking in some regard and needs to be reinvested with a 'true' cosmopolitan sense of direction. This begs the question of how we are supposed to know which direction is the right one, and who is authorized to make this decision. Whose cosmopolitanism is the best one, and how might we judge? On a more practical note, how is the EU likely to orientate itself towards a cosmopolitan future when neither the EU or European citizens conceive of themselves as cosmopolitans (let alone 'deformed cosmopolitans')?

When discussing Zielonka's work it was suggested that the main weaknesses of *Europe as Empire* are less to do with the idea of Europe as empire and mainly to do with the idea that the empire is a neo-medieval one. In the case of Beck and Grande's 'cosmopolitan empire' thesis I would say that the opposite is the case; the case can be made for a cosmopolitan Europe but that the case for this equating to a 'cosmopolitan empire' is much more difficult to sustain. The case for the empire being cosmopolitan is rather weaker, and in fact less compelling than Zielonka's case for neo-medievalism, which at least succeeds in making historical comparisons and outlining a cogent case for why the EU is more like an empire than a state. In the case of Beck and Grande's version, the case for Europe as a cosmopolitan empire is not convincing; why is 'empire' a necessary part of this formulation—why not 'cosmopolitan polity' or simply 'cosmopolitan Europe'?

Beck and Grande have attempted to rethink the EU project in ways which escape the 'methodological nationalism' of much political science and sociology literature. They are also committed to the idea that cosmopolitanism needs to be at the centre of attempts to provide a *'new critical theory of European integration'*, an aim which I would certainly endorse, with the proviso that what we should be studying is Europe in preference to European integration (Rumford, 2008a, and Chapter 2). The idea of Europe-as-empire allows them to combine a critique of statist approaches with a cosmopolitan reading of the institutionalization of the EU, and allows them also to draw upon a range of ideas which have contributed to understanding the contours of contemporary Europe: multi-level governance, the (non-)existence of a public sphere, the variable geometry resulting from enlargement, the emergence of network Europe, new core-periphery relations. Empire is a convenient umbrella term under which disparate ideas and approaches can be brought together and connected in a casual but suggestive manner.

HARDT AND NEGRI: ANOTHER KIND OF EMPIRE

Hardt and Negri's celebrated book (Hardt and Negri, 2000) outlines a very different kind of empire, which does not centre on Europe (except to the extent that they see Europe as the site of the origins of modernity). Much has been written about *Empire*, indeed it is probably the most widely debated and written about book published in recent times.[4] I do not intend to offer a comprehensive critique of *Empire*, or systematically examine key facets of their work (for example, I do not aim to give proper consideration of their use of Foucault's notion of bio-politics, nor to reflect on the important theme of resistance to empire and the role of 'multitude'), but rather seek to identify a number of important themes developed by Hardt and Negri which chime with the preoccupations of this chapter. But before proceeding to this task, it is necessary to say something about the scope of Hardt and Negri's project.

Empire has become well-known for its account of globalization-as-empire. It can also be read as an account of the transformation of the world from modernity to postmodernity, and for its attempt to "fashion a theoretical language—a toolbox—that enables us to reimagine our world and so remake our future" (Laffey and Weldes, 2004, 127). The book is best known for its account of empire as a new globalization-driven form of global domination. However, the authors make it clear that by empire they do not have in mind classic imperialism (an extension of nation-states beyond their boundaries). Rather, they are looking at "a decentred and totalizing apparatus of rule that progressively incorporates the entire global realm within its open, expanding frontiers" (Hardt and Negri, 2000, xii). This global realm is a system of all-encompassing power which operates through diffuse networks. The logic of this system is difficult to capture through conventional categories of political thought: "state and society, war and peace, control and freedom, as well as core and periphery; even the distinction between systemic and anti-systemic agency is blurred beyond recognition" (Balakrishnan, 2003b, x). Sovereignty now takes new forms (Hardt and Negri, 2000, xii) and a new imperial sovereignty has replaced nation-state sovereignty It should be noted that the United States is not seen as an imperialistic power by Hardt and Negri, although they do see the United States as occupying a key position in the hierarchy of empire (see Fitzpatrick, 2004, 47). As a result, empire is best thought of as a global system of "'governance without government' that sweeps together all actors within the order as a whole . . . the single logic of rule that now governs the world" (Urry, 2007a, 158).

The first point I wish to make about *Empire* concerns its contribution to the debates on globalization, which I think is an important and sometimes neglected dimension of the book. "*Empire* is a book about globalization . . . Empire is the form of sovereignty that exists under conditions of globalization" (Passavant, 2004, 3). However, I think it is entirely possible that despite the book's many strengths *Empire* has done fundamental damage to the image of globalization studies, the academic debates concerning its nature and dynamics, and the 'shape' of the discourse on globalization. Or rather a combination of readings of *Empire* and responses to the 9/11 attacks have done this.

Hardt and Negri provide a very interesting account of global public spaces, for example, which leads to an innovative account of global–local relations. Hardt and Negri (2000, 54–57) develop an interesting line on the idea of the global public sphere and the primacy of political communication. In their view, many contemporary political struggles are, in terms of conventional political understanding, 'incommunicable' due to their specificity and the 'local' nature of the conflict. Whether it is the Zapatista rebellion in Mexico or the events in Tiananmen Square, contemporary conflicts find it all but impossible to generate support from and link with comparable struggles elsewhere. However, they do have a global resonance and signal an increasingly important cosmopolitan dimension to political struggle: the conflict between international law and humanitarian concerns, the provisional nature of world citizenship, and the need to recognise the 'multitude' in opposition to 'empire'. In this sense, these disparate struggles are helping to forge "new public spaces and new forms of community"(Hardt and Negri, 2000, 56). Despite this sophistication however, a view of Hardt and Negri persists in which globalization is seen as an all-encompassing empire which subsumes everything to itself, permitting no exterior, and allowing no alternatives other than those directed from within. Globalization and empire become synonymous as that which progressively enfolds the world and from which there is no escape.

There is an interesting politics of space contained in *Empire*. Indeed, the question of space is central to Hardt and Negri's enterprise: "we try to capture the various ways in which space has been transformed in the transition from the modern to the postmodern" (Hardt, 2004). Hardt and Negri advance a notion of empire which is decentralized and deterritorialized, which can "incorporate the entire global realm within its open, expanding frontiers" (Hardt and Negri, 2000, xii). Empire has no boundaries. The resulting global realm is post-national and post-western (although they do not employ that term—see Chapter 7). "The distinct national colors of the imperialist map of the world have merged and blended in the imperial golden rainbow . . . the spatial divisions of the three Worlds (First, Second, and Third) have been scrambled so that we continually find the First World in the Third, the Third in the First, and the Second almost nowhere at all" (Hardt and Negri, 2000, xiii). There is a strong sense that boundaries between inside and outside no longer exist, and not only in the sense that empire comprises the entire world. As Passavant (2004, 7) points out, for Hardt and Negri, boundaries disappear in a number of contexts. The boundary between public and private has been eroded, for example, through the "privatization of public space through the rise of shopping malls and gated communities". Similarly, empire works to "eviscerate boundaries between home and factory or nation and nation" (Passavant, 2004, 7).

Although *Empire* does not directly contribute to the study of Europe, the approach to spatiality developed by Hardt and Negri resonates with many key themes in the literature on European space. In particular, the notion that empire operates in a smooth space of deterritorialized flows (Hardt and Negri, 2000, 333) resonates with the EU's self-image as a monotopia (Jensen and Richardson, 2003), a space of 'frictionless flows'. But Hardt and Negri (2000, 190) acknowledge that this smooth space "only appears as continuous uniform space". The binary divisions of modernity have given way to a multiplicity of finely grained fault lines. The correspondence between the smooth space of empire and the smooth space of the EU suggests that similar processes are at work in both. The EU is a but a tranche of empire, a postmodern space of postnationalism and deterritorilaized networks, but one where the striations and fault lines run in a slightly different direction to those in North America, Asia, or Africa. Whereas in Zielonka's account Europe has constructed an empire, Hardt and Negri hold that Europe is constructed by empire. In the first case the empire is centred on Europe and moves outwards, in the second case empire is global and Europe is very much a subsidiary consideration. Zielonka's assumptions are reproduced throughout the literature on globalization and Europe. EU integration scholars tend to see globalization as something 'out there' and perceive it as a threat to the European model. Integration then becomes a defensive mechanism in the face of globalization. Globalization scholars, on the other hand, emphasise the continuity between Europe and the rest of the world and the fact that, in many respects, the developments in Europe over the past two decades have been mirrored (or been initiated) by other regions (Meyer, 2001; Delanty and Rumford, 2005).

THE SINGULARITY OF EMPIRE, AND THE IDEA OF THE 'HIGH POINT'

> Aristotle said the best size of nation was one with borders visible from a high point in the centre
> —Alasdair Gray, 2007, 301

The most interesting aspect of empire from the perspective of this book is its singularity. As pointed out by Urry in the aforementioned quote, empire is a global order possessed with a 'single logic of rule'. There is one world, one world order, one empire. According to Hardt and Negri (2000, 9) "what used to be conflict and competition among several imperialist powers has in important respects been replaced by the idea of a single power that overdetermines them, structures them in a unitary way, and treats them under one common notion of right that is decidedly postcolonial and post-imperialist". What Hardt and Negri offer then is a global realm which has no outside and which contains the whole world within its logic of rule.

The limitations of this singularity, or what I here term the supposition of a 'high point', is revealed, for example, in Hardt and Negri's discussion of Foucault's "society of control". Foucault's work outlines the transition from disciplinary societies to the society of control, which work to regulate norms, behaviour, and culture through institutions of discipline (schools, hospitals, prisons, factories). Such societies corresponded to the period of high modernity. Nowadays we have shifted towards the society of control in which mechanisms of command are "distributed throughout the brains and bodies of the citizens" (Hardt and Negri, 2000, 23). This is the realm of what Foucault calls "biopolitics", a form of social power which "regulates social life from its interior" and which is concerned with "the production and reproduction of life itself" (Hardt and Negri, 2000, 23–4). It is not necessary to dig deeper into the Foucauldian roots of these ideas to make the point that I wish to make. Hardt and Negri make a conceptual leap from talking about individual disciplinary societies to talking of the 'society of control' which they see as being coterminous with empire. Empire, as a biopolitical machine, works on the 'whole social body', the 'entirety of social relations'. On this account, society has become global in a way not accounted for in globalization theory let alone Foucault's work and, more importantly perhaps, it has become singular and its 'oneness' can be overseen from a privileged 'high point'.

The argument to be developed here is that the idea of empire, whether in Hardt and Negri's formulation or those of Zielonka and Beck and Grande, works to sustain a particular feature associated with high modernity, namely the belief that there exists a privileged vantage point, a command centre, from which all of society can be viewed, mapped, and made intelligible. The 'high point' is the perspective from which all can be seen and all can be understood, from its vantage point all is brought together within a single domain. It is the prime location from which the entirety of a social world can be surveyed and governed. Within society, particular individuals, groups, and institutions will have only partial knowledge of political, economic, and cultural processes, unless they have access to a privileged position from which an overview can be obtained. This privileged position is what I call the 'high point', from which perspective society can be understood in entirety. The 'high point' is the place from which objectivity is possible so that knowledge can be interpreted and codified in such a way as to be understood and acknowledged by all. During modernity it was the 'high authority' of the state that occupied the 'high point' (Scott, 1998; Walters and Haahr, 2005). Empire, by bringing the whole world within its purview (at least on Hardt and Negri's account) is the latest attempt to maintain (the fiction of) a 'high point'. It could be argued that the idea of empire is popular precisely because it allows us to imagine the possibility of command over political space, a command which is looking increasingly problematic on post-modern, post-national, post-political, or cosmopolitan accounts.

Maintaining the possibility of the 'high point' in this way bestows tremendous power as it enables the creation (and ending) of epochs and fuels self-justification in the present. A perfect example is the way in which we are frequently told by our political leaders that 'everything changed on 9/11'. (It is worth noting that although the idea of Y2K failed to generate a strong sense of epochal change, the attacks of 9/11 did this with immediate effect). Since that date we have lived, apparently, in a new world, with new threats, new rules, new priorities—and new sources of political legitimacy. The idea of empire appears to chime well with the politics of the post 9/11 world. But in many ways it is the continuation of the politics of high modernity. Toulmin makes the point that modernity is preoccupied with the search for a 'scratch line' and the possibility of a clean state upon which a self-justifying new start can be made (Delanty, 2000, 61).

The argument made so far is that the idea of empire resonates with the need to maintain an analytical 'high point', a privileged position which allows for authoritative interpretation of events occurring across the broadest political and social field. The 'high point' is generally associated with the state in high modernity (or the church in earlier times) which had access, through its monopoly of expertise, to perspectives denied to others (Scott, 1998, 93). In this way it was able to consolidate the legitimacy of a singular vision and disallow other perspectives. In terms of social science perspectives we can say that the idea of empire (with its 'high point' connotations) is at odds with the critical cosmopolitanism advanced in this book. Whereas empire proposes a mono-perspective and a singular vision, cosmopolitanism offers a multi-perspectival approach.

The idea of a 'high point' is also synonymous with endings and beginnings. The contemporary 'age of empire' is also 'first past the post'— post-modern, post-Fordist, post-industrial, post-political, post-national, post-colonial, post-western, post-9/11, and so on. It is a world full of endings: the end of ideology, the end of history, the end of faith, the end of space. It is a world of loss: borderless world, McWorld, paperless office, 'mourning sickness'.[5] The old order has been swept away and new rules introduced for fresh challenges: Human rights are fetters on the 'war on terror'; torture is permissible in Guantanamo Bay and Abu Ghraib. At the same time the contemporary 'age of empire' is also a world full of beginnings: The global age, the digital age, information society, knowledge society, risk society, new world (dis)order, and network society are all heralded. History is punctuated with new beginnings and new eras: 1945, 1968, 'year zero,' Y2K, 9/11, and so on. As Bauman says, "Liquid life is a succession of new beginnings" (Bauman, 2005, 2) and "the power of identity is the power to be born again" (Bauman, 2005, 8). Ending and beginnings, epochs of past and future, are only made possible by the existence of a 'high point' around which such temporal orders can be constructed. As Terry Eagleton (1998) says, "Modernity is the era in which time speeds up because democracy and technology now allow us to fashion our own destinies instead of waiting on the *longues durees* of Nature or Providence". But not all of us have the same ability to fashion our own destinies, and for many Nature and Providence remain attractive alternatives to the statist projects of modernity.

Some points raised in the discussion of Balibar's work, particularly the ideas of polysemy, and overdetermination (Chapter 3), echo in the themes explored in this chapter. Borders are polysemic in that they present themselves differently to different people: walls or bridges, barriers or gateways. This is one of Balibar's significant contributions to border studies. As was commented earlier on Balibar's interpretation, although the border may treat people in different ways it will still be recognised as a border by all concerned. The same is true of his assumption about overdetermined borders: that contending groups will mutually recognise the important, world-defining borders. Balibar is in fact assuming the existence of a 'high point', a privileged position from which it is possible to decide upon the status of all borders, recognise them as such, and act accordingly. The idea that border can be polysemic or overdetermined presumes a common vantage point accessible to all parties, from which it is possible to construct a mutually agreed view of the location of borders and their importance. The assumption of a 'high point' precludes the idea that borders may be invisible to some groups while being reinforced by others, and denies the possibility that what are important borders to some provoke only indifference in others; in short, it denies the possibility of multiple and incommensurate perspectives.

By the same token, the earlier critique of the ubiquity of borders, in Balibar's formulation, concluded with the observation that borders can only be ubiquitous if there is a position from which this ubiquity can be determined. This, again, presumes a 'high point'. From the perspective of critical cosmopolitanism there can be no 'high point' and therefore no vantage point from which the ubiquity of borders can be demonstrated. Balibar's thinking on the polysemic nature of borders, their overdetermination, and their ubiquity stands in contradiction with his claim that no 'synoptic' vantage points exists from which politics can be observed (Balibar, 2004a, 206). As with his work on Europe-as-borderland, wherein Europe secures for itself a privileged position in the overdetermination of 'world borders', Balibar unwittingly adopts 'high point' thinking about borders. According to Balibar, borders can be viewed from a 'synoptic' vantage point which allows for a general overview and a mono-perspective. Indeed, his notions of overdetermination, polysemy, and ubiquity are only intelligible within a logic which presupposes a 'high point'.

The idea of the 'high point' will be taken up again in various ways in Chapters 7 and 8, particularly in the context of how a critical cosmopolitanism can counter the mono-perspective which the 'high point' generates. In relation to empire there are two key points that should be noted. First, it should be emphasised that asserting that empire depends upon (and works to maintain) the 'high point' does not mean that a particular actor (e.g., the United States, the European Commission, the West) must occupy this position. The important thing about the 'high point' is not that it is occupied by a particular actor or organization but that its existence is assumed. In this sense, the 'high point' is analogous to Foucault's panopticon; it is not necessary for a prison guard to occupy the central, all-seeing position from which all prisoners can be observed (without being aware that they are being so viewed). It is enough that the prisoners know that such a vantage point exists, following which they police themselves by acting as if they are being watched. If the world is viewed as singular and the belief exists that it is possible to observe it, make judgements about it, and promote policies designed to bring about change from a single, privileged vantage point then the 'high point' exists. The 'high point' is the obverse of Delanty's 'world openness'; the 'high point' represents world closure.

Cosmopolitanism and empire are antithetical, despite Beck and Grande's efforts to bring them together. Empire presumes that all diversity, a multiplicity of differences, can be housed within a single project. The value placed on diversity and difference can be universalized, and the common project of tolerating difference can work with empire; this is Back and Grande's view of the integrative potential of empire. Similarly, Zielonka views Europe's plurality as held in place by empire. Segmented public spheres and cultural diversity can be viewed as part of a single family of differences. All of this presumes a singularity and oneness which is consistent with empire but not cosmopolitanism, which stands for openness and multiplicity. In it not enough to embrace diversity; cosmopolitanism must acknowledge that a multiplicity of perspectives is possible and as such difference exceeds mere diversity.

Despite the popularity of the idea of Europe-as-empire, we should bear in mind that the resources exist for thinking about Europe in ways which do not succumb to a mono-perspectival view from the 'high point'. To conclude this chapter I turn to the work of Ruggie and his idea that the EU might be a "multi-perspectival polity". In discussing the development of the modern state, Ruggie makes the interesting point that the Renaissance technique of developing a single perspective in art was quickly translated into state-craft, and territory became viewed from a single vantage point. In the world of nation-states, political space came to be defined as it appeared from a single fixed viewpoint. In Ruggie's argument, the concept of sovereignty became "the doctrinal counterpart of the application of single-point perspectival forms to the spatial organization of politics" (Ruggie, 1993,159). In this way, Ruggie outlines the origins of the mono-perspectival viewpoint associated with modernity.

Ruggie then proceeds to outline the case for the EU being the "first multi-perspectival polity" to emerge since the advent of the modern era. By this he states he is emphasising that

> it is increasingly difficult to visualize the conduct of international politics among community members, and to a considerable measure

even domestic politics, as though it took place from a starting point of twelve separate, single, fixed viewpoints. (Ruggie, 1993, 172)

In a passage which presages ideas which have come to be associated with the work of Castells, Ruggie states:

the concept of multiperspectival institutional forms offers a lens through which to view other possible instances of international transformation today. Consider the global system of transnationalized microeconomic links. Perhaps the best way to describe it, when seen from our vantage point, is that these links have created a nonterritorial "region" in the world economy—a decentered yet integrated space-of-flows, operating in real time, which exists alongside the spaces-of-places that we call national economies. (Ruggie, 1993, 172)

The idea of 'multiperspectival institutional forms' is thus extrapolated from an EU setting to a global one. The idea of a space of places being over-taken by a space of flows, usually associated with Castells, is used to good effect; network society is a mechanism for creating multiple perspectives as territorial nation-states now exist alongside non-territorial networks which do not necessarily form an integrated whole. The possibility exists for different forms of linkages to generate different perspectives. Reading the accounts of empire offered by Zielonka and Beck and Grande in the light of Ruggie's work, we would have to conclude that although the theorists of Europe-as-empire attempt to go beyond the statist imaginary when trying to apprehend the reality of the EU, in fact they succeed in reproducing a fundamental dimension of the statist paradigm; the mono-perspective associated with the 'high point'.

7 Postwesternization

"The West" is hardly now a meaningful term, except to historians.
—J. M. Roberts, 2001, 291

What do we mean by postwesternization, and what are the implications of postwesternization for Europe? Postwesternization suggests a process, or series of processes, which is leading to the de-unification of the West, and, at the same time, a displacement of the idea of 'the West' from a central position in the way we think about self and others. Postwesternization is a designation which suggests that the West has ceased to exist as a meaningful entity, that it has been superseded, or at least that it is undergoing serious transformation. Whereas it was once possible to view the West as a coherent geopolitical presence it is no longer possible to do this. There is no longer a unity to the West, with Europe and the United States diverging in important respects, and elements of what was previously the non-West are now indistinguishable from it. But postwesternization is more than a new description of geopolitical realities. It is also a process which informs social scientific thinking in such a way as to de-universalize the West, increase awareness of other non-Western perspectives and, looking ahead to Chapter 8, points to the possibility that a multiplicity of worlds may exist.

The position advanced in this chapter is that understanding postwesternization is essential if we are to properly apprehend the 'cosmopolitan spaces' of Europe, and better appreciate Europe's relation to cosmopolitanism, which in my view has become somewhat skewed in recent years. There have of late been some worrying tendencies to emerge from debates on Europe and cosmopolitanism. In particular, these include the idea that Europe is (potentially) more cosmopolitan than any other region in the world, coupled with the notion that cosmopolitanism is, at root, a European initiative (see Chapter 1). This emerges most clearly in the anti-Americanism which has given cosmopolitanism a new complexion in recent years. European identity, with an added cosmopolitan inflection, is projected as an antidote to US unilateralism. A European cosmopolitanism (as distinct from a cosmopolitan Europe) is a chimera (Rumford, 2007c). In this context, the idea of postwesternization therefore performs an anamorphotic function, bringing the relationship between Europe and cosmopolitanism into clearer focus.

Europe is not the 'natural' site of cosmopolitanism, nor can Europe claim exclusive possession of a cosmopolitan identity. Postwesternization is a dimension of cosmopolitanism, and an important one in that it makes impossible any homology between cosmopolitanism and Europe. Postwesternization makes us aware that cosmopolitanism can contribute to understanding the transformation of Europe, but is not an expression European belonging. As such, it is an important addition to the social science 'toolkit', entering as it has at a time when studies of cosmopolitanism have begun to align it with an expression of Europe identity in the world. Postwesternization is thus an important corollary to thinking about cosmopolitanism, and is the *sine qua non* of a non-Eurocentric and critical cosmopolitanism.

There is not as yet extensive literature on postwesternization, as one would expect of a concept of such recent vintage (although see Brown, 1988). Nevertheless, the work published on this topic has begun to shape current debates on the transformation of Europe (Delanty, 2003; Delanty, 2006b; Therborn, 2006) and there have already been applications of the idea of postwesternization in social scientific analyses of Europeanization (Samson, 2006), and globalization (Rumford, 2006d; 2007a). In addition to these works, there exists a broader base of literature which does not explicitly develop the idea of postwesternization but contains analysis and argument which point in a similar direction and which serves to expand upon and bolster the thesis. After offering an introduction to postwesternization and an outline of the scope and usefulness of the concept, I advance a detailed account of the process of postwesternization in relation to Turkey, Europe, and the European Union. The argument here is that the relationship between Turkey and Europe is best understood, not in terms of Turkey's Europeanization, or the shifting boundaries (and bridges) between East and West, but through a different lens: a postwestern Turkey meeting a postwestern Europe.

POSTWESTERNIZATION: AN INITIAL DEFINITION AND OUTLINE OF CURRENT USAGE

The idea of postwestern Europe has its origins in the decline of the Cold War, although it cannot be reduced to the ending of the bipolar world. Whereas the West was once unified against the communist threat (under US hegemony) it is now more fragmented and no longer has a common enemy (although it could be argued that George W. Bush's 'war on terror' has attempted to give form to such a notion). The US-led invasion of Iraq has led to an increasing sense of Western disunity, recognized on both sides of the Atlantic with the United States aligning with 'new' Europe in opposition to 'old' Europe represented by France and Germany, and Europeans themselves suggesting a division between 'core' Europe and the rest (Levy, Pensky, and Torpey, 2005a).

However, postwestern Europe is more than a consequence of the ending of the Cold War. Reading the emerging literature on the subject, it is possible to identify several developments which have contributed to its emergence. First, the recognition that Europe is a meeting place for different modernities—western, post-communist, Islamic (Therborn, 2003)—rather than the site of a singular western modernity (Karagiannis and Wagner, 2006b). Second, the emergence of a new East shaping the continent (Delanty, 2003) means that Europe can no longer equate itself with the West when much of what used to be the Eastern bloc is now part of the European Union, for example. The incorporation of Central and Eastern Europe into the EU continues to orientate the EU around a new set of concerns, for example the idea of a European Neighborhood Policy (Rumford, 2007b), and global governance more generally (Lamy and Laidi, 2001). Third, postwesternization signals the increasing lack of unity within those countries formerly considered to have a common 'Western' world view; examples include divisions over the invasion of Iraq in 2003, or action on climate change which divided Europe from Australia and the United States, for example. This dimension of postwesternization is reproduced in the EU's project of enlargement, which not only involves becoming bigger but also means that the EU is becoming more diverse. At the same time as the EU is becoming more internally differentiated it is also becoming arguably less exclusively European in its sphere of operation, with an increasing interest in developing mechanisms of global governance, exporting its Social Model (seen as major badge of identity vis-à-vis the United States; Delanty and Rumford, 2005, 106–119), and developing what some see as a more cosmopolitan set of concerns.

Delanty's use of the concept stems from his interest in expressions of European self-understanding in the post Cold War period. For him, it is impossible to sustain the idea of the West as a coherent ideological, cultural, or geopolitical entity partly because 'Western civilization' has been globalized and partly because its underlying unity is rapidly fragmenting. "Europe, America and the West have become disentangled" (Delanty, 2006c, 1). One consequence is that Europe has come to possess an identity distinct from that of the West; it is moving eastward and is possibly developing a cosmopolitan character, which also suggests that there exists contestation over the meaning and identity of Europe (Delanty, 2006c, 2). Europe is moving eastwards as the axis shifts from the Baltic and Adriatic towards the Baltic and the Black Sea (Delanty, 2007).

In one of his earliest papers on the theme Delanty (2003) sees the emergence of postwesternization as being linked to the confluence of Europe's 'three civilizational constellations': The Occidental Christian constellation; the Byzantine-Slavic Eurasian constellation; the Ottoman Islamic constellation. These civilizational constellations allow for the possibility of multiple modernities; "European modernity has been shaped in the image of not one modernity but all three" (Delanty, 2003). Delanty thus warns against assuming the singularity of European history or origins. Europe's multi-civilizational heritage has produced different traditions of modernity, experienced as Western capitalism/liberalism, Communism, and statist Westernization exemplified by Turkey, which also offered a challenge to the dominant Western model (Delanty, 2003). Delanty's historical schema allows him to see Europe in terms of multiple modernities and the meeting place of different civilizations. He writes, "The contemporary project of Europeanization must be situated in the broader perspective of modernity and the encounter of different civilizational constellations. These modernities are coming closer together today, and not least because of the project of enlargement on which the European Union has embarked" (Delanty, 2003).

In his discussion of the opening up of Europe to the world and emerging cosmopolitan relationship between Europe and Asia, Delanty advances the claim that, "Europe may be becoming less Western at precisely the time Eurasia is becoming less Eastern and that something like a 'post-Western' Europe is emerging" (Delanty, 2006c, 4). The association between Europe and the West is being transformed and one of the most importance reference points for European identity has been undermined. If we are no longer able to work with a "unitary notion of Western civilization or by reference to a political design called the West" (Delanty, 2006c, 4) then we have to rethink some of the most basic elements of European Studies. The idea of postwesternization issues a challenge to our understanding of Europe, but also offers an opportunity to rethink Europe, and cosmopolitanism, in very productive terms.

THE DIVIDED WEST

There are two principle dimensions to postwesternization evident from the current literature. First, the separation of Europe from the West as a result of the collapse of Western unity, what Habermas refers to, in the title of a recent book, "the divided West" (Habermas, 2006). Second, the globalization of the non-west, which has become perceived as a threat by political commentators in the United States and Europe, but which is both a key dynamic of globalization in the contemporary world (alternative global networks) and a major catalyst of postwesternization (globalization provides options not represented by conventional models of development). Of the two, the first dimension has been elucidated most clearly in the literature to date. It is important to distinguish between two stands of 'divided West' thinking. One proceeds from the idea that the West no longer captures the essence of Europe's self-identity (Delanty's position). The other encapsulates the idea that Europe is deliberately shunning an association with the West, due to its negative and pejorative connotations (of association with the United States), which is Therborn's (2006) position. Let us examine the idea of the 'divided West' in more detail.

In the post Cold War period, Europe has emerged from the shadow of the West. "Instead of 'Western' values, 'Western' culture, and 'Western' civilization, the mainstream literature, sustained by EU research funding, now begins to focus on 'European' values, culture and civilization, and their roots" (Therborn, 2006, 25). The gap that has opened up between Europe and the West is partly a result of the United States usurping Europe's position as the West's 'indispensible nation' and partly as a result of Europe choosing to dissociate itself from the West, preferring the United States to take on that mantle, particularly in the wake of differences of opinion over the conduct of the 'war on terror' between the United States and several European countries. According to Beck (2007a, 47),

> Europeans and North Americans are living in different worlds. The way it looks to the Americans, the Europeans are suffering from a form of hysteria in relation to the environment, [climate change] while, to many Europeans, US Americans are paralysed by an exaggerated fear of terrorism.

Probably the best example of the 'divided West' tendency is Jurgen Habermas' call for a 'core' European response to the (Anglo-) American war in Iraq in 2003. Habermas' original newspaper article, signed also by Jacques Derrida, entitled "February 15, or, What Binds Europeans Together" (published in both *Frankfurter Allgemeine Zeitung* and *La Liberation*), appeared on the same day (31st May) as five other articles penned by European public intellectuals that were published in other European newspapers (Habermas thereby constructing, for one day at least, a European public sphere). In their article Habermas and Derrida called for a 'core' Europe constructed upon shared Enlightenment values to act as a European vanguard which could forge an EU capable of acting as a global player and opposing American aggression in Iraq.

The Habermas–Derrida intervention is founded upon some shaky assumptions: that Europe has an identity crisis because it doesn't have a singular identity; that Europe needs a common EU foreign policy; that 'core' Europe can call upon a shared set of cultural values. Furthermore, in making its case for a Europe capable of acting as a counter-weight to US-led aggression, Habermas and Derrida perpetuate some rather stereotypical dualities: between a 'weak' Europe and a 'strong' United States; between a 'core' Europe (France, Germany, and a few others) acting as a 'locomotive' of integration and a group of 'followers' (the rest of Europe) who will take their cue form this lead (thereby paralleling US attempts to polarise 'old' and 'new' Europe). In formulating the problem in these terms Habermas and Derrida fall into a familiar trap: the search for an elusive common European identity here coupled with being unable to think of the EU in terms other than that of the state. In fact they go further and posit the idea that the EU *should* become more state-like. Posing a narrowly defined sense of identity and old-style state-building as solutions to the EU's current problems, particularly its inability to become an effective actor in global politics, is a surprisingly conservative response to what is identified as an opportunity to advance a cosmopolitan solution to Europe's problems.

According to Habermas, in terms of a common political identity 'core' Europe can call upon securalization; trust in the state coupled with scepticism towards markets, what Harold James has caricatured as "anti-capitalist longing" (James, 2005, 63); sensitivity to the paradoxes of progress; preference for forms of social solidarity represented by the welfare state; desire for multilateral world order based on international law. These are indeed values that many Europeans can identify with. The problem is that they are also the values that half the world can identify with: Secular, Enlightenment , and social democratic traditions are rooted in many modern societies. More importantly in the current context, they are not values which mark off 'core' Europe from the rest. The line of argument pursued by Habermas and Derrida is that all Europeans can associate with these values. The point that needs making is not so much that New Zealanders and Canadians share them too, as Garton Ash and Dahrendorf have pointed out (Garton Ash and Dahrendorf, 2005) but that European countries can share these values and *still want to act in a different way.* Sharing an Enlightenment heritage does not make for a common foreign policy.

There is a heavy dose of Euro-nationalism in the Habermas–Derrida position, and the argument, from Enlightenment values all the way down, points to the absence of a Euro-state as the key to understanding the EU's foreign policy failures. Again, possession of 'core' European values is seen to be the key: "only the core European nations are ready to endow the EU with certain qualities of a state" (Habermas and Derrida, 2003, p. 5). So, not only do Spain, the United Kingdom, and other members of 'new Europe' align themselves with the United States in its intervention in Iraq thereby precluding a common European response but they are also holding back the development of a state-like EU. The preoccupation with state-building resonates with the Habermasian interpretation of the anti-war demonstrations of 15 February 2003 as signalling the birth of a European public sphere. In the hands of other commentators, notably Strauss-Kahn, this rhetoric can be cranked up a further notch, and signs of a nascent European public sphere can be mistaken for the wonders of nation-building: "On Saturday, February 15, 2003, a nation was born in the streets. This nation is the European nation" (quoted in Levy, Pensky, and Torpey, 2005b, xvi). Both the Habermas–Derrida article and Strauss-Kahn are happy to ignore the fact that the demonstrations of 15th February took place in many cities across the world, a point made by Iris Marion Young in her perceptive reading of the Habermas–Derrida position. That demonstrations took place in Tokyo, Sydney, Sao Paulo, Istanbul, Moscow, and many other places, "may signal the emergence of a *global* public, of which European publics are wings, but whose heart may lie in the Southern Hemisphere" (Young, 2005, 154).

Ignoring the global nature of the protest does not square with the "new European political responsibilities beyond any Eurocentrism" (Habermas and Derrida, 2005, 3) claimed by Habermas and Derrida.

Such shortcomings would be apparent under any circumstances, but are particularly glaring when the authors think of themselves (in different ways, admittedly) as cosmopolitans. Their take on European identity and state-building notwithstanding, the most significant aspect of the Habermas–Derrida rallying call to Europe is its muted cosmopolitanism. The idea that Europe's identity could ever embrace cosmopolitanism, while hinted at, is never formulated with any conviction. Moreover, cosmopolitanism, when it does appear timidly from behind the idea of EU as a putative global actor, is 'cosmo-lite'—applying to Europeans but not reaching out to the rest of the world. European identity is here conceived as a "consciousness of a shared political fate, and the prospect of a common future" (Habermas and Derrida, 2005, 7), with the emphasis very much on a European political fate and a common European future. According to Habermas and Derrida, this will allow "the citizens of one nation to 'regard the citizens of another nation as fundamentally 'one of us'" (Habermas and Derrida, 2005, 7). The cosmopolitan dimension to the 'manifesto' struggles to engage with the wider world. In its 'cosmo-lite' variety, cosmopolitanism is a badge of common European identity and an alternative to a Europe of nation states. As such, a Europe which acknowledges its internal diversity, its history of conflict (class struggle, church versus state, urban against rural), and its institutionalization of differences is a cosmopolitan Europe. Cosmopolitanism as a means of identifying with the wider world is virtually nonexistent; no more than a passing reference to the Kantian tradition and a suggestion that Europe could work to "defend and promote a cosmopolitan order on the basis of international law" (Habermas and Derrida, 2005, 8).

The cosmopolitan credentials of the Habermas–Derrida 'manifesto' are queried by Iris Marion Young who asks: "just how cosmopolitan is the stance taken?" (Young, 2005, 153). She suggests that to observers in the rest of the world "the philosophers' appeal may look more like a re-centring of Europe than the invocation of an inclusive global democracy" (Young, 2005,153). She also makes the pertinent point that invoking a European identity may inhibit solidarity with those far away (Young, 2005,156). The more exclusively European the identity, the less cosmopolitan its potential.

The difficulty for Habermas and Derrida is that, in attempting to give form to a European political identity which could lead to a common foreign policy, they have erred too far on the side of nationalist caution. By drawing so heavily on the imagery of state-building they "may reinscribe the logic of the nation-state for Europe, rather than transcend it", as Young rightly argues (Young, 2005, 156). Habermas' much vaunted cosmopolitanism is here stifled and stunted, squeezed from several sides simultaneously (between Iraq and a hard place, so to speak). This is not a vision of Europe as a post-national constellation. It is a Europe which is as solipsistic, self-obsessed, and lacking in vision as the much-criticised United States. What is absent here, as Ulrich Beck points out, is a "culture of world-political thinking . . . Europe must overcome its tendency to be self absorbed" (Beck, 2005, 197) if it is to turn into a cosmopolitan Europe. Cosmopolitanism cannot be advanced by creating two Europes; old and new, the 'core' and the rest. By framing the problem in this way, the Habermas–Derrida 'manifesto' risks being remembered only as a footnote to Donald Rumsfeld's too-easily dismissed idea that Germany and France represent 'old Europe'.

THE GLOBAL NON-WEST

The second dimension, the globalization of the non-West, is less well fleshed out in the existing literature but may well prove to be the more significant of the two themes for an understanding of postwesternization, and for this reason deserves more thorough consideration here. In his remarkable book *Landscapes of the Jihad* (Devji, 2005) Faisal Devji (who does not employ the term postwesternization) makes some very interesting observations about the post-Cold War period which resonate with the account of postwesternization outlined in this chapter. He reinforces the point that the West has become fractured or "split down the geographical middle" (Devji, 2005, 135), as evidenced by the aforementioned divisions between Europe and America over the invasion of Iraq. Simultaneously, the West has become less clearly demarcated from the East, as demonstrated by the transformation of some of the West's main institutional pillars—NATO, the EU—and their incorporation of large portions of the former East. Devji also talks about the fragmentation of the East. He writes,

> the Middle East today is a truly dispersed entity, with much of its press headquarters in London, its language used by Arab and non-Arab alike, and even its jihad originating elsewhere. Indeed, the Middle East might well be grounded in a specific territory only in its oil wells. (Devji, 2005, 71)

Another, more penetrating observation about the West is that it has "departed from its geographical moorings" and has become a global rather than territorial entity, meaning that it is "metaphysical rather than geographical" (Devji, 2005, 135). Devji is not arguing that the globalization of the West is simply another name for the hegemony of the West, or a cover for neo-imperialism (associated with the idea that globalization equals Americanization). For example Brown, in his early engagement with the notion of "a post-Western world" (Brown, 1988, 343), writes that, "many features of the westernization of the world do seem to be firmly embedded in contemporary non-western cultures, to the extent that they can be regarded as having been de-westernized and made universal".

Devji also alerts us to the fact that the prime emblems of the rhetorical unity of the West, freedom, and human rights, have been undermined by the 'war on terror'. This is something that Osama Bin Laden had drawn attention to in his ministrations on the disintegration of the West. In pursuit of the 'war on terror' the allies have curtailed individual liberties—the control orders mentioned in a previous chapter, for example. As such, the West struggles to preserve the freedom of its own citizens (and freedom slips down the hierarchy of core values). As was highlighted in Chapter 5, attacks on human rights come from within as well as without. By maintaining the 'state of exception' represented by Guantanamo Bay the US authorities give substance to Bin Laden's prediction that "freedom and human rights in America are doomed" (quoted in Devji, 2005, 138).

The global dimensions of the 'war on terror' inhere in the deterritorialization of the conflict and its separation from local peoples, movements, and politics. These developments are evident in both the global nature of jihad (Devji, 2005) and the strategy of the United States, for whom the only way to "prevent terror within the US is to prevent it taking place anywhere" (Zizek, quoted in Diken and Laustsen, 2004). Once deterritorialized, global conflict becomes an 'internal' affair (as indeed does terrorism) and threats do not take geopolitical form. The threats stemming from jihad are global but do not emanate from a particular place. Attempts by the United States and its allies to give territorial form to the 'war on terror' by for example seeking to locate Osama Bin Laden in a particular place (Afghanistan) have been unsuccessful. According to Devji (2005, xii), "jihad makes Islam into an agent as well as a product of globalization by liberating it from its specific content. Islam becomes a global fact by destroying its own traditions and recycling their fragments in novel ways". In this way, Muslims are able to reformat the terrain of global politics by highlighting an issue that national states are unable to address.

In Devji's view, jihad is based upon an ethics rather than a politics. The aims of jihadist movements are not political in the traditional sense; they do not seek to form political parties, represent an identifiable group, seize power, establish a territorial state for their people, or negotiate a settlement or compromise. The politics of jihad has 'gone global', and in doing so has vacated the traditional ground of political movements. It now operates on the terrain of ethical struggles and has more in common with those movements normally associated with civil society, environmentalism, 'anti-globalization', animal rights, and anti-abortion (Devji, 2005, 130). All share an organizational form based on 'cellular' or networked connectivity (Appadurai, 2006). Islam's globalization is possible because it is anchored neither in an institutionalized religious authority like a church, nor in an institutionalized political authority like a state. Indeed it is the continuing fragmentation and thus, democratization of authority in the world of Islam that might account for the militancy of its globalization.

The importance of de-territorialization in understanding 'global terror' is also emphasised by Appadurai. Cellular terrorist organizations work to "blur the lines between the enemies within and the enemies without" (Appadurai 2006, 108). For example, the 'homegrown' London bombers on July 2005 were young muslims who "could not have failed to make connections between 9/11 in New York, the war in Iraq and Afghanistan, the ongoing brutalization of their fellow Muslims in Palestine" (Appadurai, 2006, 112). They became terrorists because they identified themselves with "the cellular world of global terror rather than the isolating world of national minorities". They morphed "from one kind of minority—weak, disempowered, disenfranchised, and angry—to another kind of minority—cellular, globalized, transnational, armed, and dangerous" (Appadurai 2006, 113).

Just as the organizational structure of global civil society is not only appropriated by progressive and democratic forces, the term *post-political* is not only reserved for terrorists. The strategy of George W. Bush has also been described as post-political; for portraying the war on terror as a fight between 'good and evil', for example, and for creating extra-legal forms of detention (Guantanamo Bay) which aim to take the war against terror out of the political realm. According to Diken (2003), "the ultimate catastrophe, emerging from the war against terror, is the disappearance of politics" (Diken, 2003). Initiatives such as Homeland Security in the United States, Guantanamo Bay, and 'control orders' in the United Kingdom are about 'finding apolitical solutions to political problems' (Diken, 2003).

Devji's account, although necessarily skewed towards an understanding of global jihad, offers support for the postwesternization thesis because it echoes the themes associated with the idea of the 'divided west', but more so because it gives substance to the idea of a globalized East and a global Islam. These are important themes in relation to consideration of postwesternization and Turkey–EU relations, which is the theme of the rest of this chapter. Much scholarship on Turkey's fraught relationship with the EU still works with Cold War notions of Turkey's position in the world, and the dynamics of Turkey's domestic politics. It is argued here that Turkey is playing a leading role in the postwesternization of Europe and has alternative ports of entry into global politics which do not depend upon the EU as a gateway. Rather than seeing the EU as an agent of the westernization of Turkey, it would be more accurate to see Turkey as one agent of Europe's postwesternization.

In offering an account of Turkey–EU relations in terms of postwesternization, I intend not only to revise the accepted understanding of Turkey's role in the architecture of European institution-building but also allow for a different reading of the 'global non-West' as it was referred to previously. To date, accounts of the global East or globalization and Islam have tended to focus on the relation between globalization and terrorism, jihadism, fundamentalist Islam—as in the accounts offered by Devji. In other words, postwesternization and global Islam have thus far been explored via consideration of a narrow range of issues. Left unattended this might lead to the impression that it is only in extreme cases that we can point to the existence of a global East. My account of postwestern-Turkey-meets-postwestern-Europe is designed as a corrective to such thinking, demonstrating the 'ordinariness' of globality as a component of postwesternization, and situating 'global Islam' within the framework of mainstream European politics (in this context see also Devji's accounts of the Islamic protests against the 'Danish cartoons'; Devji, 2006, 2008).

POSTWESTERN TURKEY MEETS POSTWESTERN EUROPE[1]

> With the potential inclusion of Turkey and the countries in the Balkans, the European Union is bound to develop into a 'postwestern space'
> —Volker Heins, 2005, 442

Discussion of Turkey's relations with the European Union (EU) usually centres on Turkey chances of full membership and how she might eventually be incorporated within the Union's institutional architecture, that is unless the debate has not already floundered on the question of Turkey's perceived cultural differences and the problems of offering membership to a country in which respect for human rights is still perceived as less than wholehearted. This chapter takes the view that this is by no means the most productive way of framing discussion of Turkey's relation with the EU. It is proposed that a more important and productive line of enquiry proceeds from consideration of how Turkey is responding to (and contributing to) the social, political, and economic transformation of Europe, and, in turn, is managing (and reflecting upon) its own processes of transformation. It is further argued that the dynamics of these processes of transformation cannot be captured by the simple idea that what is occurring in Europe is 'integration' or even 'enlargement', notions which seek to render complex processes into familiar and accessible terms, but in doing so sacrifice much explanatory power. In the EU studies literature, the idea of integration has come to stand for the entire post-war transformation of Europe, notwithstanding the fact that mass unemployment, responses to the war in Iraq, and the European Union's democratic deficit, to take just a few examples, point to a more complex (and less teleological) process of transformation (Rumford and Murray, 2003). The transformation of Europe is more complex and wide-ranging than can be accounted for by the idea of integration. Moreover, this transformation is not limited to the economic and institutional spheres as suggested by the idea of integration; it is to be found also in the realms of societal cohesion, political communication, transnational networking, and the nature of citizenship. The account offered here focuses instead on the changing relationship between Turkey and the EU and places this within the frame of postwesternization.

Turkey's relationship with the EU has long been a puzzle for social and political scientists, except where essentialized civilizational differences are evoked (Huntington, 1996) or geopolitical clichés reinforcing east–west dichotomies are relied upon (Kramer, 2000). The difficultly of understanding Turkey from a conventional EU studies perspective stems from the persistence of an East–West dichotomy which structures thinking about European development. For example, Turkey is still seen as a bridge between East and West, despite those terms having lost much resonance over the past two decades or so. Similarly, Turkey's key position in the West's defense architecture was not consolidated by the collapse of the communist East, it was made less secure. Indeed, Turkey's uncertain position on the East–West axis has been exacerbated by the recent successes of its Islamicist government. In fact, it is no longer possible to employ an East–West model of European politics in the Turkish context. Rather, it is argued that understanding the shifting political orientations of Turkey's ruling AK Party and the Kemalist elites they have to a large extent displaced can be only understood in the context of postwesternization: Postwestern Turkey meets postwestern Europe. The process of postwesternization is of course not limited to the interactions of the EU and Turkey: It is a much wider process taking in the whole of the continent and incorporating major changes to Europe/Asia relations (Delanty, 2006b).

The idea that Turkey might be considered postwestern may be thought to be contentious by some. The secular elites who, since Ataturk's revolution in the 1920s, have dominated Turkish political life, would not wish to deviate from one of the core principles of Kemalism: Westernization. Nevertheless, the case for Turkey being postwestern is a compelling one and is not dependent upon her new, and perhaps temporary, orientation under an Islamic-leaning government.[2] Despite the best efforts of the Kemalists during the Cold War period, being Western was not a strong enough suit. The 'fast-track' accession for many former communist countries from Eastern Europe was a blow to Turkey's self-image as a highly valued ally, staunch defender of the West, and bulwark against communism. Nowadays, former Eastern bloc countries are more firmly embedded in the architecture of the emerging European Union order. Turkey remains an outsider waiting to join the EU, and the idea of a Western vocation which sustained the Kemalists throughout the Cold War has now lost its referent. Another image which has lost much of its resonance (save in travel brochures) is the idea that Turkey is a bridge between East and West. The East no longer has a fixed frontier and Turkey finds it to impossible to use this geopolitical reference point to orientate itself to the European order. As we shall see, the Kemalist fixation with points West has led to a degree of disorientation for Turkey in the post-communist world (Onis, 1995). The Islamicists in Turkey have been much more successful in projecting a new role for Turkey in a globalizing world. From their perspective an Islamicist Turkey is aligned with the universalism of European style democracy, human rights, and individual freedoms. Significantly, Turkey is seen as being simultaneously in both Europe and the Middle East. Such a concept of multiple belonging is, in essence, founded on a vision of Europe (and Turkey) as postwestern.

A concrete example of what is meant by postwesternization in the Turkish context may be useful at this point. The phenomenon of 'Islamic Calvinism' in Turkey has been the subject of some reflection in the recent past (ESI, 2005). The Christian (Protestant) values of thrift, piety, and hard work which Max Weber famously identified as underpinning capitalist emergence in Western Europe have been identified as values contributing to the rise of the Anatolian Tigers (dynamic economic centers in central Turkey, such as the regions centered on the city of Kayseri). As one commentator has noted, Kayseri demonstrates that "Islam and Western values can coexist without problems in Turkey, and Kayseri is the best answer to those who oppose Turkey's EU membership because of cultural, religious and social differences".[3] The idea of Islamic Calvinism is much contested it should be noted, not least in Turkey, where critics have argued that it is a European attempt to westernize or 'Christinize' Islam (Lodhi, 2006). Other commentators have pointed to the clear continuity between what are seen as traditional Christian values and the contemporary conservative Anatolian values which Islamic Calvanism embodies (Judson, 2005). From the perspective of this chapter, the phenomenon of 'Islamic Calvinism' can be read as a sign that Turkey is simultaneously 'eastern' and 'western', inside and outside: in short, postwestern.

SECULAR FUNDAMENTALISTS AND 'THIRD WAY' ISLAMICISTS

In the July 2007 (i.e., most recent) General Election in Turkey the Islamic-leaning Justice and Development (AK) Party won 47% of the vote (up from 34% at the 2002 election) and for the second election in succession achieved an outright majority of parliamentary seats (341 of 550 seats).[4] The continuing electoral success of AK Party is significant for several reasons. First, until AK Party's rise to dominance, previous governments had comprised fragile coalitions of often antagonistic parties. AK Party is able to pursue its policy agenda without the need for routinized parliamentary compromise. Second, that this party has a strong Islamic provenance is of continuing concern to the traditional Kemalist elites (secular politicians, the military, senior state bureaucracy) who fear a deviation from Turkey's secular, Western vocation. No such deviation has yet occurred. Third, the Kemalist political elites have been reduced to the status of a parliamentary minority and official opposition, represented by the secular-nationalist

Republican Peoples' Party (CHP), and, in the most recent election by the ultra-nationalist MHP.

The outcome of these elections is indicative of the growing challenge faced by the Kemalist vision of a modern secular Republic and a unitary and homogenous nation-state. Indeed, the Kemalists have come under pressure from a number of sources. In addition to the domestic challenge mounted by a succession of Islamicist political parties, who prior to the electoral successes of AK Party had enjoyed considerable success in local and municipal elections for more than a decade, the Kemalists have had great difficulty in adapting to the realities of the post-Cold War world, and to the demands of international organizations (the UN, the Council of Europe), particularly where these institutions seek to modify the nature of Turkey's democracy and its appreciation of human and minority rights (most evident in dealings with the European Union). It short, the Kemalists are not fully conversant with the emerging global order (Rumford, 2003). Moreover, the Islamicists have fared much better in this respect, taking advantage of opportunities provided by international organizations for increasing domestic political leverage in matters of minority and cultural rights and freedom of personal expression, and utilizing sources of political legitimacy emanating from bodies such as the EU (Arikan, 2002). It could be argued that, whereas the Kemalists have viewed globalization mainly in terms of outside interference and threats to sovereignty, the Islamicists have associated it with a range of political opportunities hitherto denied them in the domestic arena. So marked is the difference in their appreciation of globalization that one Turkish academic commentator has used this as the basis for a political classification. In the view of Onis (2007), contemporary Turkey is witnessing a struggle between 'conservative globalists' (AK Party) and 'defensive nationalists' (CHP and Kemalists more generally).

One consequence of these shifts is that the Kemalists are losing the struggle to maintain their position as the dominant political force within Turkey, and, importantly, their credibility as the bearers of modernity, civilization, and progress. One consequence of the poor electoral showing of Kemalist parties over the past two decades or so is that the Kemalist elites have sought to maintain their political dominance through domestic repression of both ethnic minorities (particularly the Kurds) and a sequence of Islamicist political parties. Party closures (and bans on opposition politicians, including current Prime Minister Erdogan for whom the ban was not lifted until after the party he led won the 2002 General Election) have been the favoured tools of political regulation. This has led to criticism that the Kemalists are in fact more fundamentalist than the Islamicists whose rise they seek to block (Buzan and Diez, 1999, 46), an interpretation reinforced by the Kemalists' hesitant embrace of the pluralism and respect for minorities required by the European Union's Copenhagen Criteria.[5]

From a Kemalist perspective, the threat posed by Islamicist political parties resides not only in their electoral successes but also in their ability to usurp Kemalist claims to embody Turkey's modernity. Islamicists, often portrayed as traditional and backwards (not least by Kemalists themselves), actually offer an alternative version of modernity, more attuned to global human rights regimes and notions of individual liberty and freedom of expression. What is often doubted (again, most vocally by the Kemalists) is the extent to which the Islamicists genuinely believe in rights and pluralism or whether they merely appropriate the language of rights for political advantage. The strategy of the current AK party government is notable for blending (conservative) social democratic initiatives with a respect for global markets in such a way as to invite comparison with the 'third way' politics developed by Prime Minister Blair in the United Kingdom and Chancellor Schroeder in Germany (Onis and Keyman, 2003). It is argued that, in part, the success of AK Party can be attributed to its ability to contest domestic politics on a global terrain, thereby evading the judicial strictures of the Kemalist elites and obviating the possibility of another 'postmodern military coup' (Bacik and Aras, 2002) such as that which terminated the coalition government led by the Islamicist Welfare Party (RP) in February 1997. Erdogan's AK Party has been determined to avoid a similar fate and has positioned itself at the centre of the spectrum of political parties in Turkey, and in doing so has won additional support from secular and nationalist constituencies. As Keyman (2006) points out, "Since the AKP emerged from the previous Islamic-oriented political parties and defined itself as a 'conservative democrat' party with moderate Islamic discourse, it has played an important role in demonstrating that in Turkey Islam can co-exist with modernity and democracy".

Before proceeding further there are two related issues that require elaboration. The first concerns the degree to which Kemalists and Islamicists both constitute relatively homogenous and cohesive groups. The second is the extent to which it is legitimate to portray them as antagonistic. In relation to the first issue, the unity of both Kemalists and the Islamicists is often overstated. There exist many divisions within the Kemalists in the military, the judiciary, business elites, and political parties in relation to particular issues—European Union membership, support for the United States, for example. There are even divisions within the military elites as regards rights for minorities and the trajectory of Turkey's Western vocation. In summary, it would be wrong to see Kemalism as a monolithic force and there are frequently clear differences between the military and political parties in terms of domestic and international priorities. Despite internal differentiation, Kemalists share a secular-statist consensus which sees Ataturk's revolution as an incomplete process in need of vigorous prosecution. For their part, the Islamicists comprise a 'broad church' within which a variety of positions can coexist, ranging from occasional fundamentalist calls for Islamic law to very moderate pro-Islamic positions (Onis, 2001, 281; Houston, 2001, 92). Currently, Islamicist positions are organized under the umbrella of AK Party, whose parliamentary successes have bestowed a good deal of authority over disparate and potentially troublesome factions.

Second, the terms of the antagonism between Kemalists and Islamicists are often misunderstood (Cosar and Ozman, 2004). For example, Kramer (2000, 86) identifies three "socio-political cleavages" in contemporary Turkey, one of which is between "Kemalist modernizers (secularists) versus religious traditionalists (Islamicists)" (the other two being Turks versus Kurds, and Sunni Muslims versus Alewites). This chapter takes issue with interpretations such as that advanced by Kramer which equate Kemalists with modernity and progress, and Islamicists with conservatism and tradition. These categorisations both reinforce a Kemalist interpretation of the terms of the conflict and over-simplify a complex reality. Islamicists advocate an alternative modernity, not a rejection of it, and the Kemalists are frequently more conservative than their opponents. Similarly, it is not possible to support the thesis that the conflict is between Kemalist universalism and the particularism of the Islamicists: The latter embed their claims for greater freedoms within universalistic discourses of human and personhood rights (Rumford, 2002; Soysal, 1997, 2001), while the former have to come to terms with the fact that they are but one group comprising Turkish society.

In short, rather than be seen as bearers of tradition (Kramer, 2000, 86), the Islamicists represent an alternative modernity, and, as we shall see, a recasting of Turkey's Western vocation. This, in part, accounts for both their popular appeal and for the threat they pose to more established elites. It is argued that what is at stake in the current contestations between Kemalists and Islamicists in Turkey is, on the one hand, the meaning of modernity and, on the other, the nature of Turkey's participation in the emerging global order. Previously modernity was associated with Kemalist dominated top-down social engineering (Sofos, 2001, 244), and globalization with Turkey taking her rightful place in an international order of nation-states. These interpretations are increasingly contested. Islamicists pose a pluralist civil society rather than authoritarian state as the marker of modernity, see no necessary link between modernity and the West, and view Turkey's entry to the post-Cold war global order as being conditioned by its embrace of human rights and tolerance of difference.

Historically, the Kemalist project has been centred on the need to modernize and Westernize: to reproduce Western civilization in Turkey. Sayyid (1994, 270–1) points out that this necessarily involved the production of an Oriental subject (as well as its repression). The Kemalists had to articulate an identity of the Orient in order to constitute themselves as Western. This was accomplished through the characterisation of the Anatolian population as backward, rural, and traditional. The Western Turk to be constructed was progressive, urban, and modern. The gap opened up by these binary divisions was to be bridged by modernization, provided by the Kemalist elite. Understood in these terms, the Kemalists operated according to a tried and tested modernisation strategy: Construct a 'bipo-larized social space' and advocate modernisation as a means of closing this very same space. In Sayyid's words;

> It is precisely this gap between the modern and traditional, between the urban and the rural, between the West and Islam, that Kemal-ism articulated, and presented itself as the only means of suturing . . . Muslim societies are seen in terms of a lack: the absence of technology, the absence of rationality, the absence of civil society, the absence of modernity. Conveniently, this lack can only be filled by imports from the West.

The idea that the Western orientation of Kemalism required an Eastern 'other' in order to give content to the concept of modernity which was at the centre of its ideology is a compelling one. As we shall see, this analysis has a contemporary relevance, and helps shed light on the ways in which contemporary Islamicists in Turkey seek to bridge the gap between East and West. However, the terms in which Sayyid describes the polarization between the West and Islam in the Kemalist imagination (as in the previous quote) are unhelpful. It is not only Muslim societies that can be accused of lacking many of the trappings of modernization. What counted as key com-ponents of modernization in other national contexts were in fact absent from Ataturk's Turkey: a national railway network; mass literacy; 'civil society'; even a bourgeoisie (Keyder, 1987).

AK PARTY IN POWER: BEYOND WEST AND EAST

It is no longer possible for political actors to maintain the boundaries that previously separated domestic from international, a reality resisted by Kemalists but embraced more enthusiastically by AK Party. Having said this, we can point to two major factors which have worked to channel the activities of both Islamicists and Kemalists onto a global terrain. First are the strictures applied to Islamicist politics through party closures imposed by the constitutional court and pressures from the military-dominated National Security Council. According to Balkir (2001, 46), this pressure encouraged the Islamicists to focus their attention on human rights, civil society, and democracy, rather than emphasise the cultural differences between Turkey and Europe. On this reading, the Islamicists came to realize that civil society issues were both safer ground for political con-testation, and areas in which substantial international support could be garnered. Second, during the 1990s the Kemalist elites came to realize that, in pursuing statist, top-down programmes, they had yielded civil society to the Islamicists who were mobilizing effectively at a 'grass-roots' level and were beginning to turn their popularity into municipal electoral victories.

In consequence, Kemalists have since turned their attention to questions of society in order to neutralize the threat. The result, according to Navaro-Yashin (2002, 153), is that "[c]ivil society was transformed into a symbolic ground on which legitimate state power was going to be based."

The rise of the governing AK Party has been associated with a more moderate version of Islamic politics in Turkey, and importantly, one which is able to win support from a broad constituency of voters not limited to the traditional Islamic electoral base developed through the 1990s by AK Party's predecessors, Refah and Fazilet. As Onis and Keyman (2003, 97) comment, prior to the 2002 general election, the AK Party were successful in shifting the political agenda away from the traditional Kemalist concerns with the state and national security and towards a more generalized concern with society and its prosperity. Moreover, their success has been attributed to their ability to present themselves not as primarily Islamic, but as centre-rightist (Keyman, 2003).

AK party has developed a distinctive interpretation of Turkey's Western vocation, generating a political discourse which incorporates key themes that were largely absent from Kemalism, such as respect for individual freedoms, human rights, and a concern for global standards of democracy. According to Prime Minister Erdogan, what is aimed for is a situation where "freedom, tolerance and mutual respect come together in a democratic environment where human rights are protected and the rule of law and good governance reign" (Erdogan, 2004). This signals an interest in themes neglected by their Kemalist predecessors: pluralism, respect for difference, and openness to global norms. Interestingly, AK Party seeks to distance itself from the type of Western orientation celebrated as a mission by the Kemalists. Now, Turkey is as much a part of the Middle East as it is of Europe, and one message that AK Party is keen to communicate is that democracy, freedoms, and rights are not incompatible with Middle Eastern politics. According to Erdogan, "people in the Middle East want democracy, though not necessarily with the Western cultural trappings" (quoted in Powell, 2004). Furthermore, he criticizes the West for adopting a 'reductionist approach' when considering Muslim societies, particularly the idea that underdevelopment and conflict are the fate of Muslim societies, and the assertion that democracy is incompatible with Muslim culture or religion. Erdogan thus seeks to counter the European perception identified by Baykan which "homogenizes Turkey into a society essentially reduced singularly to Islam" (Baykan, 2003): yet more evidence of AK Party's postwestern bent. Erdogan (2004) asserts that "Islam is a producer of, and contributor to, humanistic values that are the common heritage of civilization." In this way, Erdogan seeks to deconstruct the notion of the West that has determined Turkey's political trajectory since the 1920s. For the Kemalists, a Western vocation was the emblem of universalism necessary for Turkey to take its place in the world of nation-states. Erdogan sees an 'Eastern' orientation as no barrier to Turkey becoming a global player, because the East also shares in this global culture, and indeed, has contributed to it.

AK party's positioning of Turkey as a Middle Eastern country has possible strategic benefits. In arguing for (the potential for) greater democracy in the Middle East, Erdogan is able to narrate Turkey's position as a key player in the development of the region—a model of Islamic democracy: particularly important in strengthening relations with the United States. Equally important, Erdogan is able to satisfy his Islamic supporters at home for whom relations with the wider Muslim world—particularly the Middle East—are important, especially at a time when Turkey is moving closer to EU membership (not to mention the existence of tensions between Turkey and other Middle Eastern countries over Turkey's tradition of support for Israel). According to Erdogan, Turkey's mutually beneficial relationship with the West is based on Turkey's ability to fuse its Muslim identity with its Western orientation. In doing so, "the West and the East have been brought closer to each other" (Erdogan, 2004). Turkey "rests on a synthesis between its Moslem identity and modern values" (Erdogan, 2002). The result is that Turkey is positioned as pivotal in contemporary world politics.

> Turkey is a center that combines Asia and Europe . . . [b]y becoming a member of the European Union, Turkey will not only contribute to the economic, social and legal structure of Europe but will also become an important center for communication of the Asian countries with Europe. (Erdogan, 2005)

In Erdogan's rhetoric, Turkey's role is to promote the 'compatibility and harmony of civilization'. This is a theme that he has returned to on several occasions. For example, he has portrayed Istanbul as "not only a center combining the continents but also a central symbol combining and synthesizing the civilizations" (Erdogan, 2005), thereby reinforcing the image of Turkey as both Western and Eastern. The choice is no longer between East and West as it was for the Kemalists. It is now possible to imagine a blurring of the borders between Europe and the Middle East, East and West, with Turkey occupying a pivotal postwestern role.

The AK party message is that Turkey is a country which has formed a "vision of the world on the basis of universal values" (Erdogan, 2004). Significantly, these values are not the same universal values espoused by the Kemalists. The emphasis on the indivisibility of the nation-state, the homogeneity of the Turkish people, and the need to Westernize has given way to a privileging of democracy and a defense of tolerance and pluralism, as they underpin a "democratic, secular legal and political order that views the world of faith at the level of the individual" (Erdogan, 2002). In this formulation, religious expression and individual autonomy are virtually synonymous, which means that the freedom of religious expression sought by AK Party is not incompatible with the maintenance of the secular state. As Erdogan (2003) makes clear, the (global) "community of shared values stands tall *not* on the foundations of any religion. It's built on adherence to democratic values." Underpinning the concern with individual autonomy and democracy is the universality of human rights:

> Paramount is the need to secure human rights. The form of rule should be such that the citizen does not have to fear the State, but gives it direction and confidently participates in its administration. Similarly, gender-equality, supremacy of law, political participation, civil society, and transparency are among the indispensable elements that are the imperatives of democratization. (Erdogan, 2003)

The discourse of rights embraced by Erdogan and his Islamicist-conservative party is shaped by several concerns. First is the need to assert an alternative narrative of universalism and modernity, for so long dominated by Kemalist ideology. Their new vision of universalism and modernity is designed to allow for the participation of the Islamic world on its own terms. Second is the need to transcend East and West in order to become free of the political agenda imposed on Turkey by the Kemalists. Erdogan is not simply offering an alternative reading of Turkey's relation to modernity. Rather, he is recasting the relation between modernity and the West. The identification with universal norms of democracy and human rights and the preference for framing political contestation in terms which take it beyond the borders of the nation-state have allowed Islamicists to refashion the relationship of Turkey with the West (which is itself undergoing redefinition). This does not involve a rejection of modernity, but a reconceptualization of it. Modernity is now equated with pluralism, individual rights, and civil society rather than with 'the people,' homogeneity, and the state. Universalism has become disengaged from Westernization and is given expression by human rights and individual freedoms. Furthermore, it is consonant with Islamic aspirations: democracy without Western trappings.

Third is the need to create a niche for Turkey in global politics. The struggle for democracy, for so long depicted by Kemalists as requiring considerable domestic repression and 'top-down' direction, is recast as a question of how best to accommodate Turkey to global norms (via preparation for EU membership, for example). At the same time, AK Party has had to deal with the continuing importance of Turkey's place within the security architecture of the West, as represented by her active membership in NATO. In fact, the basis of Turkey–NATO cooperation has been changing for some time, partly as a response to the collapse of the Soviet bloc and partly as a result of ongoing US military activity in Turkey's 'neighbourhood', particularly Iraq. During this time AK Party has engineered closer political and economic links with previously hostile

Iran and Syria. AK Party has sought to contextualize Turkey's role in NATO, viewing national defence in broader, less exclusively 'Western' terms. Turkey's decision to project itself into Eastern regions—the Middle East and Central Asia—goes hand-in-hand with a shift towards a more multi-dimensional foreign policy.[6]

Fourth is the need to ensure that political contestation between Islamicists and Kemalists is not played out within national space. A focus on universal rights transposes a domestic conflict onto a public sphere which knows no national boundaries, and across which the Kemalist state instruments, particularly the judiciary and the National Security Council, have a very limited reach.

CONCLUSION: THE POLITICS OF POSTWESTERNIZATION

The global orientation suggested by the political discourse of AK Party allows an escape from Kemalist state strictures, and represents both new opportunities, political resources, and a setting in which new networks of allies can be formed. Importantly, it posits a realm where issues can be contested on the grounds of individual rights and democratic norms (more advantageous to the Islamicists), distinct from the domestic terrain which is still 'home ground' for the Kemalists and their continued dominating apparatuses of state, especially the judiciary and the military. This version of global politics offers enhanced international legitimacy—and consequent domestic political leverage—for those who embrace the universalism of human rights and global democratic norms. Furthermore, it is worth remembering that AK party has already taken Turkey into formal accession negotiations for EU membership—the Kemalist dream. Strengthening relations with the EU has helped AK party consolidate its democratic credentials, and achieve sufficient credibility (and international support) to counter the residual threat of the Kemalists embedded in state structures such as the National Security Council. Kemalists have begun, belatedly, to appreciate the opportunities to strengthen their own position that globalization entails. The July 2001 decision by the European Court of Human Rights upholding the Constitutional Court's 1998 decision to ban one of AK Party's forerunners, Refah Partesi, is a very good example. Not only has the decision of the ECHR bolstered the legitimacy of the Kemalist vision of the Turkish state, it has confirmed that Turkey's statist version of democracy (in one respect at least) is aligned with European and global norms. The ability of the Kemalists to perpetuate themselves stems less from their ability to insulate against the effects of transnational democratization and external 'interference' and more from the way an embrace of emerging global norms and standards can work to stabilize a global order of nation-states, at the same time as it works to regularize and police their activities.

That 'going global' does not only work in favour of the Islamicists can be seen in the way the AK Party has approached the issue of the Kemalist ban on women wearing the Islamic headscarf in public institutions in Turkey (Rumford, 2003). To the disappointment of many of their supporters, AK Party refrained from challenging the ban, choosing not to be drawn into a confrontation with the secular elites which would inevitably take place upon Kemalist 'home ground'. Instead, they have been content to observe the unfolding of the very same issue across France, as Chirac and the French parliament work to ban the headscarf from French schools (te Brake, 2004). In such a climate a direct confrontation over the issue in Turkey would still be ill-advised. Significantly, AK Party frames the headscarf debate as a human rights issue, not as an issue framed by narrow domestic political interests; "an AK Party spokeswoman said it considered the headscarf problem to be one of human rights—if Turkey's overall human rights record improved, the issue would be resolved".[7] The universalization of a local issue is undoubtedly a high-risk political strategy. Prime Minister Erdogan was criticized by some of his Islamic supporters in Turkey for sending his own (headscarf-wearing) daughters overseas to study "instead of properly waging a political struggle right here to lift this ban for everybody's benefit" (quoted in Gulalp, 2003).[8]

Postwestern Europe exists in a state of becoming; the broad contours can already be observed and the finer details are beginning to emerge. That a postwestern Turkey can also be discerned places Turkey at the very heart of contemporary European affairs, not on the periphery where it is normally located. More significantly, a postwestern Turkey can be an active shaper and molder of Europe in the way that a more conventionally geopolitically positioned 'Westernized' Turkey could not. An examination of Turkey's relations with the EU within this framework is valuable for several important reasons. First, it calls into question a number of accepted truths which have become ossified by European studies scholarship: the fixity of the West; the magnetic attraction represented by integration; the developmental logic of enlargement. That 'Europe's centre of gravity is shifting Eastwards' has been understood for some time. This formulation does not however do justice to the dynamics of European transformation in which the terms East and West no longer have meaningful referents. A conventional narrative of European change which places Turkey as a bridge between East and West tells a very different story from one which situates a postwestern Turkey within a postwestern Europe.

Second, the politics of AK Party can be better understood within a framework of analysis which sees Turkey as postwestern. Islamicist politics in Turkey are often accused of paying lip service to human rights, freedom of the individual, and tolerance of difference, while masking its 'real' interests: majoritarian rule and the introduction of Islamic law. What this interpretation fails to account for are the strategic political benefits that Islamlicists gain by translating domestic political contestation into the language of universal rights. Not only does this shift politics away from the favoured terrain of the Kemalists (the constitutional courts and the National Security Council) towards the realm of 'network Europe' with which Islamicists feel more comfortable, but it allows for a repositioning of Turkey within the emerging postwestern order. The skepticism towards AK Party's concern with human rights, seen as a 'smokescreen' for hidden fundamentalist intentions, and the allegations of political opportunism leveled at Prime Minister Erdogan for his pro-EU stance are examples of how Islamicist politics appear when viewed through the lens of conventional European studies thinking, which positions Turkey's on an East–West axis. The AK Party has demonstrated that there is more than one way to conceive of the West, and Turkey's relation to it. Where the Kemalists once reified the West, the Islamicists have sought to deconstruct it.

8 The World is Not Enough
Globalization Reconsidered

> The world is now one place, there is a world culture, and people, information, money, and technology all flow round the globe in a rather chaotic set of disjunctive circuits which somehow bring us all together.
>
> —Jonathan Friedman, 2007, 111

Postwesternization points to the need to rethink the relationship between globalization and cosmopolitanism, particularly the central idea of the oneness of the world that is such an important dimension of globalization. Cosmopolitanism has been referred to in this book as a politics of space precisely because it accords a central place to consideration of the relationship between the individual, the communities to which that individual belongs, and the world. In other words, a cosmopolitanism perspective necessitates a problematization of political space because it cannot be assumed that the political spaces under consideration are 'given', familiar to us, and associated with the nation-state. Following this line of reasoning, we cannot make assumptions about the spaces within which an individual acts, the extent, scope, and geographical cohesiveness of the communities with which he or she is engaged, and the globality (or otherwise) of the political realm which impacts upon or constrains an individual and/or the imagination which informs that individual's political choices.

The focus of attention in much contemporary work on cosmopolitanism is the relationship between the individual and the communities with which he or she is associated, the idea being that in a world where identity is a major political resource, the ability to embrace multiple identities, switch between them, and privilege one or more over others, and the questions pertaining to individual and collective identity formation, group loyalty, and common purpose are more necessary than ever before. We can no longer say with any certainty whether a particular collective identity will claim the allegiance of individuals who must actively choose to become a member of some groups and not others. The more traditional collective identities such as class, nation, and ethnicity cannot be certain of a top spot in a hierarchy of identities, and must vie for position with identities associated with lifestyle, politics, and consumption choices. As Beck (2003) so nicely puts it, "to belong or not to belong, *that* is the cosmopolitan question". For these reasons it is not surprising that the cosmopolitan focus normally falls on the relationship between individual and community, so much so that the third component of the cosmopolitan equation—the world—is treated as rather unproblematic or not in need of investigation. However, cosmopolitanism is more than about the shifting relationships between individuals and their communities. Nor is cosmopolitanism only a convenient means of taking us beyond national concerns. Cosmopolitanism is also concerned with how both individuals and communities are situated in relation to the world, and indeed the very nature of the world.

When I say that the world is often viewed unproblematically, I mean to say that this is the aspect of cosmopolitanism considered unimportant in relation to self/other and community. The reason for this, I suggest, is that globalization has, in recent times at least, monopolized our thinking about the world. In coming to terms with globalization we have had to get used to the idea that we live in 'one world' (Singer, 2004), indeed this is the central message contained in much globalization theorizing. A range of globalization scholars, including Robertson, Tomlinson, and Scholte, have taught us, quite rightly in many respects, that one consequence of globalization is a heightened awareness of the world as a single place, an interconnected and networked space of human activity. One key achievement of globalization scholarship has been the recognition that the globe is a viable unit of study. This achievement should not be downplayed. It may be thought of as 'common sense' now, but it was not so long ago that this idea was still seen as highly questionable in some quarters. For example, as recently as 2000, one British sociologist could state that 'the globe is a geological entity rather than a sociological one,' following this up with the caveat that the global is 'sociologically unattainable' (Fulcher 2000, 525–6). That things have moved on to the stage where no one any longer seriously challenges the appropriateness of the globe as a unit of analysis, or the right of sociologists to study it, is the result of the dogged determination of early globalization theorists, such as Robertson, Albrow, and Meyer, and of the commentators on and popularizers of their ideas on globalization who have worked to established them broadly within sociological study (Cohen and Kennedy, 2000; Holton, 1998, 2005; Lechner and Boli, 2005). That being said, it is also the case that these advances in globalization theory have also, inadvertently, over-stated the oneness of the world, so much so that it is now difficult to view it in any other way. Does it amount to globalization heresy to assert that we might not after all live in one world? Can globalization thinking accommodate the idea that a multiplicity of worlds may exist?

Roland Robertson's pioneering work is notable for emphasizing the transformed subjectivity to which globalization gives rise. One of Robertson's many contributions to the globalization debate in the 1990s was to emphasise that not only was the world becoming more interconnected but that we were increasingly becoming aware that this was so. On this reading, globalization is driven forward (in considerable part) by our realization that the world is a single place. In other words, 'global consciousness' is not only an outcome of the process but is also a motor of globalization. Despite this being a central plank of 'cultural' interpretations of globalization and one which takes globalization out of the realm of the technical or the economic, and therefore a major achievement in theorizing globalization, it is not enough, I would argue. An awareness of globality, expressed in these terms in the work of Robertson and others, works also to preclude the possibility that a multiplicity of worlds can exist. In other words, while globalization leads us to an awareness of the 'oneness' of the world, cosmopolitanism needs to allow for the possibility that we can inhabit many worlds, or that many worlds may exist simultaneously (even though we as individuals may not be able to inhabit all of them). This is why in conceiving cosmopolitanism as the relationship between the individual, community, and the world, the third part of the triad should not be treated as any less important than the other two. And because it has hitherto been treated as relatively unimportant, it deserves special attention here.

THINKING ABOUT THE WORLD

Discourses on globalization have been instrumental in providing both new opportunities for thinking about the world (as well as thinking about the importance of a global dimension when considering any space, territory or community), and also, importantly, for stimulating news ways of conceiving the world. More recently still, a range of approaches to cosmopolitanism, some contemporary and some of a more ancient lineage, have increased our awareness of the varieties of ways in which the world can be made and re-made in our discourses of belonging. Nevertheless, it seems that despite the different ways of thinking about the world that exist, the outcome of this thinking is consistently to recognise the singularity of the world. Cultural approaches to globalization perform a unique intellectual juggling act: providing a rich supply of intellectual raw material with which we can think about the world, and, at the same time, always reaching the conclusion that we live in 'one world'.

A very good example is the recent publication *Varieties of World-Making* (Karagiannis and Wagner, 2007a) an edited collection which contains excellent individual chapters by Bhambra, Halperin, and Kratochwil amongst others, but the overall thrust and direction of which is rather disappointing. In their Introduction, the editors criticise contemporary globalization theory for not paying sufficient attention to the ways the world is made by humans through their activity, and they propose a more voluntaristic, constructivist, and communitarian approach to globalization. Their interest is in shifting attention to "diverse projects of giving meaning to the world as unity" and the "plurality of ways of knowing these projects" (Karagiannis and Wagner, 2007b, 3). According to the editors' portrayal of recent intellectual trends, globalization thinking is mired in its own "futile debates"

(Karagiannis and Wagner, 2007b, 3) and this short-sightedness has allowed globalization theorists to be bested by clash-of-civilizations thinkers, and in the process the important idea that we live in a common world has failed to reap sufficient dividends. It is difficult to agree with this summary of recent intellectual history, and the editors' grasp of the core concerns of globalization studies is tenuous, as can be judged by the following statement. "In sociological terms, the promise of globalization resides in individuation seen as the liberation from socio-institutional constraints". This is a puzzling formulation and it is difficult to think of a globalization scholar who would recognise the globalization on offer here. In any case, individuation is covered well in the globalization literature—for example, in the very different approaches of Meyer and Bauman—but is always premised on various forms of institutionalism (expansion of the state form on the one hand, or marketization on the other) rather than divorced from it.

The idea of 'world-making' mapped out by Karagiannis and Wagner is introduced as a corrective to what they perceive as the weakness of globalization theory rather than a full-blown attempt to explore the ways in which globalization could lead to a plurality of worlds. In their own estimation, "world-making" is

> directed against the dominant idea of neo-liberal and mass-cultural globalization as running its course, against the revival of theories of conflicts between closed cultural communities, but also against any empty insistence on a combination of flexibility and reflexivity that will easily catapult humanity into a free and peaceful cosmopolitan future. (Karagiannis and Wagner, 2007b, 8)

This is a 'straw man' figure of globalization. That globalization cannot be reduced to either the market or Americanization is commonplace in the literature (and pretty much *de rigueur* in sociological writing). Supporters of the clash-of-civilizations thesis (outside right-wing foreign policy institutes) are extremely few and far between. No one seriously thinks that globalization will automatically lead to world peace. It is worth noting that cosmopolitans are doubly slighted in the estimation of Karagiannis and Wagner, by being portrayed as both naive and of secondary importance to globalization thinkers. In place of their characterization of globalization studies they offer a "systematic rethinking of the ways in which human beings relate to others and to the world—by emphasising the plurality of bonds between human beings" (Karagiannis and Wagner, 2007b, 8). This is a reasonable enough aim, and one which is in fact contained within globalization and cosmopolitan studies rather than being opposed to it. In fact, what the editors achieve is to reinforce the idea of the singularity of the world, thereby reproducing an assumption at the heart of the globalization studies which they otherwise wish to distance themselves from. Rather than the existence of different worlds, the book outlines different perspectives on the one world, as generated for example from US, European, or Latin American perspectives, the many bonds that hold the world together, and the ways in which calls for global justice frame the world anew. In summary, the book is concerned with the different ways in which we 'give meaning to the world as unity', and in doing so it reproduces a common trend observed in studies of globalization: the coupling of a concern with different ways of thinking about the world with the conclusion that we live in 'one world'. Such 'one-worldism'[1] needs more serious interrogation.

THE WORLD OF GLOBALIZATION

Globalization encourages us to think about a world order, a world system, or a world polity, or, where the theoretical ambitions are less totalising, a world of interconnectedness, of networks, or transnational flows and mobilities. It is generally supposed that that what makes these frameworks of interpretation 'global' is that they point to the existence of an order, a system, or a polity which is world-encompassing and/or brings the whole world within a single purview. In fact, what is most interesting is that the various interpretations of globalization all share one key facet: they concretize the world and allow us to think about the tangible 'unicity' of the world in terms which presuppose not only the oneness (interconnectedness) of the world but its singularity. Globalization thinking, particularly its sociological and cultural variants, constructs the world as unitary and indivisible and the task of social science then becomes one of elucidating that oneness and demonstrating the mechanisms that have made it that way (or threaten to unravel it). What this occludes is that there may be other ways of perceiving the globality of the world, ways that narrate the multiplicity of worlds that it is possible to inhabit and how these worlds can co-exist or enter into conflict.

Globalization studies has, over the past few years, entered a period of reflection and indecision regarding focus and direction. This is reflected in recent publications which have sought to either consolidate global studies as a (multi-disciplinary) field of enquiry—good examples are Robertson and Scholte's *Encyclopedia* (2006), and Ritzer's *Handbook* (2007)—or reorganize it through a reassessment of its main concerns and preoccupations (and continuing relevance). Good examples of the latter include the edited collections by Held and McGrew (2007a) and Rossi (2007). Global studies has been beset by doubts in the post-9/11 period, the end of the so-called honeymoon period for globalization, and has witnessed a slowdown in the development of theory (the main period of theory-building in globalization studies was the early and mid-1990s, particularly through the contributions of Robertson, Albrow, Meyer, and Held).

Held and McGrew (2007b, 2–3) in their diagnosis of the ills of global-ization theory, summarise the case being made against globalization: It has been 'oversold'.

> Critics argue that it has been oversold in at least three senses: as a description of social reality, as an explanation of social change, and as an ideology of social progress (a political project). In all of these respects, most particularly in the wake of 9/11, globalist rhetoric ap-pears rather hollow.

The world might just be witnessing a reversal of globalization. It is inter-esting that Held and McGrew see globalization as an either/or thing; you can either have more of it or less—those are the only options. Their analysis of borders, boundaries, nationalism, protectionism, localism, and ethnic-ity seem to point in the direction of "an epoch of radical de-globalization" (Held and McGrew, 2007b, 2). It could be that "the world is witnessing the demise of globalization as social ontology, explanans [explanation], and social imaginary" (Held and McGrew, 2007b, 3). What we have here is globalization measured on a sliding scale with globalization at one end and de-globalization at the other. This seems too simple a schema. Although it is not impossible to enter a period of de-globalization—Roland Robertson has always said as much (see also Holton, 2005, 49–52)—it is also worrying that Held and McGrew choose to view the possibility of de-globalization as a 'crisis'.

I do not concur with Held and McGrew's diagnosis of the ills of global-ization studies. In my opinion, the main problem with globalization studies or, to be more precise, the current direction which globalization studies is taking, is the tendency to focus on what we might term very literal readings of globalization, ones which prioritise the need to study those processes which span the globe or which give concreteness to the global by making it manifest. This focus neglects the inter-relatedness of the global and the local, and the visibility of processes of globalization in everyday experi-ence. As Jonathan Friedman comments,

> [t]he global is always about interlocal relations, not about a supralocal organism . . . Any global approach that assumes that the global is an empirical field in its own right is a victim of misplaced concreteness. Unfortunately this is precisely the nature of much of the globalization literature. (Friedman, 2007)

In the literature which reflects this trend, the global is only that which has world-wide application, which spans the globe, or which manifestly inter-connects the world. The work of Held and his colleagues is representative of this tendency. For them, globalization equates to the linking of human activ-ity over huge distances, and what is distinctive about globalization is the way social interaction can proceed across continents without hindrance. Rather than seeing the local and the global existing in a relation of mutual implication, they see the local and the global at opposite ends of a linear scale.

> Globalization can be located on a continuum with the local, national and regional. At the one end of the continuum lie social and economic relations and networks which are organized on a local and/or national basis; at the other end lie social and economic relations and networks which crystallize on the wider scale of regional and global interactions. (Held , McGrew, Goldblatt, and Perraton, 1999, 15)

On this view, processes of globalization and localization do not exist as a 'globewide cultural nexus' as they do for Robertson, but form distinct spheres of activity which operate at different levels. Local networks operate at the local level but are distinct from global or supranational networks which do not have to work within the same spatial restrictions (see Rumford, 2002, 35–38 for a critique of this aspect of Held et al.'s work).

What is absent from this type of work was hinted at earlier, that is to say a developed sense that the local and the global are interconnected, that processes of globalization also work in local settings (and can perhaps best be observed there), and that globalization can work from the inside out, or bottom up. In the words of Bauman (2006b):

> Globalization is not a process taking place somewhere far away in some exotic place. Globalization is taking place in Leeds as well as in Warsaw, in New York, and in any small town in Poland. It is just outside your window, but inside as well. It is enough to walk down the street to see it.

Another good example would be Beck's idea that cosmopolitanization should be conceived of as globalization from within, as internalized globalization. On this reading, globalization both breaks down the inside–outside distinction and works at the local and global levels. This stands in opposition to what Beck and Sznaider describe as the 'onion model' of globalization, of which Held's work is a good example. Whereas globalization presupposes, cosmopolitanization dissolves the 'onion model' of the world, where the local and the national form the core and inner layer and the international and the global form the outer layers" (Beck and Sznaider, 2006, 9).

ROBERTSON AND THE ONENESS OF THE WORLD

I want now to explore in more depth the point that globalization thinking, in pursuing the 'oneness of the world' neglects to acknowledge the possibility of multiple worlds. I have chosen to begin by looking at aspects of Roland Robertson's seminal work *Globalization: Social Theory and Global Culture* (Robertson, 1992), which I assume to be representative (if not the source) of the idea of the unicity of the world.

Consider the following, taken from Robertson's discussion of the 'cultural turn' in sociology and the impact of the global system on individual societies. He writes, "globalization involves pressure on societies, civilizations and representatives of traditions . . . to sift the global-cultural scene for ideas and symbols considered to be relevant to their own identities" (Robertson, 1992, 46). There are many ways that this insight can, and has, be used to understand cultural and political developments; the influence of reggae music and style on punk rock in Britain in the mid 1970s (Hebdige, 1979), or the adoption of William 'Bravehart' Wallace and Ghandhi as heroic icons by the regionalist Lega Nord movement in Italy in the 1990s, for example. In each case, a symbol has been lifted out of context and appropriated by another group or cultural movement who have seen something of themselves in the actions, aspirations, or identities of distant others.

My favourite example, which I have previously used to illustrate the global search for identity (Rumford, 2007a), is the Taliban (back in 2001) seeking ICC (International Cricket Council) recognition for cricket in Afghanistan, a country with little tradition of domestic cricket and where the majority of current players have lived in exile in Pakistan for many years (McCarthy, 2001). For the Taliban, sporting participation was viewed as a vehicle for wider international diplomatic recognition. The conventional interpretation of Islamic fundamentalism poses it in opposition to globalization. The Taliban's policies have certainly been viewed in this way, with its efforts to ban recorded music, preventing its people from watching TV, and outlawing the education of women, for example. But the Taliban did not attempt to avoid global modernity *per se*, rather, they attempted to create a space for themselves within global culture *on their own terms*. As Beyer points out, writing about Islam and globalization more generally rather than the Taliban in particular, "the central thrust is to make Islam and Muslims more determinate in the world system, not to reverse globalization. The intent is to shape global reality, not to negate it" (Beyer, quoted in Robins, 1997, 42). For the Taliban, cricket was considered a sport which could be both compatible with Islam *and* their global aspirations, and therefore viewed as a portal allowing entry into the wider world of international relations. Cricket was the beneficiary of this global cultural imperative in large part because it satisfied the Taliban's strict interpretation of the Islamic dress code; "Mullah Omar had decreed that, unlike athletics, football or swimming, playing cricket did not require any part of the body to be revealed to the public" (Guha, 2001). Afghanistan is now an affiliate member of the ICC and in 2006 its fledgling national team completed a first tour of England (BBC News, 11 June 2006).

My interpretation of Robertson's insight that globalization encourages us to "sift the global-cultural scene for ideas and symbols relevant to our identities" reinforces an assumption lodged at the heart of the sociological study of globalization: The oneness of the world makes it amenable to exploration and elements of world culture can be appropriated for use in identity construction. I now want to explore this assumption, suspecting that its seductiveness may beguile us into certain ways of thinking about the world. Speaking as one who may already have been beguiled, I would now say that Robertson's idea that imagining the world as a single place permits a global sifting of cultural elements needs to be held up to greater scrutiny. On Robertson's reading, the whole world is placed within the grasp of individuals and groups who become empowered by an awareness of their global reach to 'discover' something of themselves in other cultures, and to use the world of cultural differences as a resource in the construction of identity and lifestyle choices. We are all invited to shop at the global supermarket of style. The corollary of this is that the act of finding 'authenticity' in the melange of global culture (Pieterse, 2003) is at the same time an enactment of globality. The global search for ideas and elements of identity is at the same time a way of consolidating and expanding circuits of globalization. My initially satisfying conclusion that even the Taliban shop at the same global supermarket of style as the rest of us is possible only because of the prior assumption, which has worked to structure my line of reasoning, that the world is one and somehow accessible to all who wish to view it in terms of a 'global-cultural scene'. The oneness of the world makes it inviting to even the most sceptical cultural consumers.

Pursuing this theme further we can identify other staples of globalization thinking and assumptions about the nature of the world which are contained in the idea that the global-cultural scene can be 'sifted' for useful raw material. First, there is the assumption that the world is 'made' by globalization. A combination of the increasing interconnectivity of the world, coupled with an increasing awareness of its 'unicity', is what makes the world into an entity which can be understood, communicated, and traversed. Put simply, the world, conceived as a single world, is the outcome of globalization, a series of processes which both knit it together through webs of connectivity and 'open it up' and reveal it to the gaze of all interested parties. Second, it is assumed that there are multiple dimensions to globalization; economic, cultural, political, technological, and so on (see McGrew, 2007, 24–45) but that there is one resulting world order. In other words, globalization has many facets which all contribute to the construction of a unified world. This reveals a paradox; all processes of globalization contribute to the unicity of the world yet the mechanisms which permit this harmonious and singular outcome are unspecified. Put another way, we may claim to understand the motors of globalization (Robertson, 2001, 461–2) but have not explained the navigation systems which direct its multiple processes towards the same destination. Another assumption is that everyone is included in the same processes of globalization, whether as an active player or as a passive recipient. Globalization has no outside (which incidentally is probably why Hardt and Negri's work, which chimes so well with 'cultural' variants of globalization thinking, has made such an impact on thinking about the 'global system') and this means that everyone must work to situate themselves in relation to globalization and the resulting world order. You cannot opt out of globalization (even so-called anti-globalization protesters adopt a position in respect of globalization). Being 'against' globalization does not change the fact that you exist in the world, defined by your relation to everyone else in the world. This is one thing that we all have in common: We are positioned in relation to the world as a whole. Moreover, the 'inescapability' of globalization tends not to be seen as a concern by globalization thinkers. In fact it, "is not a problem so much as it is a desired condition" (Boli and Petrova, 2007, 104).

IMAGES OF WORLD ORDER

To pursue this yet further, we can usefully give consideration to Robertson's notion of world order. It is argued here that Robertson's position in relation to the oneness of the world resulting from globalization is the most sophisticated position on offer, and that his work provides some extremely useful insights which can help us work through the issue of one world versus the possibility of multiple worlds. One of Robertson's central ideas (Robertson 1992, 69) is that under conditions of globalization definitions of the global situation proliferate, particularly so as the global search for national identity "encourages conflicts within societies, because the increasing significance of the problem of societal order in relation to global order almost automatically means that political-ideological and religious movements arise in reference to the issue of defining societies in relationship to the rest of the world and the global circumstances as a whole." Stated in different terms, this means that identity claims and the positioning of actors in relation to the world as a whole are circumscribed by the global situation or global order or the global-human condition, as he terms it. Similarly, Robertson highlights the fact that "the problem of individual identity can be raised not merely vis-à-vis a particular state but also vis-à-vis the global circumstance" (Robertson, 1992, 73). This stimulates a multiplicity of 'relations to globalization', as Robertson specifies: "the global field is highly 'pluralistic' in that there is a proliferation of civilizational, continental, regional, societal, and other definitions of the global-human condition as well as considerable variety in identities formed in those respects without direct reference to the global situation." (Robertson, 1992, 70). The key idea here is that different groups and individuals, because of their different perspectives and preoccupations, will construct different relationships to globalization and, consequently, construe the 'global situation' in different terms (which may include choosing not to acknowledge globality).

Robertson (1992, 75) talks about 'world images' which he frames in terms of 'images of global order'. He posits 'four types of image of world order' (Robertson, 1992, 78–83). It will be instructive to look at these in some detail. The first version of world order he terms "Global Gemeinschaft 1", which refers to a vision of the world as a series of "relatively closed societal communities" (Robertson, 1992, 78). Examples of such a vision can be found in the politics of ethnic revival, for example. The second image of world order is termed "Global Gemeinschaft 2" and consists of the idea that global order emerges from a "fully globewide community". Examples include religious movements which aim for the "global organization of the entire world". The third image is termed "Global Gesellschaft 1" and posits the world "as a series of open societies, with considerable sociolcultural exchange between them" (Robertson, 1992, 79). This vision of a world-system can lead to international collaboration or a hegemonic arrangement among states. "Global Gesellschaft 2" on the other hand represents a "formal, planned world organization", in other words a "strong world government" (Robertson, 1992, 82). Robertson makes clear that, although in this discussion he has suggested images of world order, he does not wish to over-emphasise the order that exists or could exist in the world. He states, "I am just as much concerned with the 'order of global disorder' as I am with global order per se" (Robertson, 1992, 83). For Robertson the world as a single place is the product of the systematic tension between the local and the global.

To conclude this discussion we can draw together some of the 'one-world' strands of thinking emerging from discussion of different aspects of Robertson's work. The quote in the above paragraph is a useful starting point. Robertson does not advance a vision of a 'world system' resulting from globalization. There is a world order of sorts, and certainly a 'global-human condition', but his ambition is to neither offer a normative vision of the world or argue that the world is 'hard-wired' according to some overarching global organizational plan. On the contrary, it is not 'world order' which is important, 'world disorder' will do just as well. Globalization has resulted in a circumstance in which we have all come to see ourselves, albeit in many different ways, as existing in some relation to the global. What 'the global' is will differ from account to account; we do not all see the global in the same way. As Robertson says, "definitions of the global situation proliferate", but what is common to all definitions is that there exists a singular global situation in relation to which we are all required to adopt a position in. Whether we see ourselves as belonging to an ethnic group in a world of ethnic groups, as a member of world community of believers, or belonging to a world community of cooperative states, or even as existing in a world of morally equal individuals, what we have in common with all others is our sense of fitting into a world of something, a world which, in its globality, gives meaning to our existence in it, and helps us understand the perspectives, struggles, and community attachments which sustain others. The oneness of the world is not incommensurate with our different understandings of it; rather it is a precondition for such a multiplicity of perspectives.

WORLD-MAKING: THE HETEROCOSMIC IMAGINATION

We can no longer (if we ever could) take for granted what is meant by the idea of 'the world' in political discourse. The world can be *inter alia*, a fragile ecological system, a tourist playground, a religious community, the setting for a sporting competition, a communications network, a giant market place. The world can be thought of as incredibly large (containing an infinite variety of natural habitats, species, landscapes, peoples, etc.) and as a global village. Some visions of the world combine the two: Books such as '1000 places to see before you die' (Schultz, 2003) portray the world as both within the range of the average (if ambitious and affluent) tourist and simultaneously as overwhelmingly vast (1000 places, most of which you are unlikely to visit in a lifetime). The world can be cast as under threat or under control; the idea of the disappearing world (extinction of species, loss of habitats) jostles for attention with the idea of a networked world accessible to those with an internet connection (or even a mobile phone).

This serves as an introduction to a critique of the idea, explored earlier at length and associated with the work of Robertson, amongst others, that globalization results in the singularity of the world. But the point here is not simply that there are many ways of imagining the world—there is nothing new in asserting this. The important point is that the 'heterocosmic imagination'—a term derived from the thinking of the nineteenth century romantics and which refers to the ability to construct the world afresh on the basis of new subjectivities (Rumford and Inglis, 2005)—has become a key component of everyday political (and non-political) discourse. The world is forever being made and remade in the imaginations of our politicians, policy makers, advertising executives, and social movements. Thus, it is not the existence of a multiplicity of meanings accorded the world which is interesting or important, or even the power of the imagination to conjure up yet another vision of the world. What is particularly noteworthy is the belief that we live, not in 'one world' but in a multiplicity of worlds, or that many worlds are possible. What needs to be explored then are the ways in which the idea that many worlds are possible sits alongside (or in tension with) the strong conclusion which has emerged from studies of 'cultural' globalization that we live in 'one world'.

Introducing the idea of the 'heterocosmic imagination' requires that we give consideration to two themes. One is the multiplicity of words that are possible, and this idea has already been introduced. The other is the imagination itself, a theme covered in interesting ways in some current thinking on globalization. One writer who has sought to explore the relationship between globalization and the imagination is Arjun Appadurai, particularly his ideas on the democratization of the work of the imagination (Appadurai, 1996, 31). He says that global cultural processes rely upon imagination as a social practice. Imagination is now a form of work and the means by which individuals connect with the possibilities opened up by globalization. He summarises his ideas on work and the imagination in the following terms:

> No longer mere fantasy (opium for the masses whose real work is elsewhere), no longer simple escape (from a world defined principally by more concrete purposes and structures), no longer elite pastime (thus not relevant to the lives of ordinary people), and no longer mere contemplation (irrelevant for new forms of desire and subjectivity), the imagination . . . is now central to all forms of agency, is itself a social fact, and is the key component of the new global order.

John Tomlinson (2007, 357), writing about cultural globalization, asserts that imagining the world as a single place, which, as we have already noted, is a central component of contemporary sociological imaginings of globality, is automatically also an attempt to universalize a particular view of the world. This is an assumption which does not bear up to scrutiny. It is an assumption which goes unchallenged in much global studies work but which needs confronting. Why should we assume that every world-view must have universalist ambitions? In contrast, I believe that there are different ways of viewing the world which cannot be understood adequately within the cultural globalization paradigm with its emphasis on the 'oneness' of the world. A critical cosmopolitan approach, I wish to argue, emphasises that worlds are constructed, multiple, and not necessarily compatible.

The point to be made is that it is not satisfactory to assume that globalization leads to one world, when there is plenty of evidence to suggest that responses to an awareness of globalization (an awareness that the world is increasingly interconnected, in Robertsonian terms) can include the assertion of new, separate, or incommensurate worlds. In other words, one consequence of the impact of globalization on our lives is to encourage the belief that it is possible to imagine a number of worlds. This stands more as a corollary to Robertson's view of globalization than as a corrective: Globalization leads to an increased awareness of the oneness of the world at the same time as it increases the possibility that we can imagine multiple worlds. To explore these ideas further I have selected four examples of ways in which many or different worlds are imagined. These examples are deliberately chosen from the world of 'everyday' politics and culture in order to demonstrate the ordinariness of the idea that different worlds exist. While it contradicts a central tenet of cultural globalization, this idea seems fairly obvious to a range of commentators, here drawn from politics, current affairs, and popular culture.

The first example highlights the ways in which politicians invoke images of the world in order to justify policy choices, what I term *heterocosmic pre-emption*, particularly apposite in the case of Tony Blair. The second example looks at how pivotal dates in world history can be deployed to construct a narrative of a new world. The third example explores the imagery of 'many worlds' which underlies some contemporary thinking emanating from 'global civil society' movements. The fourth example draws attention to another world envisioned as a result of a sophisticated understanding of globalization advanced by the 'slow' movement. It is suggested that these examples point to ways in which the 'one-worldism' of globalization theory denies the reality of much popular thinking on globalization, and, as such, acts as a fetter on our ability to understand the range of possible political responses to globalization.

BLAIR'S HETEROCOSMIC PRE-EMPTION

In order to develop the argument just introduced, I offer a critical reading of foreign policy speeches made by Tony Blair during his time as UK Prime Minster. Blair's concern to frame political decisions with reference to the 'new world order', the needs of humanity, and the future of the planet echo themes in the recent revival in cosmopolitan political thought (although this is certainly not to argue that Blair is a cosmopolitan but perhaps does suggest another legacy of the 'third way'). The political speeches of Tony Blair reveal a strategy of advancing a particular understanding of the world (rather than a set of core personal beliefs) to justify political decisions. This suggests that the ability to advance a world vision has advantages over holding to an ideology (worldview) in contemporary politics. Whereas an ideology enables one to make sense of and give meaning to world events (imposing order on the world), a 'world vision' is about imaginatively constructing a new world (within which events obtain a preferred meaning). Blair engages in what I call *heterocosmic pre-emption*: the political project of constructing the most plausible world vision within which to 'make sense' of a world which often doesn't 'make sense' (Runciman, 2004).

In a speech given in Chicago in 1999, which subsequently became known as 'The Doctrine of the International Community' Prime Minister Blair defended NATO intervention in Kosovo on the grounds that 'we', the West, have a duty to put an end to the ethnic cleansing, mass murder, and systematic rape being perpetrated there. Blair cautions against seeing conflict in the Balkans as a local affair: "Kosovo cannot be seen in isolation'. He makes the point that previously we might have turned our backs on Kosovo but we can no longer do this so easily. The world has changed, and not just because of the end of the Cold War and technological innovation. "I believe that the world has changed in a more fundamental way. Globalization has transformed economies and our working practices. But globalization is not just economic, it is also a political and security phenomena" (Blair, 1999). Economic developments in one part of the world can cause job losses in other places; conflicts in distant lands can impact upon domestic security. "Acts of genocide can never be a purely internal matter. When oppression produces massive flows of refugees which unsettle neighbouring countries, then they can properly be described as 'threats to international peace and security'" (Blair, 1999). In short, "we are all internationalists now, whether we like it or not" (Blair, 1999), and the upshot is that "we are now in a new world", a world which demands "new rules for international cooperation and new ways of organizing our international institutions" (Blair, 1999), a key dimension of which is deciding when to intervene. Blair also emphasised the 'world has changed' message on other occasions too. For example, in a speech to the Labour Party conference in 2004 he said,

> There are two views of what is happening in the world today. One view is that there are isolated individuals, extremists, engaged in essentially isolated acts of terrorism . . . The other view is that this is a wholly new phenomenon, worldwide global terrorism . . . If you take this view, you believe September 11th changed the world; that Bali, Beslan, Madrid and scores of other atrocities . . . are part of the same threat. (Blair, 2004)[2]

This examination of elements of a selection of Blair's speeches is not intended to suggest that his insights on global politics should inform our work in building new theories of globalization, or that they contain a 'truth' which has eluded social scientists. Rather it is to draw attention to the way in which the world can be made and remade in political discourse and, in the case of Tony Bair's 'world vision', the positing of a new or changed world can drive policy choices and political priorities. The 'world has changed' motif has been utilized by politicians of every stripe in recent years and it has become a routinized way of making reassurances in the face of dramatic change (see Chapter 5). Nevertheless, beneath the clichés, there lies a real attempt to wrest thinking about the global situation out of the grasp of accounts which emphasise the unfolding of a pre-existing logic, towards a narrative that posits the existence of a separate world of possibility.

THE DIFFERENCE A YEAR MAKES

It was 'the year that changed everything' according to a recent issue of *Newsweek*: 1968 was the "year that made us who we are" (Adler, 2007). In Chapter 6 we looked at the ways in which epoch-making and epoch-ending dates are related to ways of thinking and seeing which depend upon the existence of a 'high point', a privileged vantage point from which society can be understood and interpreted, and hence managed and directed. Ending and beginnings are woven into the fabric of the heterocosmic imagination. This is the context within which we should view the claims in *Newsweek* that 1968 was "a global season of rude awakenings" (Dickey, 2007, 50)—it contained the events associated with the Paris uprising, the 'Prague Spring' and anti-Vietnam protests in the United States. "In Europe and the United States, the generation of 1968 had an idealistic core expressed in culture, politics and a distinct way of looking at the world. Its legacy lives on" (Dickey, 2007, 50). The article makes a (rather unconvincing) case for the continued, or even growing, influence of the '68ers in Europe; focussing on the activities of Joschka Fischer in Germany and Bernard Kouchner in France. Nevertheless the more general point that epoch-making events can colour or give shape to a vision of the world is a valid one. For the '68ers, the world is still a different place (even if what is exactly different about it may be difficult to establish with any certainty) and will always be viewed with a degree of idealism. But as another article in the same issue of *Newsweek* makes clear "many years are jostling for staring roles in history" (Adler, 2007, 64), and indeed in world history. The author of *The Times Complete History of the World* does not include 1968 in his list of "the 50 key dates of world history" (Overy, 2007), despite the fact that most of the important events in the past 1000 years appear to have their origins in Europe or the European sphere of influence. The point here is that the processes of epoch-making, determining starting and ending points, and narrating perspectival histories can fuel the 'heterocosmic imagination'. Such activity can result in different perspectives on the same tranche of 'global history'; or it can result in the construction of conflicted worlds whose histories do not fit together to form a whole.

WORLDS WITHIN WORLDS

In the context of a discussion on the possibility of global justice Naomi Klein draws attention to how the Zapatistas see the world we live in (a world of neoliberalism, global institutions of governance, and US hegemony) as one of many possible worlds. They call it 'one world with many worlds in it' (Klein, 2001). This has become something of a motif for transnational social movements and global civil society actors more generally as a way of expressing both the possibility of living according to a set of values different from those propagated by neoliberalism, and their resistance to the 'one-worldism' associated with globalization, which they insist obscures the many worlds that exist, or can exist, alongside it. The idea that 'different worlds exist and co-exist' is not easily accommodated within mainstream sociological accounts of globalization. But for global civil society movements this assertion is a prerequisite to imagining a better world.

In the world vision of the International Forum on Globalization (International Forum in Globalization, 2004, 439), corporate capitalism creates one world, citizens' movements create another one entirely. Similarly, the slogan of the World Social Forum is 'Another World is Possible'. This suggests that one important response to the experience of globalization is to celebrate the many worlds which comprise the world. In the words of Subcomandante Marcos, as a result of the actions of the Zapatistas, "A world made of many worlds opened a space and established its right to exist, raised the banner of being necessary, stuck itself in the middle of the earth's reality to announce a better future" (Marcos, 2004, 433).

THE WORLD OF SLOW

The Slow Movement, born in Italy as a response to the spread of 'fast food' but now extending through its various networks (slow food, slow cities) to more than 100 countries worldwide (Miele, 2008), is a measured response to the experience of globalization (the 'global everyday') not a denial of it, or naïve desire to return to 'the good old days'. What is particularly interesting about the Slow Movement is that the self-awareness and reflexivity required to embrace a world of slow exists as a direct consequence of a global consciousness: "practices of slow living arise from, and in response to, processes of globalization" (Parkins and Craig, 2006, 9). But this should not be taken to imply that the Slow Movement is a retreat into the local. Rather, it is "part of a reconfiguration of social relations and identities in new reflexive ways which 'utilize, criticize and even contribute to globalization, while developing new senses of locality and community'" (Parkins and Craig, 2006, 11). In other words, to embrace slow living, one must first define oneself in relation to the 'global situation' to use Robertson's phrase. Slow living is a form of 'ethical cosmopolitanism' according to Parkins and Craig (2006, 26) "in which people are aware of the global connections which bind them to distant others". These connections are sustained by a shared desire to 'create a better world' through alternative modes of producing and consuming food.

CONCLUSIONS: WORLD VISIONS

In contrast to the global studies emphasis on the 'oneness of the world', what these examples demonstrate is that the world is not to be 'found' emerging fully formed as a result of global interconnectedness. Rather, the world we construct is one of many possibilities which can co-exist. We do not all see the same world when we look at globalization. In this sense, the heterocosmic imagination or 'world visions' outlined here are significantly different from many sociological perspectives on globalization. They exhibit this difference in the following ways. First, the world is not constituted by globalization and ready to offer itself to us 'fully-formed' so that we may easily apprehend its global and interrelated nature. The world as a meaningful entity is narrated and constructed by those possessing a vision of the world. In the resulting narratives it is not necessarily the case that the world thus envisioned is the only world possible. Second, the world can exist independently of any processes of globalization. World-making is not necessarily linked to globalization, and certainly cannot be reduced to it. Third, the multiplicity of processes contributing to globalization do not have to be viewed as leading to one world which can be seen from different perspectives. It is possible to have many worlds, bespoke worlds, incommensurate worlds, which cannot be viewed from a singular or unifying vantage point. A world vision does not necessarily lead to consciousness of globality. Fourth, sociological and cultural theories of globalization emphasise that we have the opportunity to re-position ourselves in relation to the global whole; we can all map our shifting positions in relation to the dimensions of globality. In stark contrast, the heterocosmic imagination suggests that worlds can be circumscribed and delineated (they have origins and limits). Such worlds are not open and inclusive, they can be fragmented, discontinuous, and exclusive.

Globalization and critical cosmopolitanism promote different ways of viewing the world. In the case of the former, the world is interconnected, systemic, unified, singular. In the case of the latter, it is possible to imagine a plurality of worlds which are multiple, simultaneous, and perspectival, and their construction can become a site of political contestation. Globalization theory does not dismiss contestation and contention as unimportant, but it has its own way of dealing with it: giving the world a common language and agenda for political disputes, for example. The diffusion of global norms which pattern the world of nation-states also engenders some fundamental debates about the identity and purpose of nation-states, debates which also generate norms: economic liberalism versus social justice; equality versus security; economic growth versus welfare.

We are familiar with the idea that many Europes exist (whether in terms of the various institutional versions of Europe; the Council of Europe, the European Union, Schengenland, etc., or in terms of cultural constructions of Europe; Western, Eastern, Central), and indeed that many modernities co-exist (Delanty, 2003; Delanty and Rumford, 2005). It is also well-established that globalization comprises a multiplicity of processes (economic, political, cultural). So why then do we have a problem with the idea that globalization leads to not one world but several? Globalization thinking has produced its array series of certainties and expectations and these can and should be challenged by new perspectives. Critical cosmopolitanism suggests that we know the world less well than we think.

This chapter has focussed on one such certainty, that globalization renders the world into a unified and comprehensible whole. I began this chapter with a quote from Jonathan Friedman (2007, 111) which captures this need to investigate the 'givens' of sociologically inspired globalization thinking. Friedman floats the familiar notion that "the world is now one place"—what I have here termed one-worldism—and then proceeds to unpick its logic, tossing it up in order to shoot it down. Globalization comprises the flows of culture, people, information, money, and technology—which we are aware work chaotically, in other words in a rather unpredictable and unsystematic manner, forming 'disjunctive circuits' (in a nod to Appadurai, perhaps)—but which at the same time lead us to the conclusion that they work to 'somehow bring us all together'. It is the 'somehow' in this sentence which sparks Friedman's critique. As I stated earlier in the chapter, this is one of the great mysteries of globalization thinking, and one of its unexplored theoretical realms. There exists a large gap between our understanding of what drives globalization and the guidance systems which propel its multiple processes towards a common destination. Friedman allows us to see that the 'one-worldism' characteristic of sociological approaches to globalization is an article of faith (and borderline normative prescription) which sits uncomfortably alongside empirical accounts of the world.

9 Concluding Thoughts
The Spaces of Critical Cosmopolitanism

> The cosmopolitan outlook . . . begins where notions of 'one world' in which everything could have its proper place, at least in principle and in theory, have been forever shattered.
>
> —Beck and Grande, 2007, 120

The above epigraph serves a useful purpose at the start of this short concluding section. Much as I would like to agree with Beck and Grande—in the sense that they are 'fellow travellers' determined to offer an interesting account of 'cosmopolitan Europe'—I find it difficult to do so, despite sharing their sense of the inadequacy of 'one-worldism'. There are at least three reasons why I find myself in disagreement with them. The first is their conclusion, contained in the epigraph, that the 'one-worldism' found within sociological approaches to globalization has been 'forever shattered' by the cosmopolitan outlook. As I see it, the feathers of 'one-worldism' have hardly been ruffled, although the identification of this way of thinking as a problem is certainly a step in the right direction.

The second reason centres on their conclusion that the EU project is best thought of in terms of cosmopolitan empire. The third is that their 'methodological cosmopolitanism' leads them to a 'cosmopolitan realist' vision of the world. All of which is rather too cosmopolitan for my taste for reasons outlined in detail in Chapters 1 and 6, but to recap I would agree with Philip Schlesinger's (2007) observation that Beck's work succumbs to the 'cosmopolitan temptation'—the tendency to see cosmopolitanism everywhere and thereby precluding clear-headed analysis.

The result of this 'cosmopolitan realism' is rather unfortunate in as much as researchers wishing to explore Europe from a cosmopolitan perspective are now obliged to navigate not only around Habermas' attempt to make cosmopolitanism a European value but also away from Beck and Grande's idea that cosmopolitan Europe is the unintended outcome of the EU's project of integration. The upshot is that a generation of scholars is faced with the task not of demonstrating the applicability of cosmopolitan thinking to the study of Europe, but demonstrating that Europe is less cosmopolitan than leading public intellectuals would have us believe.

This discussion recalls the concerns voiced at the opening of this book, particularly that the study of cosmopolitanism and Europe has taken an unfortunate turn and is becoming associated with the desire to forge a European identity vis-à-vis the United States and/or recast the EU as a cosmopolitan project, irrespective of what the EU's own view of this might be. Robert Fine (2007) has found the 'new' cosmopolitan to not be cosmopolitan enough. However, from my perspective there is rather too much of it, and the high profile public interventions of its leading adherents (newspaper articles, interviews, media coverage) have given cosmopolitan a distinctive complexion and steered debate on cosmopolitanism and Europe down one particular path. The cosmopolitan spaces explored in this book are neither cosmopolitan in the realist sense understood by Beck, nor European in the way Habermas would prefer. Separating 'cosmopolitan' and 'Europe' by a colon in the title of this book may well turn out to be an inspired decision. Europe does not possess cosmopolitan spaces, nor should the EU be seen as a 'cosmopolitan space'. Following the line of argument developed throughout this book, cosmopolitan spaces exist to the extent that spaces, borders, and networks can be apprehended from different vantage points and which emerge as a result of multiple perspectives being brought to bear.

Moreover, the idea of 'cosmopolitan spaces' challenges the accepted relationship between spaces and borders. It is usually assumed that borders are of secondary importance, spaces forming sites of political action and the connecting tissue out of which networks can be formed. In conventional thinking, borders are merely the limits to the spaces which contain politics and serve as dividing lines between polities. Following Balibar (2004a, 220) we might wish to invert the relationship between territory and borders. This is not simply to suggest that borders are everywhere or alternatively emphasise their spatiality, although this is in itself a worthwhile task. Rather the inversion points to the dynamism of borders which, freed from their sole task of containing the nation-state, have become a key site for understanding the dynamics of political transformation in Europe (and elsewhere), the politics of identity and belonging, and the 'deep grammar' of spatiality in an age of globalization. In this sense, borders are the pre-eminent 'cosmopolitan spaces'.

I have argued in this book that it is meaningful to talk of cosmopolitan borders, but can we also speak of global borders? While the distinction between cosmopolitan and global borders is seldom made, at least in the existing literature, the issue of whether borders can be global is a vexed one around which intellectual debate is only now beginning to cohere. Balibar, to turn to him again, argues that borders can be global. As we saw in Chapter 3, for Balibar local borders are also endowed with a global function. What he means is that a border may separate two localities, be of importance only to local people, and be low down in a national hierarchy of borders, for example. This local significance does not mean however that it does not have a global role. At the same time as being 'merely local', such a border also works to 'partition the world'. Any dividing line, no matter how local, serves to divide the whole world into inside–outside, us and them. As Balibar says, "every map in this sense is always a world map, for it represents a 'part of the world'" (Balibar, 2004a, 220–1).

I do not think this is the best position from which to launch an investigation of global borders. For a border to be global in the sense advanced by Balibar the map of the world would have to be recognised as such by all peoples. A local border can be a global border as well only if the map that it appears on is universally recognised. I do not think we live in circumstances for which one map of the world will serve. Who would draw up this map, and how would it come to be recognised as *the* map of the world. Put another way, are the Palestinians, the US Homeland Security Agency, Kurds in Northern Iraq, and African migrants crossing the Mediterranean by boat all reading from the same map of the world? It is problematic to assume that any border, even a border accorded key international status such as the Mexico–US border, or the wall between the West Bank and Israel, Turkey's eastern border with Iraq, or Balibar's 'Great Wall of Europe' is or could be a global border. Such observations raise many interesting issues which require further study. At the present time it is only possible to say that for a long time it has been assumed that such a map can exist. We now need to think in ways which do not rely upon this 'one-worldist' assumption. In other words, Balibar's account of global borders only works within a frame of reference that assumes that the world is a single place: A global border requires a 'high point' perspective (see Chapter 6) from which all borders can be viewed and their positions relativized.

What I would offer in place of global borders is the idea of cosmopolitan borders. This is much more than a semantic preference. Borders can be cosmopolitan in a way that they can never be global. In addition to cosmopolitan borders not necessarily being under the control of the nation-state, which was the thrust of Chapter 4, borders can also be cosmopolitan in other important ways. We can also say that a border is cosmopolitan when it is viewed from a variety of perspectives, resulting in people interpreting its function and meaning in different ways, possibly disagreeing on its significance, and perhaps not even noticing that it exists at all.

Such a view of borders stems not from 'cosmopolitan realism', taking the view that a border has been cosmopolitan all along but that its true nature was obscured by 'methodological nationalism'. Such a view stems from the 'critical cosmopolitan' advanced here, of which there are three main components. The first is summarised by the idea of post-westernization (Chapter 7) which prevents cosmopolitanism from being yoked to European identity. The second, closely related to the first, is the idea of multiplicity. There exist not only multiple perspectives and multiple voices but also a multiplicity of Europes and indeed of worlds. Following on from this we can say, third, that critical cosmopolitanism is engaged in a critique of globalization thinking, specifically the idea that we live in one world.

In the novel *Against the Day*, Thomas Pynchon introduces us to a device called an anamorphoscope, "or more properly no doubt a *para*morphoscope because it reveals worlds which are set to the side of the one we have taken, until now, to be the only world given us" (Pynchon, 2007, 249). My conclusion in this book is that what is required in order to better study globalization is a 'paramorphoscopic sociology' which prioritizes the study of worlds which exist in addition to the one given to us by theorists of cultural globalization. This is essentially the task of what I am calling 'critical cosmopolitanism', which like Pynchon's paramorphoscope, "when placed on or otherwise near a deliberately distorted picture, and viewed from the appropriate direction, would make the image appear 'normal' again" (Pynchon, 2007, 249).

Notes

NOTES TO CHAPTER 1

1. Cosmopolitanism and Europe' held in the Department of Politics and International Relations, Royal Holloway, University of London, 22–23April 2004 http://www.chrisrumford.org.uk/cosmopolitanism.html

NOTES TO CHAPTER 2

1. The European Neighbourhood Policy covers Belarus, Ukraine, Moldova, Georgia, Armenia, Azerbaijan, Morocco, Algeria, Tunisia, Libya, Egypt, Israel, Jordan, Lebanon, Syria, the Palestinian Authority.

NOTES TO CHAPTER 3

1. A neglect more marked in Anglophone than continental scholarship. I am grateful to Luiza Bialasiewicz and Claudio Minca for this point.
2. See the essays on 'citizens and borderwork' published in the special issue of *Space and Polity* (Volume 12, Number 1, 2008) of which I am guest editor.
3. Bailbar's work is replete with italicised phrases and words placed in quotation marks. When quoting from Balibar's work I have taken the decision to leave the italicised passages in their original form, even though at times these may read slightly strangely when taken out of context.
4. "The trainers that mark a drug gang's territory" by Glen Owen and Oliver Wadeson, *The Mail on Sunday*, 21 April, 2007.
5. According to Beck (2007a, 47), "Europeans and North Americans are living in different worlds. The way it looks to the Americans, the Europeans are suffering from a form of hysteria in relation to the environment, [climate change] while, to many Europeans, US Americans are paralysed by an exaggerated fear of terrorism".
6. The German word Graussraum can be translated as 'geopolitical space'.

NOTES TO CHAPTER 4

1. "M15 trains supermarket checkout staff" by Sophie Goodchild and Paul Lashman, *The Independent*, 4 March 2007 http://news.independent.co.uk/uk/crime/article2326211.ece
2. http://www.frontex.europa.eu/

3. Holton (2008, 23) suggests that the idea of the EU as a network state or society is too simplistic. He quotes Barry who states that it is more profitable to see the EU as a "political institution in which the model of the network has come to provide a dominant sense of political possibilities".
4. "Trans-border Trans-Dniester", Simon Reeve, BBC News, 10 May 2005 http://news.bbc.co.uk/1/hi/programmes/this_world/4532267.stm
5. "EU operation begins monitoring Ukrainian–Moldovan border" Jan Maksymiuk, Radio Free Europe/Radio Liberty, 30 November 2005 http://www.rferl.org/featuresarticle/2005/11/99eeadea-763e-454e-845f-9e6e20d09c89.html
6. "Does dispersal mean order?" BBC News, 15 July 2005 http://news.bbc.co.uk/1/hi/england/london/4683123.stm
7. Congestion Charging applies to cars entering the central zone between 7.00a.m. and 6.30p.m., Monday to Friday. The cost is £8 per day. See https://www.cclondon.com/
8. See for example, "No Borders @ Harmondsworth Detention Centre, Sat 8 April" http://www.indymedia.org.uk/en/2006/03/335158.html and the website of the No Border network http://www.noborder.org
9. "'Pie zone' battle goes to Europe" BBC News 14 March 2006 http://news.bbc.co.uk/1/hi/england/leicestershire/4806322.stm
10. I am not trying to answer the question of what attracts people to life in a gated community in definitive terms. Clearly many people will not be motivated by perceptions of insecurity, and may choose to live in a gated community because a prestige value may be attached to such property, for example. Equally important, reasons for living in gated communities may differ from place to place, country to country.
11. "Spain offers boats to Mauritania" BBC News 15 March 2006 http://news.bbc.co.uk/1/hi/world/europe/4809814.stm
12. "Police say violence ban working" BBC News 22 December 2005 http://news.bbc.co.uk/1/hi/wales/south_west/4552956.stm

NOTES TO CHAPTER 5

1. "US fears home-grown terror threat" BBC News 24 June 2006 http://news.bbc.co.uk/2/hi/americas/5112354.stm
2. "Chicago plot suspects denied bail" BBC News 5 July 2006 http://news.bbc.co.uk/2/hi/americas/5152652.stm
3. "Chicago plot suspects denied bail" BBC News 5 July 2006 http://news.bbc.co.uk/2/hi/americas/5152652.stm
4. "US fears home-grown terror threat" BBC News 24 June 2006 http://news.bbc.co.uk/2/hi/americas/5112354.stm
5. James Coomarasamy "Home front fears in war on terror" BBC News 24 June 4 2006 http://news.bbc.co.uk/2/hi/americas/5108582.stm
6. "US fears home-grown terror threat" BBC News 24 June 2006 http://news.bbc.co.uk/2/hi/americas/5112354.stm
7. "Terror controls 'may get tougher'" BBC News 17 October 2006 http://news.bbc.co.uk/2/hi/uk_news/6057562.stm
8. See for example, "Control orders breach human rights, law lords say" *The Guardian* Wednesday October 31 2007 http://www.guardian.co.uk/terrorism/story/0,,2202266,00.html
9. "Marriage visa age to rise to 21" BBC News, 28 March 2007 http://news.bbc.co.uk/2/hi/uk_news/politics/6501451.stm
10. "Reid makes Nazi terror comparison" BBC News 31 October 2006 http://news.bbc.co.uk/2/hi/uk_news/6102508.stm

11. "Reid makes Nazi terror comparison" BBC News 31 October 2006 http://news.bbc.co.uk/2/hi/uk_news/6102508.stm
12. "Britain facing 'most sustained threat since WWII', says Reid" Matthew Tempest, *The Guardian*, 9 August 2006 http://politics.guardian.co.uk/terrorism/story/0,,1840482,00.html
13. Tony Blair, Speech to the World Affairs Council in Los Angeles, California http://news.bbc.co.uk/2/hi/uk_news/politics/5236896.stm
14. John Reid, The Times 13 May 2007 http://www.timesonline.co.uk/tol/news/politics/article1782106.ece

NOTES TO CHAPTER 6

1. In March 2003 the European Commission published a Communication entitled 'Wider Europe–Neighbourhood: A New Framework for Relations with Eastern and Southern Neighbours' (European Commission, 2003)
2. See note 1 Chapter 2, above
3. http://ec.europa.eu/world/enp/index_en.htm
4. See for example the essays in the edited volumes by Balakrishnan (2003a) and Passavant and Dean (2004).
5. "Mourning sickness is a religion" http://news.bbc.co.uk/1/hi/uk/3512447.stm

NOTES TO CHAPTER 7

1. A version of the following section was published as Rumford (2006d).
2. The Islamic nature of the AK Party is the subject of some dispute, as is the usefulness of the designation 'Islamic' as an attempt to capture the essence of their political orientation. On this point see for example Turunç (2007), Onis (2007).
3. Gurkan Zengin quoted at www.esiweb.org/index.php?lang=en&id=114
4. Despite AK Party's increased share of the vote they received fewer seats in parliament (341 rather than 363). This is a quirk of the electoral system in Turkey which allows only parties which secure 10% of the national vote to take up seats in parliament. In 2002 only one other party (CHP) crossed the 10% threshold, in 2007 two other parties, CHP with 21% and MHP with 14%, did so.
5. The Copenhagen Criteria require candidate counties to ensure stable political institutions guaranteeing democracy, the rule of law, human rights, and the protection of minorities; a functioning market economy and the capacity to handle competitive pressure from the EU's internal market; public authorities capable of implementing and enforcing EU law.
6. I am grateful to Hasan Turunc for information on Turkey–NATO relations.
7. 'Scarf conundrum grips Turkey' http://news.bbc.co.uk/1/hi/world/europe/3513259.stm
8. At the time of this writing (January 2008), AK Party was working with the opposition MHP to secure parliamentary approval for a lifting of the headscarf ban in universities in Turkey. Interestingly, even the ultra-nationalist MHP are starting to talk about the headscarf issue in terms of human rights. "It is a question of rights and freedoms", MHP leader Devlet Bahceli quoted by the BBC. See "Turkish MPs plan headscarf reform" BBC News. Wednesday 30 January 2008 http://news.bbc.co.uk/2/hi/europe/7214827.stm

NOTES TO CHAPTER 8

1. The usage of 'one-worldism' here should not be confused with its connotations in American foreign policy in the early part of the twentieth century.
2. There are of course many attempts to portray the attacks on the United States of September 11, 2001 as a major switch-point in history (Runciman, 2004).

References

Adler, J. 2007. A century of destiny. *Newsweek*, 19 November.

Alexander, J. 2004. 'Towards a theory of cultural trauma.' In *Cultural Trauma and Collective Identity*. eds. Alexander, J., Eyerman, R., Giesen, B., Smelser, N. and Sztompka, P. 2004: 1–30. Berkeley: University of California.

Alexander, J., R. Eyerman, B. Giesen, N. Smelser, and P. Sztompka, P. 2004. *Cultural trauma and collective identity*. Berkeley: University of California Press.

Amin, A. 2004. Multi-ethnicity and the idea of Europe. Theory, Culture and Society 21(2):1–24.

Amoore. L. 2006. Biometric borders: Governing mobilities in the war on terror *Political Geography* 25(3): 336–51.

Anderson, J. 1996. The shifting stage of politics: New medieval and postmodern territorialities? *Environment and Planning D: Society and Space* 14(2): 133–153.

Andreas, P. 2000. Introduction: The wall after the wall. In *The Wall Around the West: State Borders and Immigration Controls in North America and Europe*, eds. P. Andreas and T. Snyder, 1–14. Lanham Maryland; Rowman and Littlefield.

Andreas, P. 2003. Redrawing the line: Borders and security in the twenty-first century. *International Security* 28(2);78–111.

Appadurai, A. 1996. *Modernity at large: Cultural dimensions of globalization.* Minneapolis: Minnesota University Press.

Appadurai, A. 2006. *Fear of small numbers: An essay on the geography of anger.* Durham: Duke University Press.

Archibugi, D. 1998. Principles of cosmopolitan democracy. In *Re-imagining political community: Studies in cosmopolitan democracy*, eds. D. Archibugi, D. Held, and M. Kohler, 198–230. Cambridge: Polity Press.

Arikan, H. 2002. A lost opportunity? A critique of the EU's human rights policy towards Turkey. *Mediterranean Politics* 7(1):19–50.

Ash, T. G., and R. Dahrendorf, 2005. The renewal of Europe: Response to Habermas. In *Old Europe, New Europe, Core Europe: Transatlantic Relations after the Iraq War, eds.* D. Levy, M. Pensky, and J. Torpey, 141–145. London: Verso.

Atkinson, R. 2001. The emerging "urban agenda" and the European spatial development perspective: Towards an EU urban policy? *European Planning Studies* 9(3): 385–406.

Axford, B. 2006. The dialectic of borders and networks in Europe: reviewing "topological presuppositions". *Comparative European Politics* 4(2/3):160–182.

Axford, B. 2007. Editorial: Borders and networks in the global system. *Globalizations* 4(3):321–326.

Bache, I., and M. Flinders, eds. 2005. *Multi-level governance.* Oxford: Oxford University Press.

Bacik, G., and B. Aras, 2002. Exile: A keyword in understanding Turkish politics. *Muslim World* 92(3/4):387–406.

Balakrishnan, G., ed. 2003. *Debating empire*. London: Verso.

Balakrishnan, G. 2003. Introduction. In *Debating empire*, ed. G. Balakrishnan, vii–xix. London: Verso.

Balibar, E. 1998. The borders of Europe. In *Cosmopolitics: Thinking and feeling beyond the nation*, eds. P. Cheah, and B. Robbins, 216–229. Minneapolis: Minnesoto University Press.

Balibar, E. 2002. *Politics and the other scene*. London: Verso.

Balibar, E. 2003. Europe, an "unimagined" frontier of democracy. *Diacritics* 33(3–4):36–44.

Balibar, E. 2004a. *We, the people of Europe? Reflections on transnational citizenship*. Princeton: Princeton University Press.

Balibar, E. 2004b. Europe as borderland: The Alexander von Humboldt Lecture in Human Geography. Lecture given at University of Nijmegen, Netherlands

Balibar, E. 2006. Strangers as enemies: Further reflections on the aporias of transnational citizenship. Globalization. Working Papers 06/4, Institute on Globalization and the Human Condition, McMaster University, Canada.

Balkir, C. 2001. Turkey and the question of European identity. *European Urban and Regional Studies* 8(1):39–47.

Barry, A. 2006. Technological zones. *European Journal of Social Theory* 9(2):239–54.

Batt, J. 2003. The EU's new borderlands. Working paper, London Centre for European Reform.

Bauman, Z. 1998. *Globalization: The human consequences*. Cambridge: Polity Press.

Bauman, Z. 1999. *In search of politics*. Cambridge: Polity Press.

Bauman, Z. 2002. *Society under siege*. Cambridge: Polity Press.

Bauman, Z. 2004. *Wasted lives: Modernity and its outcasts*. Cambridge: Polity Press.

Bauman, Z. 2005. *Liquid life*. Cambridge: Polity Press.

Bauman, Z. 2006a: *Liquid Fear*. Cambridge: Polity Press.

Bauman, Z. 2006b. The unwinnable war: An interview with Zygmunt Bauman. *Eurozine*. www.eurozine.com/articles/2006-12-13-bauman-en.html

Bauman, Z. 2007. *Liquid times: Living in an age of uncertainty*. Cambridge: Polity Press.

Baykan, A. 2003. Turkey: From Empire to Integration. *The European Union Centre and Centre for West European Studies Newsletter* (University of Pittsburg), February: 1/7. http://www.ucis.pitt.edu/euce/pub/newsletter/2003/feb03nwslt.pdf

Beck, U. 1992. *Risk society: Towards a new modernity*. London: Sage.

Beck, U. 2000. *What is globalization?* Cambridge: Polity Press.

Beck, U. 2003. Towards a new critical theory with cosmopolitan intent. *Constellations* 10(4): 453–468.

Beck, U. 2004, The cosmopolitan turn. In *The Future of Social Theory*, ed. N. Gane, 143–166. London: Continuum.

Beck, U. 2005. 'Power and weakness in a Word Risk society' in *Old Europe, New Europe, Core Europe: Transatlantic relations after the Iraq war*, eds. D. Levy, M. Pensky and J. Torpey, London: Verso.

Beck, U. 2006. *Cosmopolitan vision*. Cambridge: Polity Press.

Beck, U. 2007a. Reinventing Europe—a cosmopolitan vision. In *Cosmopolitanism and Europe*, ed. C. Rumford, 39–50. Liverpool: Liverpool University Press.

Beck, U. 2007b. Cosmopolitanism: A critical theory for the twenty-first century. In *The Blackwell companion to globalization*, ed. G. Ritzer, 162–176. Oxford: Blackwell.

Beck, U. 2008, forthcoming. Understanding the real Europe: A cosmopolitan vision. In *Handbook of European Studies*, ed. C. Rumford, . London: Sage.

Beck, U., and A. Giddens. 2003. Discovering real Europe: A cosmopolitan vision. http://www.policy-network.net/php/article.php?sid=2&aid=471.

Beck, U., and E. Grande. 2007. *Cosmopolitan Europe*. Cambridge: Polity Press.

Beck, U., and N. Sznaider. 2006. Unpacking cosmopolitanism for the social sciences: A research agenda. *British Journal of Sociology* 57(1):1–23.

Berezin, M. 2003. Introduction: Territory, emotion and identity: Spatial recalibration in a new Europe. In *Europe without borders: Remapping territory, citizenship and identity in a transnational age*, eds. M. Berezin, and M. Schain, 1–32. Baltimore: Johns Hopkins University Press.

Berezin, M., and M. Schain eds. 2003. *Europe without borders: Remapping territory, citizenship and identity in a transnational age*. Baltimore: Johns Hopkins University Press.

Bhambra, G. 2008. Forthcoming. Postcolonial Europe: Or, understanding Europe in times of the postcolonial. In *Handbook of European Studies*, ed. C. Rumford. London: Sage.

Bialasiewicz, L., C. Minca. 2005.Old Europe, new Europe: For a geopolitics of translation. *Area* 37(4): 365–372.

Blair, T. 1999. Doctrine of the international community. Speech by the UK Prime Minister, Economic Club of Chicago, Hilton Hotel, Chicago.

Blair, T. 2004. Speech to Labour Party Conference, Brighton, UK.

Bleiker, R., M. Leet. 2006. From the sublime to the subliminal: Fear, awe and wonder in international politics. *Millennium: Journal of International Studies* 34(3): 713—737.

Boli, J., and V. Petrova. 2007. Golabalization today. In *Blackwell companion to globalization*, ed. G. Ritzer, 103–124. Oxford: Blackwell.

Borocz, J., and M. Sarkar. 2005. What is the EU? *International Sociology* 20:2.

Bourne, A., and M. Cini. 2006. Introduction: Defining boundaries and defining trends in European Union studies. In *Palgrave Advances in European Studies*, eds. M. Cini, and A. Bourne, 1–18. Houndmills: Palgrave.

Brenner, N. 2003, Rescaling state space in western Europe: Urban governance and the rise of glocalizing competition state regimes (GCSRs). In *Europe without borders: Remapping territory, citizenship, and identity in a transnational age*, eds. M. Berezin, and M. Schain, .Baltimore: Johns Hopkins University Press.

Brenner, N. 2004. *New state spaces: Urban governance and the rescaling of statehood*, 140–168. Oxford: Oxford University Press.

Brown, C. 1988: The modern requirement? Reflections on normative international relation theory in a post-Western world. *Millennium* 17(2):339–48.

Butler, J. 2004. *Precarious life: The powers of mourning and violence*. London: Verso.

Buzan, B., and T. Diez. 1999. The European Union and Turkey. *Survival*, 41(1): Spring: 41–57.

Calhoun, C. 2003. The democratic integration of Europe: Interests, identity, and the public sphere. In *Europe without borders: Remapping territory, citizenship, and identity in a transnational age*, eds. M. Berezin, and M. Schain, 243–274. Baltimore: Johns Hopkins University Press.

Calhoun. C. 2006. The emergency imaginary: Humanitarianism, states, and the limits of cosmopolitanism. Inaugural Lecture, University Professorship, NYU, New York.

Castells, M. 2000. *The rise of the network society. The information age: Economy, society and culture*. vol. 1. 2nd ed. Oxford: Blackwell.

Cheah, P. 2006. Cosmopolitanism. *Theory Culture and Society* 23(2–3):486–949.

Chernilo, D. 2006. Social theory's methodological nationalism: myth or reality? *European Journal of Social Theory* 9(1):5–22.

Coaffe, J. 2004. Rings of steel, rings of concrete and rings of confidence: designing out terrorism in Central London pre and post-September 11th. *International Journal of Urban and Regional Research* 28(1):201–11.

Cohen, R., and P. Kennedy. 2000. *Global sociology*. Houndmills: Palgrave.

Colas, A. 2007. *Empire*. Cambridge: Polity Press.

Cosar, S., and A. Ozman. 2004. Centre-right politics in Turkey after the November 2002 general election: Neo-liberlaism with a Muslim face. *Contemporary Politcs*, 10(1):57–74.

Delanty, G. 2000 *Modernity and postmodernity*. London: Sage.

Delanty, G. 2003. The making of a post-western Europe: A civilizational analysis. *Thesis Eleven*, 72:8–24.

Delanty, G. 2006a. The cosmopolitan imagination: critical cosmopolitanism and social theory. *British Journal of Sociology* 57 (1):25–47.

Delanty, G., ed. 2006b. *Europe and Asia beyond east and west: Towards a new cosmopolitanism*. London: Routledge.

Delanty, G. 2006c. Introduction: The idea of a post-western Europe. In *Europe and Asia beyond east and west*, ed. G. Delanty, 1–8. London: Routledge.

Delanty, G. 2007. Peripheries and borders in a post-western Europe. *Eurozine*. *www.eurozine.com/articles/2007-08-29-delanty-en.html*

Delanty, G., and C. Rumford. 2005. *Rethinking Europe: Social theory and the implications of Europeanization*. London: Routledge.

Delanty, G., and C. Rumford. 2007. Political globalization. In *Blackwell companion to globalization*, ed. G. Ritzer, 414–428. Oxford: Blackwell.

Devji, F. 2005. *Landscapes of the Jihad: Militancy, morality, modernity*. London: Hurst and Company.

Devji, F. 2006. Back to the future: The cartoons, liberalism, and global Islam. *OpenDemocracy*, 13 April. www.opendemocracy.net/conflict-terrorism/literalism_3451.jsp

Devji, F. 2008 (forthcoming). The mountain comes to Muhammad: Global Islam in provincial Europe. In *Handbook of European Studies*, ed. C. Rumford, . London: Sage.

Dickey, C. 2007. 1968: The year that changed everything. *Newsweek*, 19 November.

Diez, T. 2006. The paradoxes of Europe's borders. *Comparative European Politics* 4 (2):235–52.

Diken, B. 2003. *The comedy of (t)errors*. www.lancs.ac.uk/fss/sociology/papers/diken-comedyofterrors.pdf

Diken, B. and C. Laustsen, 2004. 7/11, 9/11, and post-politics. Department of Sociology On line papers. www.lancs.ac.uk/fass/sociology/papers/diken-lausten-7-11-9-11-post-politics.pdf

Dinan, D. 2004. *Europe recast: A history of European Union*. Houndmills: Palgrave.

Donnan, H., and T. Wilson. 1999. *Borders: Frontiers and identity, nation and state*. Oxford: Berg

Doty, R. L. 2006. Fronteras Compasivas and the Ethics of Unconditional Hospitality. *Millennium: Journal of International Studies*, 35(1):53–74.

Duffield, M. 2005. Governing the borderlands: Decoding the power of aid. In *The global governance reader, ed. R. Wilkinson, 204–216. London: Routledge.

Eagleton, T. 1998. Newsreel history. *London Review of Books* 20(22); www.lrb.co.uk/v20/n22/eagl01_.html.

Entrikin, N. 2003. Political community, identity, and cosmopolitan place. In *Europe without borders: Remapping territory, citizenship, and identity in a transnational age*, eds. M. Berezin, and M. Schain, 51–63. Baltimore: Johns Hopkins University Press.

Erdogan, R.T. 2002. Speech at the centre for strategic and international studies, Washington D.C., December 9. http://www.theturkishtimes.com/archive/02/12_15/f_erdogan.html.

Erdogan, R.T. 2003. Democracy in the Middle East, pluralism in Europe. Speech at Harvard University, Kennedy School of Government, January 30. http://www.mfa.gov.tr/Harvard.htm.

Erdogan, R.T. 2004. Turkey, Islam and the West. *Global Agenda.* http://www.globalagendamagazine.com/2004/receptayyiperdogan.asp.

Erdogan, R. T. 2005. Speech to 38th Annual Meeting of the Board of Directors of the Asian Development Bank, Istanbul, May 5. http://www.adbistanbul.org/annualmeeting/Speeches/prime-minister-speech.html.

Etzioni, A. 1965. *Political unification: A comparative study of leaders and forces.* New York: Holt, Rinehart and Winston.

European Commission. 2003. *Communication from the Commission to the Council and the European Parliament: Wider Europe—Neighbourhood: A New Framework for Relations with our Eastern and Southern Neighbours' COM(2003) 104 Final.* Brussels: Commission of the European Communities.

European Stability Initiative (ESI). 2005. *Islamic Calvinists: Change and Conservatism in Central Anatolia.* www.esiweb.org.

Favell, A. 2007. Sociological Perspectives on EU Politics. In *Handbook of European Politics*, eds. K. Jorgensen, M. Pollack, and B. Rosamond, 122–128. London: Sage.

Fine, R. 2007. *Cosmopolitanism.* London: Routledge.

Fitzpatrick, P. 2004. The immanence of empire. In *Empire's new clothes: Reading Hardt and Negri*, eds. P. Passavant, and J. Dean, 31–55. New York: Routledge.

Friedman, J. 1990. Being in the world: Globalization and localization. In *Global culture: Nationalism, globalization and modernity*, ed. M. Featherstone, . London: Sage.

Friedman, J. 2007. Global systems, globalization, and anthropological theory. In *Frontiers of Globalization research: Theoretical and methodological approaches*, ed. I. Rossi, 109–132. New York: Springer.

Fulcher, J. 2000. Globalisation, the nation-state and global society. *The Sociological Review* 48(4): 522–543.

Furedi, F. 2004. The politics of fear. http://www.frankfuredi.com/index.php/site/article/88/.

Gillan, A. 2005. Europe condemns UK's terror control orders. *The Guardian*, 9 June.

Gillingham, J, 2003. *European Integration 1950–2003: Superstate or new market economy?* Cambridge: Cambridge University Press.

Gray, A. 2007. *Old men in love.* London: Bloomsbury.

Guha, R. 2001. A man from Kabul. *The Hindu*, 2 September.

Guiraudon, V., and A. Favell. 2007. The sociology of European integration. Paper presented at EUSA Conference, Montreal.

Gulalp, H. 2003. Whatever happened to secularization? The multiple Islams in Turkey. *The South Atlantic Quaterly* 102(2/3): 381–95.

Habermas, J. 2006: *The Divided west.* Cambridge: Polity Press.

Habermas, J. and J. Derrida. 2003. February 15, or, what binds European together. In *Old Europe, new Europe, core Europe: Transatlantic relations after the Iraq War*, eds. D. Levy, M. Pensky, and J. Torpey, 3–13. London: Verso.

Hardt, M. 2004. Intermezzo: The "Theory and Event" interview. Sovereignty, multitudes, absolute democracy: A discussion between Michael Hardt and Thomas L. Dumm about Hardt and Negri's Empire. In *Empire's new clothes: Reading Hardt and Negri, eds.* P. Passavant, and J. Dean, 163–173. New York: Routledge.

Hardt, M., and A. Negri. 2000. *Empire*. Cambridge, MA: Harvard University Press.

Hartley, E. 2006. *Did David Hasselhoff end the Cold War? 50 facts you need to know: Europe*. Cambridge: Icon Books.

Hassner, P. 2002. Fixed borders or moving borderlands? A new type of border for a new type of entity. In *Europe unbound: Enlarging and reshaping the boundaries of the European Union*, ed. J. Zielonka, 38–50. London: Routledge.

Harvey, D. 1989. *The condition of postmodernity: An enquiry into the origins of cultural change*. Oxford: Blackwell.

Hebdige, D. 1979. *Subculture: The meaning of style*. London: Routledge.

Hedetoft, U. 2003. *The global turn: National encounters with the world*: Aalborg: Aalborg University Press.

Hein, C. 2006. European spatial development, the polycentric EU capital, and Eastern enlargement. *Comparative European Politics* 4(2): 253–71.

Heins, V. 2005. Orientalising America? Continental intellectuals and the search for Europe's identity. *Millennium: Journal of International Studies* 34(2):433–48.

Held, D., and A. McGrew, eds. 2007a. *Globalization theory: Approaches and controversies*. Cambridge: Polity Press

Held, D.,and A. McGrew. . 2007b. Globalization at risk? In *Globalization theory: Approaches and controversies*, eds. D. Held, and A. McGrew, . Cambridge: Polity Press.

Held, D., A. McGrew, D. Goldblatt, and J. Perraton. 1999. *Global transformations: Politics, economics and culture*. Cambridge: Polity Press.

Holton, R. 1998. *Globalization and the nation-state*. Houndmills: Palgrave.

Holton, R. 2005. *Making globalization*. Houndmills: Palgrave.

Holton, R. 2008. *Global networks*. Houndmills: Palgrave.

Home Office, 2007. *Securing the UK border: Our vision and strategy for the future*. www.bia-homeoffice.gov.uk/sitecontent/document/managingourborders/securingtheukborder/

Houston, C. 2001. The brewing of Islamist modernity: Tea gardens and public space in Istanbul. *Theory, Culture and Society* 18(6): 77–97.

Huntington, S. 1996. *The clash of civilizations and the remaking of world order*. New York: Simon and Schuster.

Huysmans, J. 2006. *The politics of insecurity: Fear, migration and asylum in the EU*. London: Routledge.

Ignatieff, M. 2001. It's war—but it doesn't have to be dirty. *The Guardian*, October 1st.

Imig, D.,and S. Tarrow, S. 2001. *Contentious Europeans: Protest and politics in an emerging polity*. Lanham, MA: Rowman and Littlefield.

International Forum of Globalization. 2004.A better world is possible! In *The Globalization reader (Second Edition)*, eds. F. Lechner, and J. Boli, 438–448. Oxford: Blackwell.

Jachtenfuchs, M., and B. Kohler-Koch. 2003. Governance and institutional development. In *European integration theory*, eds. A. Wiener, and T. Diez. Oxford: Oxford University

James, H. 2005. Foreign policy turned inside out. In *Old Europe, new Europe, core Europe: Transatlantic relations after the Iraq War*, eds. D. Levy, M. Pensky, and J. Torpey, 59–63. London: Verso.

Jensen, O., and T. Richardson. 2003. *Making European space: Mobility, power and territorial identity* London: Routedge.

Judson, D. 2005. "Islamic Calvinism" a paradoxical engine for change in conservative Central Anatolia. *Turkish Daily News* 30 September 2005 www.turkishdailynews.com.tr/article.php?enewsid=24704

Karagiannis, N., and P. Wagner. eds. 2007a. *Varieties of world-making beyond globalization.* Liverpool: Liverpool University Press.

Karagiannis, N., P. and Wagner. 2007b. Introduction: globalization or world-making? In *Varieties of world-making beyond globalization,* eds. N. Karagiannis, and P. Wagner, 1–13. Liverpool: Liverpool University Press.

Kehlmann, D. 2007. *Measuring the world.* London: Quercus.

Keyder, C. 1987. *State and class in Turkey: A study in capitalist development.* London: Verso.

Keyman, F. 2003. A political earthquake in Turkey. *Eurozine.* http://www.euro zine.com/article/2003–01–08-keyman-en.html.

Keyman, F. 2006. Turkey between Europe and Asia. In *Europe and Asia beyond east and west: Towards a new cosmopolitanism,* eds. G. Delanty London: Routledge.

Klein, N. 2001. Reclaiming the commons. *New Left Review* 9 (May-June): 81–89.

Kofman, E. 2005. Figures of the cosmopolitan: privileged nationals and national outsiders. *Innovation: the European Journal of Social Science Research* 18(1):83–98.

Koopmans, R., and P. Statham. 2000. *Challenging immigration and ethnic relations politics: Comparative European perspectives.* Oxford: Oxford University Press.

Kramer, H. 2000. *A changing Turkey: The challenge to Europe and the United States.* Washington: Brookings Institution Press.

Laffey, M., and J. Weldes. 2004. Representing the international: Sovereignty after modernity? In *Empire's new clothes: Reading Hardt and Negri,* eds. P. Passavant, and J. Dean, 141–142. New York: Routledge.

Lahav, G., and V. Guiraudon. 2000. Comparative perspectives on border control: Away from the border and outside the state. In *The wall around the west: State borders and immigration controls in North America and Europe,* eds. P. Andreas, and T. Snyder, . Lanham: Rowman and Littlefield.

Lamy, P., and Z. Laidi. 2001. Governance or making globalization meaningful. www.laidi.com/papiers/governance.pdf.

Lavenex, S. 2004. EU external governance in "wider Europe". *Journal of European Public Policy* 11(4):680–700.

Lechner, F. and J. Boli. 2005. *World culture: Origins and consequences.* Oxford: Blackwell.

Le Gales, P. 2002. *European cities: Social conflicts and governance.* Oxford: Oxford University Press.

Leonard, M. 1999. *Network Europe: The new case for Europe.* London: The Foreign Policy Centre.

Levy, D., M. Pensky, and J. Torpey. eds. 2005a. *Old Europe, new Europe, core Europe: Transatlantic relations after the cold war.* London: Verso.

Levy, D., M. Pensky, and J. Torpey. 2005b. Editors' introduction. In *Old Europe, new Europe, core Europe: Transatlantic relations after the Iraq War,* eds. D. Levy, M. Pensky, and J. Torpey, xi–xxix. London: Verso.

Lodhi, A. 2006. Turkish toil brings new form of faith. BBC News, 13 March. http://news.bbc.co.uk/2/hi/business/4788712.stm.

Maas, W. 2005. Freedom of movement inside "fortress Europe" In *Global Surveillance and Policing: Borders, Security, Identity,* eds. E. Zuriek, and M. Salter, 233–246. Portland: Willan Publishing.

Massumi, B. ed. 1993. *The politics of everyday fear.* Minneapolis: University of Minnesota Press.

Makdisi, S. 1996. *Romantic imperialism: Universal empire and the culture of modernity* Cambridge: Cambridge University Press

Marcos, Subcomandante 2004. Tomorrow begins today. In *The globalization reader (Second Edition)*, eds. F. Lechner, and J. Boli, 430–434. Oxford: Blackwell.

Marks, G., F. Scharpf, P. Schmitter, and W. Streek 1996. *Governance in the European Union*. London: Sage.

McCarthy, R. 2001. Afghan applause just isn't cricket. *Guardian*, 18 May.

McGrew, A. 1995. World order and political space. In *A global world? Re-ordering political space*, eds. J. Anderson, C. Brook, and A. Cochrane, 11–64. Oxford: Oxford University Press.

McGrew, A. 2007. Globalization in hard times: Contention in the academy and beyond. In *The Blackwell companion to globalization*, ed. G. Ritzer, 29–53. Oxford: Blackwell.

McNeill, D. 2004. *New Europe: Imagined spaces*. London: Arnold.

McNeill, D. 2006. Europe and the globalised city: The case of London. *Comparative European Politics* 4(2): 218–34.

Mestrovic, S. 1994. *The Balkanization of the west: The confluence of postmodernism and postcommunism*. London: Routledge.

Mestrovic, S. 1997. *Postemotional society*. London: Sage.

Meyer, J. W. 2000. Globalization: Sources and effects on national states and societies. *International Sociology* 15(2): 233–248.

Meyer, J. W. 2001. The European Union and the globalization of culture. In *Institutional approaches to the European Union*. ARENA Report No. 3/2001, ed. S. S. Andersen, . Oslo: ARENA.

Meyer, J. W., J. Boli, G. M. Thomas, and F. O. Ramirez. 1997. World society and the nation-state. *The American Journal of Sociology* 103(1): 144–181.

Miele, M. 2008. CittàSlow: Producing slowness against the fast life. *Space and Polity* 12(1): 135–156.

Mignolo, W. D. 2000a. The many faces of cosmo-polis: Border thinking and critical cosmopolitanism. *Public Culture* 12(3): 721–48.

Mignolo, W. D. 2000b. *Local histories/global designs: Coloniality, subaltern knowledges, and border thinking*. Princeton, NJ: Princeton University Press.

Milward, A. 1993. *The European rescue of the nation-state*. London: Routledge.

Naim, M. 2005. Broken borders *Newsweek*, October 24, 55–66.

Naim, M. 2006. *Illicit: How smugglers, traffickers and copycats are hijacking the global economy*. London: Heinemann.

Nash, K. 2007. Out of Europe: Human rights and prospects for cosmopolitan democracy. In *Cosmopolitanism and Europe*, ed. C. Rumford. Liverpool: Liverpool University Press.

Navaro-Yashin, Y. 2002. *Faces of the state: Secularism and public life in Turkey*. Princeton: Princeton University Press.

Newman, D. 2003. On borders and power: A theoretical framework. *Journal of Borderlands Studies* 18(1):13–25.

Novoa, A. and M. Lawn eds. 2002. *Fabricating Europe: The formation of an education space*. Amsterdam: Kluwer.

O'Dowd, L. 2003. The changing significance of European borders. In *New borders for a changing Europe: Cross-border cooperation and governance*, eds. J. Anderson, L. O'Dowd, and T. Wilson, . London: Frank Cass.

Offe, C. 2002. Is there, or can there be, a "European society". In *Demokratien in Europa. Euopaissche Integration, Institutionenwandel und die Zukunft des demokratischen Verfassungsstaates*, eds. I. Katenhusen, W. Lamping. 71-90. Opladen: Leske and Budrich.

Onis, Z. 1995. Turkey in the post-cold war era: In search of identity. *The Middle East Journal* 49(1):48–68.

Onis, Z. 2001. Political Islam at the crossroads: From hegemony to coexistence. *Contemporary Politics* 7(4):281–98.

Onis, Z. 2007. Conservative globalists versus defensive nationalists: Political parties and paradoxes of Europeanization in Turkey. *Journal of Southern Europe and the Balkans* 9(3):247–61.

Onis, Z., and F. Keyman 2003. Turkey at the polls: A new path emerges. *Journal of Democracy* 14(2):95–107.

Outhwaite, 2005. *The Future of society.* Oxford: Blackwell.

Outhwaite, W. 2006a. Etienne Balibar, *New Formations* 58:9–9, Summer.

Outhwaite, W. 2006b. The state (and society) of Europe. *New Formations* 58, Summer, 31–38.

Outhwaite, W., and L. Ray. 2005. *Social theory and postcommunism.* Oxford: Blackwell.

Overy, R. 2007. The 50 key dates of world history. *The Times*, October 19. http://entertainment.timesonline.co.uk/tol/arts_and_entertainment/books/article2687623.ece

Parkins, W. and G. Craig. 2006. *Slow Living.* Oxford: Berg.

Passavant, P. 2004. Postmodern republicanism. In *Empire's new clothes: Reading Hardt and Negri*, eds. P. Passavant, and J. Dean, 1–20. New York: Routledge.

Passavant, P., and J. Dean. eds. 2004. *Empire's new clothes: Reading Hardt and Negri.* New York: Routledge.

Persson, H., and B. Strath. 2007. *Reflections on Europe: Defining a political order in time and space.* Frankfurt Peter Lang.

Pieterse, J. 2003. Hyperpower exceptionalism: Globalization the American way. In *Global America?: The cultural consequences of globalization*, eds. Beck, Sznaider, and Winter, 67–94. Liverpool: Liverpool University Press.

Powell, A. 2004. Erdogan calls for cooperation. *Harvard University Gazette*, February 5. http://www.news.harvard.edu/gazette/2004/02.05/03-turkey.html.

Prodi, R. 2001. The European Union and its citizens: A matter of democracy » Speech to European Parliament Strasbourg, 4 September 2001. http://europa.eu.int/rapid/pressReleasesAction.do?reference=SPEECH/01/365&format=HTML&aged=1&language=EN&guiLanguage=en.

Pynchon, T. 2007. *Against the day.* New York: Penguin.

Reid, J. 2006. Speech at Kings College, London, 20 February. http://politics.guardian.co.uk/iraq/story/0,,1713992,00.html

Rifkin, F. 2000. *The age of access: How the shift from ownership to access is transforming capitalism:* London: Penguin

Rifkin, J. 2004a. *The European dream: How Europe's vision of the future is quietly eclipsing the American dream.* New York: Tarcher/Penguin.

Rifkin, J. 2004b. This is the first attempt to create a global consciousness. *The Guardian* 16 November. http://www.guardian.co.uk/politics/2004/nor/16/eu.world

Ritzer, G. 2007. *The Blackwell companion to globalization.* Oxford: Blackwell.

Roberts, J. M. 2001. *The triumph of the west: The origin, rise, and legacy of western civilization.* London: Phoenix Press.

Roberston, R. 1992. *Globalization: Social theory and global culture.* London: Sage.

Robertson, R. 2001. Globalization theory 2000+: Major problematics. In *Handbook of social theory*, eds. G. Ritzer, and B. Smart, . London: Sage.

Robertson, R. 2007. Open societies, closed minds? Exploring the ubiquity of suspicion and voyeurism. *Globalizations* 4(3): 399–416.

Robertson, R., and J. A. Scholte. eds. 2006. *Encyclopedia of globalization.* London: Routledge.

Robertson, R., and K. White. 2007. What is globalization? In *The Blackwell companion to globalization*, ed. G. Ritzer, 54–66. Oxford: Blackwell.

Robin, C. 2004. *Fear: The History of a political idea.* Oxford: Oxford University Press.

Robins, K. 1997. What in the world's going on? In *Production of culture/cultures of production,* ed. P. Du Gay, . London: Sage.

Rossi, I. ed. 2007. *Frontiers of globalization research: Theoretical and methodological approaches.* New York: Springer.

Ruggie, J. G. 1993. Territoriality and beyond: Problematizing modernity in international relations. *International Organization,* 47(1): 139–74.

Rumford, C. 2000a. *European cohesion? Contradictions in EU integration.* Houndmills: Palgrave.

Rumford, C. 2000b. European cohesion? Globalization, autonomization, and the dynamics of EU integration. *Innovation: The European Journal of Social Science Research* 13(2):183–97.

Rumford, C. 2002. *The European Union: A political sociology.* Oxford: Blackwell.

Rumford, C. 2003. Resisting globalization? Turkey–EU relations and human and political rights in the context of cosmopolitan democratization. *International Sociology* 18(2): 379–94.

Rumford, C. 2004. Organizing European space: Regions, networks and EU integration. *International Journal of Urban and Regional Research* 28(1):225–9.

Rumford, C. 2005. Cosmopolitanism and Europe: Towards a new EU studies agenda? *Innovation: The European Journal of Social Science Research* 18(1): 1–9.

Rumford, C. 2006a. Theorizing borders. *European Journal of Social Theory* 9(2):155–70.

Rumford, C. 2006b. Borders and rebordering. In *Europe and Asia beyond east and west: Towards a new cosmopolitanism,* ed. G. Delanty, . London: Routledge.

Rumford, C. 2006c. Rethinking European spaces: Territory, borders, governance. *Comparative European Politics* 4(2/3):127–40.

Rumford, C. 2006d. Rethinking Turkey's relationship with the EU: Postwestern Turkey meets postwestern Europe. Politics and International Relations Working Paper No. 3, November. http://www.rhul.ac.uk/politics-and-IR/Working-Papers/RHUL-PIR_Working_Paper-03_Chris_Rumford_Postwestern_EU.pdf.

Rumford, C. 2006e. The European Union. In *Encyclopedia of globalization,* ed. R. Robertson, and J. A. Scholte, 417–422. London: Routledge.

Rumford, C. 2007a. More than a game: Globalization and the post-Westernization of world cricket. *Global Networks* 7(2): 202–214.

Rumford, C. 2007b. Does Europe have cosmopolitan borders?' *Globalizations* 4(3): 327–339.

Rumford, C. 2007c. *Cosmopolitanism and Europe.* Liverpool: Liverpool University Press.

Rumford, C. 2008a. Introduction: The stuff of European studies. In *Handbook of European studies, ed.* C. Rumford, . London: Sage.

Rumford, C. 2008b. Introduction: Citizens and borderwork. *Space and Polity* 12(1): 1–12.

Rumford, C., and D. Inglis. 2005. The cosmopolitan sublime: Romanticism, subjectivity, and the infinities of nature. Paper presented at the Millennium Annual Conference "Between Fear and Wonder: International Politics, Representation and 'the Sublime'", London School of Economics, London.

Rumford, C. and P. Murray. 2003. Do we need a core curriculum in European Union studies? *European Political Science* 3(1):85–92.

Runciman, D. 2004. *The Politics of good intentions: History, fear and hypocrisy in the new world order.* Princeton: Princeton University Press.

Samson, R. 2006. The cultural integration model and European transformation— The case of Romania. PhD diss., Copenhagen Business School, Denmark.

Sayyid, B. 1994. Sign o'times: Kaffirs and infidels fighting the ninth crusade. In *The making of political identities*, ed. E. Laclau, 264–286. London: Verso.

Scholte, J. A. 2004. Globalization and governance: From statism to polycentricity. *GSGR Working Paper No. 130/04*, http://www.csgr.org.

Schlesinger, P. 2007. A cosmopolitan temptation. *European Journal of Communication* 22(4):413–26.

Scott, J. 1998. *Seeing like a state: How certain schemes to improve the human condition have failed*. New Haven, CT: Yale University Press.

Scott, J. W. 2005. The EU and "wider Europe": Towards an alternative geopolitics of regional cooperation. *Geopolitics*, 10:429–54.

Singer, P. 2004. *One world: The ethics of globalization*. New Haven, CT: Yale University Press.

Smelser, N. 2004. Epilogue: September 11, 2001 as cultural trauma. In *Cultural Trauma and Collective Identity*, eds. J. Alexander, R. Eyerman, B. Giesen, N. Smelser, and P. Sztompka, 264–282. Berkeley: University of California Press.

Sofos, S. 2001. Reluctant Europeans? European integration and the transformation of Turkish politics. In *Europeanization and the southern periphery*, eds. K. Featherstone, and G. Kazamias, 243–260. London: Frank Cass.

Soysal, Y. 1994. *The limits of citizenship*. Chicago: University of Chicago Press.

Soysal, Y. 1997. Changing parameters of citizenship and claims-making: Organized Islam in European public spheres. *Theory and Society* 26(4): 509–527.

Soysal, Y. 2001. Changing boundaries of participation in European public spheres: reflections on citizenship and civil society., In *European citizenship between national legacies and postnational projects*, eds. K. Eder, and B. Giesen, 159–179. Oxford: Oxford University Press.

Spruce, D. 2007. The cosmopolitanization of the EU's borders' *Portal. Journal of Multidisciplinary Studies* 4(2): 1–17.

Stevenson, N. 2006. European cosmopolitan solidarity: Questions of citizenship, difference and post-materialism. *European Journal of Social Theory* 9(4): 485–500.

Strydom, P. 2002. *Risk, environment and society: Ongoing debates, current issues, and future prospects*. Buckingham: Open University Press.

te Brake, W. 2004. King Chirac: Off with their scarves! *History News Network*, January 21. http://www.hnn.us/articles/2991.html.

Tempest, M. 2006. Britain facing "most sustained threat since WWII" says Reid. *The Guardian*, 9 August: www.guardian.co.uk/politics/2006/aug/09/immigrationpolicy.uksecurity

Therborn, G. 1995. *Beyond European modernity: The trajectory of European societies*. London: Sage.

Therborn, G. 2003. Entangled modernities. *European Journal of Social Theory* 6(3): 293–305.

Therborn, G. 2006. Post-Western Europe and the plural Asias. In *Europe and Asia beyond east and west: Towards a new cosmopolitanism*, ed. G. Delanty, . London: Routledge.

Thomson, R. 2005. *Divided kingdom*. London: Bloomsbury. http://www.divided kingdom.co.uk/.

Tomlinson, J. 2007. Cultural globalization. In *The Blackwell companion to globalization*, ed. G. Ritzer, . Oxford: Blackwell.

Turunc, H. 2007. Islamicist or democratic? The AKP's search for identity in Turkish politics. *Journal of Contemporary European Studies* 15(1):79–91.

Urry, J. 2007a. Global complexities. In *Frontiers of globalization research: Theoretical and methodological approaches*, ed. I. Rossi, . New York: Springer.

Urry, J. 2007b. *Mobilities*. Cambridge: Polity Press.

van Houtum, H., and R. Pijpers. 2003. Towards a gated community. *Eurozine*. http://www.eurozine.com/articles/2005-01-12-houtumpijpers-en.html.

Vaughan-Williams, N. 2008. Borderwork beyond inside/outside? Frontex, the citi-zen-detective and the war on terror. *Space and Polity* 12(1): 63–79.

Walters, W. 2004. The frontiers of the European Union: A geostrategic perspective. *Geopolitics* 9(3): 674–98.

Walters, W. 2006a. Rethinking borders beyond the state. *Comparative European Politics* 4(2/3): 141–59.

Walters, W. 2006b. Border/control. *European Journal of Social Theory* 9(2): 187–204.

Walters, W., and J. Haahr. 2005. *Governing Europe: Discourse, governmentality and European integration*. London: Routledge.

Young, I. M. 2005. De-centring the project of global democracy. In *Old Europe, new Europe, core Europe: Transatlantic relations after the Iraq War*, ed. D. Levy, M. Pensky, and J. Torpey, . London: Verso.

Zielonka, J. ed. 2002. *Europe unbound: Enlarging and reshaping the boundaries of the European Union*. London: Routledge.

Zielonka, J. 2007. *Europe as empire: The nature of the enlarged European union*. Oxford: Oxford University Press.

Index

A

Aberdeen, 57
Abu Ghraib, 74, 81, 82, 106
'actually existing cosmopolitanism', 4, 100
Afghanistan, 118, 119, 140
Against the Day, 154
airports, 37, 42, 52, 67, 79, 80
  See also Gatwick Airport, 80
AK Party, 121–124, 126–132
Albrow, Martin, 134, 137
Al Qaeda, 76, 82, 83
Alexander, Jeffrey, 85, 86
alterity, 71, 72
Amin, Ash, 69
Anatolian Tigers, 122
Anderson, John, 96
Andreas, Peter, 56, 79
'annihilation of space', 15, 70
apartheid, 24, 38, 50
Appadurai, Arjun, 119, 145, 151
Arabs, the, 117
Archibugi, Daniel, 4, 7, 10
Ash, Timoth Garton, 115
Asia, 46, 64, 104, 113, 128, 130
'asymmetric membrane', 41, 60, 64
Ataturk, Kemal, 121, 124, 126
Australia, 112

B

Bakhtin, 74
Bali, 147
Balibar, Etienne, 16, 24, 34, 37–51, 52, 54, 68, 72, 75, 81, 107, 153–154
Balkans, The, 120, 146
Basra, 87
Bauman, Zygmunt, 64, 65, 67, 71, 74, 78, 80, 81, 106, 136, 139

Beck, Ulrich, 1, 3, 7, 8, 9–12, 13, 18, 19, 21, 22, 59, 73, 87, 90, 98–101, 105, 108, 109, 114, 117, 133, 139, 152, 153, 157n
Belarus, 56, 57, 157n
Beslan, 147
Berezin, Mabel, 32
Berlin Wall, 59, 64, 65
Beyer, Peter, 140
Bhambra, Gurminder K., 25, 135
Bin Laden, Osama, 118
biometrics, 79, 80
biopolitics, 102, 105
Black Sea, 112
Blair, Tony, 75, 76, 77, 82, 84, 124, 146–147
'border thinking', 12, 51
'border sickness', 66
'borderless world', 15, 17, 38, 43, 49, 60, 75, 79, 106
borders, 37–51, 53–68, 78–84, 153–154
  See also 'asymmetric membrane', 'border sickness', 'fuzzy borders', 'invisible borders', 'juxtaposed borders', 'networked borders', 'offshore borders', 'polysemic borders'
'borderwork', 17, 39, 42, 54, 56–59, 61–65, 68, 157n
borderlands, 30, 31, 34, 44, 54, 61
  See also 'global borderlands'
Borders and Immigration Authority, 80
Borocz, Jozsef, 19, 23–25
Bosnia, 91
Brenner, Neil, 31, 32, 35
'Brides without Borders', 65
Brown, Christopher, 111, 117
Bush, George W., 119
Butler, Judith, 77–78

Byrne, Liam, 79

C
Camp Breadbasket, 82
Canary Islands, 67
Castells, Manuel, 21, 22, 27, 32, 45, 55, 109
CCTV, 71
'cellular politics', 118–119
Ceuta, 50, 72, 81
Chakrabarti, Shami, 77
Channel Tunnel, 58
Cheah, Pheng, 7–8, 15
Chicago, 76
Chirac, Jacques, 131
christian values, 58, 122
citizenship, 20, 21, 48
    See also post-national citizenship
civil society, 22, 63, 65, 93–94, 118, 125, 126, 129
    See also global civil society
'Clash of civilizations', 44–45, 136
Cold War40, 45, 47, 54, 66, 111, 112, 114, 117, 119, 121, 123, 125, 146
'collar of steel', 58
colonialism, 24
    See also post-colonialism
congestion charging, 42, 58, 158n
Constitutional Treaty, 23
control orders, 76, 77–78, 118, 119
Copenhagen Criteria, 123, 159n
'core Europe', 111, 114, 115
core-periphery relations, 30, 35, 44, 46, 55, 95, 97, 99, 100, 101, 102, 131
'cosmo-lite', 116
'cosmopolitan border', 52–68, 153–154
'cosmopolitan empire', 98–101, 152
'cosmopolitan realism', 10, 152, 154
cosmopolitan spaces, 3, 110, 153
'cosmopolitan turn', 5
cosmopolitanism,
    See 'actually existing cosmopolitan-ism', 'cosmo-lite', 'cosmopolitan borders', 'cosmopolitan empire', 'cosmopolitan realism', 'cosmo-politan turn', cosmopolitaniza-tion, 'critical cosmopolitanism', 'methodological cosmopolitan-ism', 'new' cosmopolitanism
cosmopolitanization, 10, 11, 13, 27, 67, 68, 98, 101, 139
Council of Europe, 54, 77, 123, 150

cricket, 140
'critical cosmopolitanism', 1, 2, 4, 7, 11–13, 16. 51, 106, 107, 111, 150, 154–155
'cultural trauma', 85–86
Cyprus, 40

D
Dahrendorf, Ralf, 115
'dangerousness', 75–78
'Danish cartoons', 120
Davis, Norman, 29
Delanty, Gerard, 7, 9, 11–12, 11–113
Derrida, Jacques, 114–116
Devji, Faisal, 117–118, 120
Dinan, Desmond, 28, 29
dispersal zones, 57, 65
'diversality', 13
Divided Kingdom, 66
'divided West', 113–114, 119
Doctrine of the International Commu-nity, 146
Donnan, Hastings, 61–62
drug smuggling, 56, 60

E
e-borders, 80, 88
ECHR (European Court of Human Rights), 130
ECSC (European Coal and Steel Com-munity), 98
EEA (European Economic Area), 54
empire, 16, 18, 31, 90–109
    see also 'cosmopolitan empire', 'europe-as-empire'
enlargement, 10, 30, 40, 47, 57, 91–92, 94–95, 101, 112, 113, 120, 131
Erdoğan, Recep Tayyip, 123, 127–129, 131, 132
Etzioni, Amitai, 20
Eurocentrism, 51, 116
Euroland, 36
Eurostar, 56, 58, 79
'Europe-as-empire', 31, 101, 108, 109
Europe of the regions, 6
European Commission, 46, 107, 159n
European Journal of Social Theory, 36
Europeanization, 18, 23, 28, 30, 58, 97, 111
European Neighbourhood Policy, 34, 81, 94, 157n
European Social Model, 112
'ever closer union', 20, 23
'everyday fear', politics of, 63–64

exclusion zones, 59, 67, 68
'extremist shoppers', 52

F

Favell, Adrian, 19, 20–22, 25, 26–27
Fear, 69, 73–75, 85–86, 88
  See also 'everyday fear'
Fine, Robert, 9, 153
firewall, 64
Fischer, Joschka, 148
'fortress Europe', 17, 47, 53, 55, 61
Foucault, Michel, 105
France, 33, 79, 111, 114, 117, 131,
  148
Friedman, Jonathan, 133, 138, 151
'frisk society', 52
Fronteras Compasivas, 65
Frontex, 40, 54, 81, 94, 157n
frontier, 34, 63, 88, 121
Furedi, Frank, 88
'fuzzy borders', 91

G

gated communities, 60–65, 71, 89, 103,
  158n
Gatwick Airport, 80
Gauss, Carl Freidrich, 25, 26
Germany, 40, 111, 114, 117, 124,
  148
Gil-Robles, Alvaro, 77
Gillingham, John, 28, 29
'global borderland', 4, 50, 75, 81, 82,
  84
global civil society, 64, 65, 94, 119,
  146, 148
'global frontierland', 50
global governance, 9, 72, 81, 112
'global non-West', 117–120
'global supermarket of style', 141
globalization, 133–151
  See also 'global borderland', 'global
    civil society', 'global frontier-
    land', 'global governance',
    'global non-West', 'global
    supermarket of style'
'governance turn', 30, 31
governmentality, 27
Grande, Edgar, 3, 8, 9, 18, 90, 98–101,
  109, 152
'Great wall of Europe', 40, 50, 72, 81,
  154
Guantanomo Bay, 74, 77, 81, 106, 118,
  119
Guiraudon, Virginie, 19, 26–27, 63

H

Habermas, Jurgen, 3, 7, 113, 114–117,
  152
Halperin, Sandra, 135
Hardt and Negri (*Empire*), 70, 101–
  105
headscarf, 131, 159n
Hedetoft, Ulf, 41, 60
Held, David, 7, 10, 137–139
'heterocosmic imagination', 144, 148,
  149, 150
'heterocosmic pre-emption', 81, 146
'high point', 13, 90, 104–109, 148, 154
Hitler, Adolf, 83
Hobbes, Thomas, 74
Home Office, 79, 80
Homeland Security, 119, 154
humanity, 5, 14, 146,
human rights, 9, 14, 24, 77, 82–89,
  106, 118, 120, 124, 126, 127,
  129–132, 159n
Human Rights Act, 88
Humboldt, Alexander von, 25–26
'humpty dumpty' view of society, 85,
  88
Huntington, Samuel P., 45, 121
Hurricane Katrina, 73
Huysmans, Jef, 70, 74
hybridity, 27

I

ICC (International Cricket Council), 140
identity politics, 47–48, 112–114,
  140–142, 153
Ignatieff, Michael, 87
'inner mobility', 66
International Criminal Court, 84
International Forum on Globalization,
  149
'invisible borders', 39, 42
IRA, 58
Iraq, 82, 97, 111, 112, 114, 119, 129,
  154
Iron Curtain, 30, 40. 56
Islam, 118–120, 122, 124, 126, 127, 140
'Islamic Calvinism', 122
Israel, 72, 128, 154, 157n
Istanbul, 115, 128

J

James, Harold, 29, 115
Jensen, Ole B., 27, 32, 33
Jews, the, 53
Jihad, 118–119

Judt, Tony, 29
July 7 bombings, 87
'juxtaposed borders', 79

K
Kaliningrad, 33, 57
Kant, Immanuel, 9, 116
Karagiannis, Nathalie, 135–136
Kayseri, 122
Kehlmann, Daniel, 25
Kemalism, 121, 124, 126, 127
Keynsianism, 35
Kings College, 82, 83, 87
Klein, Naomi, 148
Kosovo, 91, 146
Kouchner, Bernard, 148
Kratochwil, Freidrich, 135
Kurds, the, 123, 125, 154

L
Labour government, 57, 77
Lahav, Gallya, 63
Landscapes of the jihad, 117
Latin America, 137
Latvia, 57
Lille, 79
Live 8, 64
London, 42, 47, 57, 58, 73
Lord Haw-Haw, 84
Luxembourg, 34

M
Madrid, 47, 73, 147
Massumi, Brian, 64
McGrew, Tony, 70, 138–139
McNeill, Donald, 32, 58
McNulty, Tony, 80
McWorld, 106
Measuring the World, 25
Mediterranean, the, 46, 81, 154
Melilla, 50, 72
Melton Mowbray, 59
Mestrovic, Stjepan G., 86–87
Methodological cosmopolitanism, 7, 10, 152
Methodological nationalism, 1, 8, 10, 11, 21, 98, 101, 154
Metropolitan Police, 58
Meyer, John. W., 24, 134, 136, 137
Mexico-US border, 65, 154
MI5, 52
Middle Ages, 100
Middle East, 95, 122, 127, 128, 130
Mignolo, Walter D., 12–13, 51

migration, 20, 21, 58, 63
Milward, Alan. S., 28, 29
mobility, 30–33, 53–56, 60, 67, 70, 81, 99
   See also 'inner mobility'
Moldova, 56, 57, 157n
Monnet, Jean, 28
'monotopia', 32, 33, 104
Morocco, 72, 157n
Moscow, 115
Mullah Omar, 140
multi-level governance, 31, 101
multiperspectival polity, 90, 108, 109
multiperspectival social science, 6, 13, 16, 106

N
Naim, Moises, 57
nationalism, 89, 115, 138
   See also 'methodological national-
      ism', 'statistical nationalism'
National Security Council (MGK), 126, 130, 132
NATO, 24, 117, 129, 130, 146
natural law, 9
Nazism, 82–84, 87, 89
neo-Medievalism, 16, 91–99, 101
'network Europe', 27, 30, 31, 36, 46, 47, 53, 55–56, 101
'networked border', 56
'New' cosmopolitanism, 2, 6–11, 153
New Orleans, 73, 74
New York, 119, 139
Newman, David, 59
'No borders', 58, 65, 158n
'no cold calling zones', 59, 65
North Africa, 50, 81, 95

O
O'Dowd, Liam, 62
'offshore borders', 4, 79–80, 89
'old Europe', 111, 117
'one worldism', 2, 137, 146, 148, 151–152, 160n
'Onion model of globalization', 139
Oniş, Ziya, 123, 127, 159n
'open society', 71
Organized Crime and Police Act, 58
Overdetermination, 39–41, 47–48, 107

P
Pakistan, 140
Palestine, 91, 119
Pan-European networks, 31, 36

'Paramorphoscopic sociology', 155
Paris, 58, 79, 148
'people power', 63–65
Pijpers, Roos, 60
Poland, 40, 57, 139
'politics of space', 5–6, 13–15, 90–91,
    97, 103
polycentricity, 30, 34–35, 91
polysemic borders, 41, 44, 54
Pope, the, 58
Pork pies, 59
post-colonialism, 23, 47
post-communism, 92, 112
postemotionalism, 84, 85–88
post-Fordism, 106
postmodernity, 27, 96, 102, 103, 104,
    124
post-national citizenship, 3, 5, 27, 36
post-political, 77, 119
post-secularism, 36
postwesternization, 16, 26, 51,
    110–132
Prodi, Romano, 46, 55, 95
public sphere, 20, 21, 92–93, 103, 114,
    115, 130
Pynchon, Thomas, 154, 155

R
rebordering, 31, 39, 47, 48, 55, 63
Red Crescent, 67
Reid, John, 75, 82–84, 87–88
'remote control', 63, 80
Richardson, Tim, 27, 33
Rifkin, Jeremy, 3, 52, 65
'ring of steel', 58
risk society, 14, 27, 64, 73, 106
Robertson, Roland, 71, 89, 134, 135,
    137, 138, 139–145
Robin, Corey, 74, 85
Rossi, Ino, 137
Ruggie, John Gerald, 90, 108–109
Rumsfeld, Donald, 117
Runciman, David, 76, 160n
Russia, 57

S
Sao Paolo, 115
Sarkar, Mahua, 19, 23–25
Sassen, Saskia, 45
Schain, Martin, 32
Schengenland, 36, 53, 55, 99, 150
Schlesinger, Philip, 11, 152
Scholte, Jan Aart, 134, 137
Schroeder, Gerhardt, 124

Sears Tower, 76
secularism, 115, 121, 122, 123, 124,
    129, 131
    See also post-secularism
security, 52, 55, 56, 58, 60, 63, 64, 72,
    74, 84, 99, 147
September 11th, 43, 73, 75, 85, 87, 88,
    102, 106, 160n
Sheffield, 57
'sieve Europe', 47
single market, 28, 30, 32, 36, 47, 55, 62,
    81, 95
'smart borders', 67, 79, 80
social science, 1, 4, 6, 7, 9–13, 14, 19,
    26, 106, 111
social theory, 18–29, 33, 36, 50
Southampton, 57
slow movement, the, 146, 149
'spaces of wonder', 17, 69–89
Spain, 33, 67, 115
spatial turn, 14, 15, 29, 30, 31–32, 44
'statistical nationalism', 21
St. Pancras, 79
'strangeness', 4, 69–75, 82, 84, 86, 88–89
Strauss-Kahn, Dominique, 115
Subcommandante Marcos, 149
sublime, the, 74, 88
surveillance, 52, 71
SUVs, 71
Swansea, 67
Sydney, 115
Sznaider, Natan, 9, 10, 139

T
Taliban, The, 140–141
'territorial cohesion', 30, 35
terror, 14, 73, 74, 77–78, 88
    See also 'terrorism', 'war on terror'
terrorism, 39, 75, 81, 83, 118, 157n
    See also 'terror', 'war on terror'
Thompson, Rupert, 66
'Titanic syndrome', 74
Tokyo, 115
Tomlinson, John, 134, 145
'tortilla curtain', 65
transborder regions, 30
transdneister, 57
tsunami, 64
Turing, Alan, 83
Turkey, 58, 111, 119–132, 159n

U
Ukraine, 40, 56, 57, 91, 157n
'unicity', 1, 137, 140, 141

Urry, John, 52, 102, 104
USA, 87, 111, 112, 114, 118, 129, 154, 157n

V
van Houtum, Henk, 60
variable geometry, 31, 99, 101
victimhood, 85, 87

W
Wagner, Peter, 135–136
Wallis, Barnes, 83
Walters, William, 27, 32, 41, 64
'war on terror', 77, 81, 84, 87, 89, 106, 111, 114, 118–119
   See also 'terror', 'terrorism'
Warsaw, 34, 81, 139
Weber, Max, 122
welfare, 99, 115, 150

Welfare Party (Refah Partisi), 124
West, the, 107, 110–114, 117–118, 121, 125–129, 131, 132, 146
West Bank, 72, 154
White Cliffs of Dover, 79
Wilson, Thomas M, 61–62
'world openness', 11, 12, 108
World polity, 14, 137
World Social Forum, 64, 149
World Systems Theory, 23

Y
Y2K, 106
Young, Iris Marion, 115–116

Z
Zapatistas, 148–149
Zielonka, Jan, 90–98, 108
'zombie categories', 10

CPSIA information can be obtained at www.ICGtesting.com
Printed in the USA
LVOW12s0827160514

385980LV00008B/170/P